Sexing *La Mode*

Sexing *La Mode*

Gender, Fashion and Commercial Culture in Old Regime France

Jennifer M. Jones

Oxford • New York

English edition
First published in 2004 by
Berg
Editorial offices:
1st Floor, Angel Court, 81 St Clements Street, Oxford, OX4 1AW, UK
175 Fifth Avenue, New York, NY 10010, USA

Berg is the imprint of Oxford International Publishers Ltd.

Library of Congress Cataloging-in-Publication Data
A catalogue record for this book is available from the Library of Congress.

British Library Cataloguing-in-Publication Data
A catalogue record for this book is available from the British Library.

ISBN 1 85973 830 3 (hardback)
1 85973 835 4 (paperback)

Typeset by JS Typesetting Ltd, Wellingborough, Northants.
Printed in the United Kingdom by MPG Books Ltd, Bodmin.

www.bergpublishers.com

To Melisande and Gerald Skillicorn

Contents

List of Illustrations

List of Illustrations

Abbreviations and Measurements

Libraries and Archives

AN	Archives nationales (Paris)
AS	Archives de la Seine (Paris)
BA	Bibliothèque de l'Arsenal (Paris)
BHVP	Bibliothèque historique de la ville de Paris
BM	Bibliothèque Mazarine (Paris)
BN	Bibliothèque nationale (Paris)

Money and Measurements

livre	The standard unit of currency in early-modern Paris, equal to 20 *sous*
écu	Equal to 3 *livres*
aune	A unit of length equal to 1.18 meters

Acknowledgments

This book took shape in the stimulating environment produced by the community of Early Modern and European historians at Princeton University in the 1980s. I thank Natalie Zemon Davis for directing my doctoral thesis, Robert Darnton for making the culture of the French Enlightenment come alive in his classes and books, Philip Nord for generously and carefully reading my thesis and convincing me of the importance of politics in the history of fashion, and Joan Scott for her path-breaking analysis of gender history.

The Rutgers University History department made possible the completion of this project by providing a semester of research leave when I was an assistant professor. I am thankful to Victoria de Grazia, whose leadership of the Rutgers Center for Historical Analysis during my first two years as an assistant professor brought together an unusually congenial group of scholars of consumer culture. I give thanks to fellow colleagues at the RCHA, Belinda Davis, David Kuchta, Ellen Furlough, and Erika Rappaport. I could not have finished this book without the encouragement and inspiration of many of my colleagues at Rutgers: Rudy Bell, Alastair Bellany, Ziva Galili, John Gillis, Donald Kelley and Phyllis Mack. My colleagues Bonnie Smith and Paul Clemens deserve thanks for reading the whole manuscript and offering invaluable professional advice. Nicole Pellegrin's warm collegiality during her visits to Rutgers and her inspiring scholarship on the history of clothing and material culture played an important role in shaping my project from start to finish.

I thank the Mellon foundation for its generous support of my doctoral studies and the French government for supporting a full year of research in France with a Chateaubriand Fellowship. In addition, I am indebted to all of the scholars who offered advice on my project while I was conducting research in Paris, presenting portions of the book at conferences, and soliciting advice from outside reviewers; Margie Beale, Joshua Cole, Rene Marion, Mary Louise Roberts, Dena Goodman, Lynn Hunt, Suzanne Desan, Elborg Forster, Mary Sheriff, Jeffrey Merrick, and Jim Johnson all deserve thanks. At the very final stage of the project, the anonymous outside reviewer for Berg Press helped me immeasurably, with advice about both small factual details and conceptualizing the relationship of my book to the new scholarship on women, gender, and theatricality. Kathleen May and the editorial staff at Berg publishers have been models of professionalism and have made the final stage of the very long process of writing this book remarkably efficient and pleasurable.

Acknowledgments

My greatest debt is to my family, who has lived with this project for many years. My mother and my stepfather, to whom I dedicate this book, have offered much needed support and inspiration through their lifelong love of learning and writing. My two wonderful sons, Soren and Lars, have grown up with this book, keeping me happily distracted and, as they have grown older, proudly focused, on being their scholar-mother. My husband, Chris Rasmussen, has been a model intellectual companion and fellow historian throughout this project. He has read and edited more drafts of this book than either of us would care to admit, each time, still finding ways to make the argument clearer and the prose more elegant.

Prologue: The Morning *Toilette*, circa 1785

A young Parisian woman wearing a dressing gown of gaily printed cotton sits down before a mirror and begins her morning *toilette*. She peruses a small booklet titled *The Friend of Ladies* she has purchased the day before while strolling in the Palais-Royal while her maid arranges her hair. A knock at the door and a merchant is announced, a *revendeuse à la toilette* making the rounds of the neighborhood with a basket full of ribbons. The young woman strokes her dog and asks her maid, "dove gray or violet trim for my new bonnet?" The maid heats an iron and begins to curl and coif the young woman's hair. A bell rings and a servant announces a male tailor (*tailleur de corps*), ready to take measurements for a new whalebone bodice (*corps à baleines*) to wear under the *robe à la française* being prepared for next week's court ball. The bust, the waist, the hips, the length of the back – all must be precisely measured for a perfect fit.

Time at last to get dressed. The woman removes her dressing gown, revealing a white linen chemise beneath. The maid brings a cotton corset, a fresh chemise, silk stockings and helps the young woman put them on. Together they select a dress, a simple *robe à l'anglaise* printed with blue flowers on a white background. A large white scarf laced around the shoulders, a straw hat tied under the chin, white gloves, and a parasol – thus adorned, the young woman is ready to venture out into the beckoning streets of Paris. Private ritual gives way to public promenade. Although this woman is clearly a member of elite society, on a smaller scale and with humbler textiles and accessories, rituals such as this one took place hundreds of times over, each day, in eighteenth-century Paris.

How do we begin to interpret the meaning of such a commonplace, even banal, act as the daily adornment of the female body? A series of questions about the personal, subjective experience of dressing race through the mind of any woman who has ever stood before a mirror contemplating her clothing, her body, and her identity: White muslin or blue silk? Which is more practical, or more flattering? How did she imagine the contours of the body when wearing a ceremonial *robe à la française* with its ballooning paniers? Whom did she dream of while dressing – her husband, her child, the crowds who would admire her at the ball? In what ways did aesthetics and the erotic overlap and mingle – the brush of linen against the skin, the firm press of whale bone around the waist, the sheen of silk, transparent gauze billowing around white shoulders – in the art of dressing? How did clothing permit her to become the woman she longed to be? How did it restrict the possible

Figure 1 *La toilette*, Jean-Baptiste Pater, courtesy of the National Museums of France (RMN).

postures she might take? How might a hat, carefully selected, provide both the allure of novelty and the reassurance of social station?

Ultimately, the questions we long to ask this young Parisian woman are modern questions, predicated on the belief that in the act of dressing we clothe the psyche and step out into the world as individuals. But identities cannot be put on and taken off at will like a new hat; and in the eighteenth century, even more than now, men and women did not have complete freedom to choose or create their identities. We need to ask then, not what this young woman thought about while she dressed, but how she thought about the act of dressing itself. How did she perceive the connection between her personal identity, her public performance as a privileged woman of leisure, and the clothing that she wore?

These questions matter to historians because the eighteenth century marked a major turning point in how men and women thought about the meaning of clothing and the connection between public and private, society and the subjects. Eighteenth-century French men and women were concerned about the ways in which identities were constructed by clothing, by the ways in which one's gender and social identity were marked and constructed by what one wore in an emerging "society of taste." More than other commodities, clothing became the problematic emblem of modernity; in particular, the emerging Parisian culture of fashion – from hoopskirts and hats to shops and shop girls – focused attention on the difficult relationship between femininity and modernity. A culture that was increasingly obsessed by the private realm of the family and the public realm of politics focused on and debated the meaning of clothing, that middle ground between private and public, between psyche and civilization, between the human body and the body politic. An act as simple as selecting and buying a hat and showing it off in public placed the consumer in a tangled web of economic, aesthetic, erotic and even political significance: how could citizens be sovereign, if they were the subjects of *la mode*?

Discerning the meaning of the unique subjective performance of personal identity staged in the wearing of a particular hat or dress lies beyond the scope of the historian – traditional historical documents fall silent here. But by ranging widely over scientific treatises and fashion magazines, from the workshops to the boutiques of Paris, we can begin to set the stage, to imagine the social and cultural backdrop of that dynamic moment when the subject takes the props available to her and begins to construct her identity piece by piece with stockings and shoes, corsets and dresses, wigs and hats. "Backdrop" and "foreground," "actor" and "audience," "scenery," "props," "performance" and "costumes" – these theatrical metaphors permit us to remove ourselves from our modern psychoanalytic understanding of identity and, in the language that eighteenth-century men and women used, to think about the relationship between the real and the imaginary, the individual and the role, the private person and the public stage, clothing and costume.

Our imaginary lady at her morning *toilette* smiles beguilingly at us from across the centuries, brought to life for us by dozens of eighteenth-century engravings and paintings. But she is either mute or deaf to our queries. She smiles but does not speak. We will have to move beyond her to broader social and cultural contexts to answer the questions we long to ask about the meaning of her dress. Yet, silent as she is, I dedicate this story to her, to her maid, to her dressmaker, her hairdresser, and to all the women of eighteenth-century Paris who participated, however

Figure 2 *Portrait d'une femme à sa toilette*, Friedrich Heinrich Fuger, courtesy of RMN.

unknowingly, however grudgingly, in the making of the modern meaning of dress. For the modern culture of fashion which these women helped to create still permeates our lives as twenty-first century women, still linking fashion with femininity and frivolity, and still warning us that while women should delight in clothing and may primp and preen, it would be frivolous to believe that any meaning of real importance could possibly be ascribed to a woman's *toilette*.

Introduction

An immoderate fondness for dress, for pleasure, and for sway, are the passions of savages; the passions that occupy those uncivilized beings who have not yet extended the dominion of the mind, or even learned to think with the energy necessary to concatenate that abstract train of thought which produces principles. And that women, from their education and the present state of civilized life, are in the same condition, cannot, I think, be controverted. To laugh at them then, or satirize the follies of a being who is never allowed to act freely from the light of her own reason, is as absurd as cruel.

Mary Wollstonecraft, *Vindication of the Rights of Woman* (1792)

In 1792 when Mary Wollstonecraft traveled to Paris to witness the French Revolution she had the opportunity to observe a great many French women and their fashions. Knowing her contempt for women's pursuit of *la mode*, she would have denounced many of these fashions as ridiculous and found their interest in clothing and adornment at best puerile and at worst a barbarous remnant of savagery. Wollstonecraft was not the first visitor to Paris to comment on French women's pronounced interest in fashions nor would she be the last. Just two decades earlier, another English visitor, James Rutledge, had charged, "every French woman believes herself to be, while at her toilette, the genius of taste and of elegance in all of her apparel, and she imagines that there is no ornament that one could invent to embellish the human figure that does not belong to her as an exclusive right."[1]

In denouncing women's interest in fashion as the product of an uncultivated mind, Wollstonecraft attacked both the luxury of the aristocratic women of the *ancien régime* and Jean-Jacques Rousseau's new-model bourgeois housewife, Sophie, whose love of clothing was celebrated in his educational novel, *Émile*. Queens and courtiers may have elevated dress and adornment to a high art, paying homage to the creative genius of their *marchandes de modes*, but for Wollstonecraft this "artistry" was merely the external mark of a depravity shared with slaves, whose "savage desire for admiration" spurred them to spend their meager earnings on "a little tawdry finery."[2] As for Rousseau's contention that Sophie's coquettish desire to please men through adornment evinced an innate feminine fondness for dress, Wollstonecraft found it ridiculous, declaring,

I am unable to comprehend what either [Dr. Gregory] or Rousseau means when they frequently use this indefinite term. If they told us that in a pre-existent state the soul was fond of dress, and brought this inclination with it into a new body, I should listen to them with a half-smile, as I often do when I hear a rant about innate elegance.[3]

For Wollstonecraft an interest in fashions was neither laudable nor natural; only "ignorance and the mistaken cunning that Nature sharpens in weak heads as a principle of self-preservation, render women very fond of dress, and produce all the vanity which such a fondness may naturally be expected to generate, to the exclusion of emulation and magnanimity."[4]

Living in an age in which satires of women's hairstyles and hoopskirts were commonplace, Wollstonecraft must be commended for de-naturalizing the link between femininity and fashion and her earnest desire to understand the social practices that rendered women so fond of dress. Nevertheless, one might ask whether Mary Wollstonecraft got it completely right concerning French women and their fashions. Could an Englishwoman whose taste was for utterly plain and nondescript dresses possibly understand French women's interest (supposed or real) in fashions? Just as daughters have throughout the centuries dared to question their mother's fashion advice, one might ask if the mother of modern feminism went far enough in her examination of contemporaries' beliefs concerning women and fashion.

If only one could have had the opportunity to meet with Wollstonecraft, perhaps to peruse the latest issue of the *Journal de la mode et du goût* or to stroll through the arcades of the Palais-Royal, one might have asked, if Rousseau was so mis-guided, why did Sophie's interest in fashion seem so right to legions of French women? One would also have liked to push Wollstonecraft to explore, not only the ways in which femininity and fashion were linked in eighteenth-century thought, but also the ways in which femininity and fashion were linked to frivolity. For Wollstonecraft's assertion that fashions are naturally frivolous is as open to question as Rousseau's contention that an interest in fashion is innately feminine: both claims are part of a distinctly modern discourse that took shape in the eighteenth century. In addition, one might have asked Wollstonecraft to be a bit more charit-able to her contemporaries and to consider whether other factors were involved in women's interest in fashion besides a "want of cultivation of mind." For example, what role did an expanding commercial culture filled with window displays, clothing merchants, fashion plates, and fashion journalists play in encouraging women's pursuit of fashions? And, how did contemporary notions of the French-ness of fashion and the frivolity of the French shape both men's and women's consumption of clothing and conceptions of *la mode*? In the ensuing exploration of the roles of women and gender in the making of Parisian fashion culture between the late seventeenth and late eighteenth centuries, I will attempt to answer these questions as I consider the social, economic, political, and cultural implications of the eighteenth-century commonplace that there was an intrinsic link between fashion, frivolity, Frenchness and femininity.

The most obvious way to begin a study of "the sexing of *la mode*" is with an examination of the growing dimorphism of middle- and upper-class male and female clothing in the period between 1750 and 1850. Not only fashion historians, but also social and cultural historians have made much of this sartorial dimorphism as a fitting symbol of transformations of masculinity and femininity in this period. In 1750 aristocratic men's elaborately embroidered vests, lace cuffs, heels, buckles, and powdered wigs seemed of a piece with their wives' and daughters' embroidered skirts, lace neckerchiefs and dainty shoes. Although men wore breeches, vests and jackets and women wore skirts and dresses, both sets of apparel seemed to share a symbolic language in which luxury, ostentation, and fashion displayed social prestige and political power. By 1850, however, the sober three-piece suit of the bourgeois and upper-class man stood diametrically opposed to the expansive hoopskirts, ornate fabrics, and glittering accessories worn by his wife, sisters, and daughters. This "Great Masculine Renunciation" (in J.C. Flugel's famous phrase) seemed perfectly to reflect the logic of a gender revolution begun in the eighteenth century and founded on a new biology of incommensurability, which culminated in the articulation of increasingly separate male and female spheres.[5] New notions of masculine and feminine biological and social difference and complementarity found their sartorial parallel in the contrast between the dour suits in which men strode out into public each morning to pursue profits and power and the frivolous dresses which encased, protected, and adorned their wives at home.[6]

Whether patriotic fashions in the French Revolution, the garb of bourgeois domesticity in the mid nineteenth century, or the reformed dress of the "modern woman" in the 1920s, fashions provide evocative representations of transformations of gender systems, social orders, and political ideologies. But comparing illustrations of the dress of a couple in 1750 with illustrations of the dress of their great-grandchildren a century later can tell us only so much about the multiple ways in which fashion informed identities and daily lives and the powerful ways in which fashion, gender systems, and social and economic practices were mutually constructed. When dress is reduced to illustration, and treated as a mere "reflection" of larger social and cultural transformations, it tells us little that we could not discover from a variety of other cultural artifacts, ranging from medical encyclopedias, prescriptive literature, and political treatises to novels.

In this study I will focus less on men's and women's clothing styles and how they diverged in the latter eighteenth century than on how men's and women's relationship to fashion itself – to commercial culture, the production of commodities, and to matters of aesthetics and taste – was transformed over the course of the eighteenth century, as the production and consumption of clothing were increasingly conceptualized as feminine/effeminate and *la mode* was conceived as a female goddess. This transformation stood at the heart of a major re-evaluation of what clothing and adornment meant in early-modern French culture and partici-pated in the construction of what historian Daniel Roche has termed a new "culture of appearances."[7] In the seventeenth century, the culture of fashion was predicated on a simple elite/popular distinction, whereby fashion was a realm in which only the aristocracy could participate. In a society of orders, aristocrats displayed their rank and position through luxury consumption and the king and his court stood at the pinnacle of the fashion culture. The new fashion system which arose in eight-eenth century added to the older elite/popular polarity three new assumptions: first, that women are essentially more interested than men in fashion; second, fashion is inherently frivolous, belonging to the world of the decorative rather than the fine arts or practical sciences; and third, good taste, rather than ostentatious luxury, should determine what people wear. In addition, the seventeenth-century common-place that fashion particularly obsessed the French people was elaborated into a new discourse that hailed Paris as the fertile center from which all fashions are born

An examination of how these axioms of the modern fashion system were constructed in the eighteenth century will require an investigation of changing understandings of masculinity and femininity, the nature of commercial culture, and the power of material objects to mark social standing and express subjectivi-ties. My subjects will be a diverse group of men and women ranging from kings and royal mistresses, to dressmakers and fashion retailers, to journalists and philosophes who used an existing cultural repertoire of ideas about women, commerce, and fashion to help shape a new model of femininity, a new national identity, and new aesthetic and moral distinctions between art and craft, taste and luxury, timeless virtues and modish frivolities.

Part I, "*La Cour*: Absolutism and Appearance," focuses on the aristocratic culture of fashion that existed in France between the 1670s and 1715. Chapter 1, "Courting *La Mode* and Costuming the French," examines the construction of a court-based, fashion system during the reign of Louis XIV and the relationship between this fashion culture and Louis's mercantilist and absolutist ambitions. The chapter relies on the *Mercure galant*, one of the first journals to report on fashion, to explore how this courtly fashion culture was both disseminated to and resisted by a public of merchants and elite consumers. Chapter 2, "Objects of Desire, Subjects of the King," elaborates on Chapter 1's broad discussion of fashion and court culture by examining the attitudes of Louis's sister-in-law, Elisabeth Char-lotte, toward clothing, particularly focusing on her effort to resolve the tension between court and commercial culture and between legitimate and illegitimate sexuality.

Part II, "*La Ville*: Clothing and Consumption in a Society of Taste," moves from Versailles to Paris, exploring the ways in which the burgeoning commercial culture of eighteenth-century Paris shaped a new culture of fashion, particularly focusing on the ways in which a new dynamic of gender and class hierarchies shaped production and consumption. Chapter 3, "A Natural Right to Dress Women," explores the ways in which clothing production was shaped by rivalries between male and female fashion workers, particularly focusing on seamstresses, linen drapers, ladies' hairdressers and fashion merchants. Chapter 4, "The Problem of French Taste," focuses on the ways in which new distinctions between art and craft, artists and artisans, and male and female capacities for taste and genius shaped practices and discourses of production and consumption of fashions. Chapter 5, "*Coquettes* and *Grisettes*," takes up the topic of consumption, examining the perceived dangers posed for (and by) female buyers and sellers in bustling cities such as Paris. In this chapter I argue for the centrality of the *marchande de mode* to the new commercial culture as fashion merchants par excellence and the proto-type of the modern, urban woman. Finally, Chapter 6, "Selling *La Mode*," discusses the role that the fashion press played in the construction of new ideas about femininity and fashion in the 1780s and early 1790s. Together these chapters chart a general movement from the *la cour* to *la ville*, from a court-based, aristocratic fashion culture in which costume was an outward mark of rank to a more inclusive fashion culture in which clothing expressed a range of new subjectivities, including new attitudes toward femininity and novelty.

From the shop floors of Paris to the ballrooms of Versailles, I have tried in this project to listen to men and women in Old Regime France discussing the meaning of *la mode*. I have found that there was as much dissonance as agreement and no single, unified narrative as French men and women crafted a "new regime of looks" in the eighteenth century. Although by the eve of the French Revolution a new hegemonic discourse on fashion, frivolity, and femininity had emerged that clearly supported the economic, aesthetic and political requirements of the new, Enlightened "society of taste," many practical and theoretical issues regarding the relationship of gender, markets, and *la mode* remained unresolved. The gendered commercial culture of fashion that had emerged by the late eighteenth century established the foundations for nineteenth-century commercial culture and dom-estic ideology, but many men and women – producers as well as consumers – wore their modernity (sartorial and otherwise) uneasily. Thus, to capture the complex reality of Old Regime fashion culture requires acknowledging that by the late eighteenth century *la mode* was clearly sexed, and grounded in women's nature, and that ultimately there could be no final word on so fickle a goddess. From the seventeenth-century court to the eighteenth-century city, *la mode* may have maddened and perplexed contemporaries, but it is precisely her unstable, roving, and slippery nature that makes her so useful for historians, forcing us to hound her from the realm of politics, to economics, to the arts as we try to pin her down to expose the flagrant artifice of her gendered nature.

Notes

1. James Rutledge, *Essai sur le caractère et les moeurs des François* (London, 1776): 165. All translations from French to English in the book are my own unless otherwise indicated.
2. Mary Wollstonecraft, *Vindication of the Rights of Woman* (London, Penguin, 1985 [1792]): 310.
3. Ibid., 111.
4. Ibid., 309.
5. John Carl Flugel, *The Psychology of Clothes* (London: Hogarth Press, 1950 [1930]). For an insightful discussion on the social and political history of men's clothing in early-modern England, see David Kuchta, *The Three-Piece Suit and Modern Masculinity: England, 1550–1850* (Berkeley: University of California Press, 2002). On the biology of incommensurability, see Thomas Laqueur, *Making Sex: Body and Gender from the Greeks to Freud.* Cambridge, MA: Harvard University Press, 1990.
6. On nineteenth-century French fashion, see Philippe Perrot, *Fashioning the Bourgeoisie: A History of Clothing in the Nineteenth Century* (Princeton: Princeton University Press, 1994).
7. Daniel Roche, *The Culture of Clothing: Dress and Fashion in the Ancien Regime* (Cambridge: Cambridge University Press, 1994); originally published as *La culture des apparences* (Paris: Fayard, 1989).

Part I
La Cour: Absolutism and Appearance

Louis XIV devoted much of his long reign (1654–1715) to harnessing the artifice, the inconstancy, and the Frenchness of *la mode* as he strove to extend his power – politically, economically, and culturally – throughout France and across Europe. He did so by asserting a distinctively French style, by deploying the artifice of fashion for the purpose of court spectacles, and by disciplining fickle fashion into a fixed court costume as he attempted to yoke the theatricality of fashion to the theater of absolutism. In this performance, to be sure, there were different roles and costumes for men and women and *la mode* was presented as a female deity, the "mother of change," and "daughter of inconstancy." Grammatically, *la mode* was gendered female, yet the social and political meanings of men's and women's costumes in elite society were more similar than different and the logic of *la mode* was relatively "gender neutral" compared with later eighteenth-century thought: in the seventeenth century, *la mode* had not yet been saturated by sex and fixed by femininity.[1] The gendered nature of clothing and fashion was of much less concern to Louis XIV than marking distinctions between privileged orders, fostering solidarity among the French aristocracy, and instilling desire throughout Europe for French commerce, culture and clothing as he attempted to harness a protean *mode* to the mercantilist and iconic interests of the centralizing, absolutist state.

Louis XIV's concern to control the etiquette of court dress and costume was deeply connected to his theatrical understanding of kingship. As studies of court culture remind us, French absolutism was a theater-state in which Versailles was the stage and Louis the playwright and principal player. The royal drama of absolutism was enacted daily through rituals, courtly etiquette, and architecture and staged for the French people at large through public statuary, royal entries, and royal gazettes.[2] Historian Joseph Klaits has written that, "As a virtuoso performer in the elaborate piece of baroque stagecraft that was his reign, he [Louis] wanted Europe to believe that he also had composed the script, built the set, designed the costumes, and directed the action. By identifying himself totally with his role of monarch, Louis gave dynamic life to absolutist ideology."[3] In the past two decades, scholarship on absolutism has focused on the importance of court rituals, cere-monies, statues and paintings in the creation of Louis's iconic image as father-king and absolute monarch.[4] As such, this scholarship highlights the role of symbolism, theatricality, and spectacle in early-modern politics and suggests that blurring the line between signified and signifier stood at the heart of the ideology and practice of absolutism.[5]

In the *ancien régime* power and the symbols of power had a very different relationship to one another than they do in modern democratic societies in which sovereignty is located in the nation, rather than in the body of a king. Ballets staged at court, in addition to battles staged in the Netherlands, enacted royal power; courtiers masquerading as Turkish sultans at court balls proclaimed Louis's imperial designs as surely as did French merchant fleets in the Mediterranean; and wigs and golden brocade supplemented ancient titles as markers of one's rank in the court hierarchy. Political power was predicated, to be sure, on noble birth, landed wealth, and purchased offices, but it was based as well on an economy of visual, iconic display. In a political culture centered on Versailles, politics became a hall of mirrors, a world in which he or she who stood physically closest to the king, holding up the mirror which reflected his image, shone by association; in the political culture of the Sun King, Louis's power shone more brightly the more Versailles, and France at large, mirrored his radiance. As the social critic Montesquieu observed, "The magnificence and splendor which surround kings form part of their power."[6]

Courtly sartorial splendor was not only indispensable to Louis's self-representation as king, but also to his attempt to extend his power by creating an aristocracy dependent on the crown and court. As the duc de Saint-Simon famously observed,

> [Louis] loved above all splendor, magnificence, profusion. This taste he turned into a political maxim, and inspired his whole court to adopt it. It was to please him that one had to throw oneself into gambling, into clothes, into carriages, into buildings and gaming. These were the occasions when he spoke to people. The result was that he tried and succeeded to squeeze the whole world into putting luxury as a point of honor, and for some parties a necessity, and so little by little reduced society to depend entirely upon his favors to survive.[7]

Mandating a culture of clothing at Versailles based on the sartorial display of power and rank not only helped Louis control the aristocracy by literally encasing their bodies in yards of silk, gold brocade, and silver trimmings, but was also an explicit part of his program to extend his royal glory and French civilization throughout Europe. Bolstering French textile and lace making industries, forbidding his courtiers to wear foreign fashions and imported textiles, and dispatching fashion mannequins from the French court to disseminate French fashions throughout the courts of Europe were central to building not only a mercantilist, but also an absolutist French state. Both for contemporaries, such as the duc de Saint-Simon, and for modern costume historians, Louis XIV occupies center stage in discussions of French fashions, with fashion either being set by Louis himself or seemingly changing each time he bedded a new woman, with robes "à la Montespan" giving way to hair ribbons "à la Fontanges." Yet, the dazzling reflection of diamonds and gold and silver brocade encasing the king's body may blind us to the fact that not only did the king possess "two bodies," but there were private bodies filled with personal desires beneath the stage costumes of courtiers as well.[8] Focusing exclusively on the glittering iconic economy at Versailles obscures the commercial economy growing within the absolutist state. Although an absolutist monarch could "decree" court costume, Louis was less successful in marshaling an elusive and capricious *mode*.

Recent scholarship argues that absolutism was never as absolute as its image suggested.[9] A historical approach which focuses on the "virtuoso" soliloquy of the king not only ignores the protests of the audience and the rumblings backstage, but also risks blinding us to the female actors who played supporting roles on the stage of absolutism.[10] Just as *la mode* might slip from Louis's grasp, following instead a commercial logic at odds with absolutist and mercantilist imperatives, so too, within a political system that firmly excluded women from legitimate political rule through the Salic law, illegitimate channels of female sexuality nevertheless created politically privileged positions for women at court.[11] The options were restricted and the stakes high, but women at court nevertheless negotiated within Louis's economy of visual display and his politics of absolutism; the power of the male absolutist gaze, seemingly so lofty, fixed and autonomous, was fundamentally predicated on the female subject's willingness to dance, occasionally improvising, around the king. In this courtly dance, illegitimate liaisons might procure certain women riches, titles, or even the status of "official mistress."

From Mme de Montespan and Mme de Maintenon in the seventeenth century to Mme de Pompadour and Mme du Barry in the eighteenth, the "official mistress" to the king played a prominent role in the political culture of absolutism and in the iconic world of court: as sartorial, sexual, and state power conjoined, the official mistress of the king became unofficial mistress of *la mode* as well. The role of mistress was so central to the politics of absolutism that when Louis XVI chose to rule without the services of a mistress, his wife, Marie Antoinette, was forced to fill the void, becoming in the popular imagination both queen and mistress, and thereby threateningly joining, as only the male monarch should, both reproductive and sexual power. Her expenditures on dresses became evidence of her excessive sexuality, while her trouble conceiving a royal heir signaled, in popular imagination, the trouble that loomed at court when the male monarch's gaze grew weak and myopic.[12]

While Marie Antoinette suffered from her perceived dual reproductive and sexual roles as wife and "mistress" to the king, from Henri IV ("the Vert Galant") onward, the power of the male monarch rested at the apex of two iconic systems, two "economies" – one of reproduction, another of sexuality. By his dual potency the king distinguished himself from ordinary fathers, whose sexual and reproduct-ive rights were restricted, at least in theory, to their own wives, and became the father above all fathers, the all-powerful father-king.[13] But while the father-king's power was expressed, in part, by his ready sexual access to the women at court, could he ever make *la mode* his mistress? Could he wed an absolutist economy of visual display to the flux and flow of France's commercial economy? In theory, as Louis's former mistress, Mme de Montespan, was keenly aware, the king might simultaneously yoke both women and *la mode* to his absolutist and mercantilist politics. Montespan knowingly remarked when she introduced the beautiful Mlle de Fontanges to Louis, "She comes from the provinces, just like silk, silver, and gold."[14] Yet, just as an absolutist polity predicated on highly regulated reproductive roles for wives also contained an alternate sub-economy based on extramarital sexuality, so too the *ancien régime* mercantilist economy predicated on a highly-regulated production and consumption of clothing and textiles contained as well the less predictable aesthetic impulses, libidinal drives, and economic fluctuations of *la mode*. At the very heart of the absolutist system they supported and contra-dicted, women and fashion proved irresistible to the absolutist gaze; yet ultimately neither women nor the commercial economy could ever be completely ordered and controlled by the iconic vision of masculine power and absolutist politics.

Both the coverage of fashion in *Le Mercure galant* and the private letters of the king's sister-in-law, Elisabeth Charlotte, duchess d'Orléans, reveal the ways in which aristocratic women participated in the construction of French fashion culture, and the ways in which the burgeoning French commercial economy played a part in the theater of absolutism, the world of court, and the lives of aristocratic women. Despite Louis XIV's vision of a court fashion culture based exclusively on masculine, royal control, a more complicated mix of gender, class, absolutism and commerce shaped the distinctive court culture of fashion that emerged between the 1670s and 1720s. The relationship of aristocratic women at court to costume and dress marked the enduring ideological power of Louis's sartorial system and the cracks and fissures that were already, in the late seventeenth century, beginning to mar the glittering surface of the Old Regime of looks and to foreshadow a new fashion culture in which femininity would eclipse absolutism as the ruling principle.

Notes

1. On the phrase and concept "saturated by sex," see Denise Riley, *"Am I That Name?" Feminism and the Category of "Women" in History* (Minneapolis: University of Minnesota Press, 1989).
2. The most influential study of the ceremony of theater-states remains Clifford Geertz, *Negara: The Theater State in Nineteenth-Century Bali* (Princeton: Princeton University Press, 1980). Guy Debord's theoretical treatment of "society of the spectacle" may also be applied to Louis XIV's Versailles. See Guy Debord, *La société du spectacle* (Paris: Champ libres, 1967).
3. Joseph Klaits, *Printed Propaganda under Louis XIV: Absolute Monarchy and Public Opinion* (Princeton: Princeton University Press, 1976): 13.
4. See Louis Marin, *Le portrait du roi.* (Paris: Minuit, 1981); Jean-Marie Apostiolidès, *Le roi-machine: Spectacle et politique au temps de Louis XIV* (Paris: Minuit, 1981); Peter Burke, *The Fabrication of Louis XIV* (New Haven: Yale University Press, 1992).
5. On the connection between absolutist politics and theatricality, see Paul Friedland, "Parallel States: Theatrical and Political Representation in Early Modern and Revolutionary France," in *The Age of Cultural Revolutions: Britain and France, 1750–1829*, ed. Colin Jones and Dror Wahrman (Berkeley: University of California Press, 2002) and Paul Friedland, *Political Actors: Representative Bodies and Theatricality in the Age of the French Revolution* (Ithaca: Cornell University Press, 2002). On the relationship between the theater, theatricality and French culture in the old regime, see Jeffrey S. Ravel, *The Contested Parterre: Public Theater and French Political Culture, 1680–1791* (Ithaca: Cornell University Press, 1999).
6. Charles de Montesquieu, *De l'esprit des lois*, ed. J. Berthe de la Gressaye (Paris: Les belles-lettres, 1950): t. 1: 108. See Joan Landes, *Women and the Public Sphere in the Age of the French Revolution* (Ithaca: Cornell University Press, 1988) for a discussion of the iconic or visual structure of the absolutist public sphere. Recently, Landes has revised her earlier arguments in *Women and the Public Sphere* by underscoring the continuing importance of visual culture into the Revolutionary period. See *Visualizing the Nation: Gender, Representation, and Revolution in Eighteenth-Century France* (Ithaca: Cornell University Press, 2001).
7. Saint-Simon, quoted in Diana de Marly, *Louis XIV and Versailles* (New York: Holmes and Meier, 1987): 38–9. On Saint-Simon's presentation of hierarchy and etiquette at court, see Emmanuel Le Roy Ladurie, *Saint-Simon and the Court of Louis XIV* (Chicago: University of Chicago Press, 2001).
8. On the metaphor of the "king's two bodies" in medieval and early-modern political thought, see the classic study by Ernst Kantorowicz, *The King's Two*

Bodies: A Study in Medieval Political Theology (Princeton: Princeton University Press, 1957). For a compelling critique of Kantorowicz that focuses on the queen's body and nuptial imagery, see Abby Zanger, *Scenes from the Marriage of Louis XIV: Nuptial Fictions and the Making of Absolutist Power* (Stanford: Stanford University Press, 1997). For a rich collection of essays on the politics of the royal body, see Sara E. Melzer and Kathryn Norberg eds. *From the Royal to the Republican Body: Incorporating the Political in Seventeenth- and Eighteenth-Century France* (Berkeley: University of California Press, 1998).

9. See William Beik, *Absolutism and Society in Seventeenth-Century France: State Power and Provincial Aristocracy in Languedoc* (Cambridge: Cambridge University Press, 1985) and Jay Smith, *The Culture of Merit: Nobility, Royal Service, and the Making of Absolute Monarchy in France, 1600–1789* (Ann Arbor: University of Michigan Press, 1996).

10. In *The Fabrication of Louis XIV* Peter Burke offers a careful study of the popular reception of and dissatisfaction with Louis's royal image in the latter years of his reign. On opponents of Louis XIV, see Lionel Rothkrug, *The Opposition to Louis XIV* (Princeton: Princeton University Press, 1965).

11. Illegitimate sexuality also created privileged positions for men at court. See the example of Monsieur, the king's brother, and his male favorites. For an important study of the impact on the Salic law on women's rule, see Sarah Hanley, "The Monarchic State in Early Modern France: Marital Regime Government and Male Right," in *Politics, Ideology and the Law in Early Modern Europe*, ed. Adrianna E. Bakos (Rochester: University of Rochester Press, 1994).

12. On images of Mme de Pompadour, see Colin Jones, *Madame de Pompadour: Images of Mistress* (London: National Gallery, 2002). On Marie Antoinette as the "bad queen" see Lynn Hunt, *The Family Romance of the French Revolution* (Berkeley: University of California Press, 1992), Jacques Revel, "Marie Antoinette in Her Fictions: The Staging of Hatred," in *Fictions of the French Revolution*, ed. Bernadette Fort (Evanston, Ill.: Northwestern University Press, 1991), and Chantal Thomas, *La reine scélérate: Marie-Antoinette dans les pamphlets* (Paris: Seuil, 1990).

13. On the power of Louis's sexual and masculine body, see Abby Zanger, "Lim(b)inal Images: 'Betwixt and Between' Louis XIV's Martial and Marital Bodies," and Thomas Kaiser, "Louis *le Bien-Aimé* and the Rhetoric of the Royal Body," in *From the Royal to the Republican Body*, ed. Melzer and Norberg.

14. Françoise Athénaïs de Rochechouart, Marquise de Montespan, *Memoirs of Madame la Marquise de Montespan* (Boston: L.C. Page and Co., 1899): vol. 2, 91.

–1–

Courting *La Mode* and Costuming the French

In the late seventeenth century, Antoine Furetière's *Dictionnaire universel* succinctly defined *la mode* as "the manner of dressing that follows the received usage at court."[1] Yet, the clarity of Furetière's dictionary entry obscures the difficulty with which monarchs such as Louis XIV courted *la mode* and reigned over appearance. For much of the seventeenth century French men and women had not yet resolved if fashion was an orderly goddess of civility whose mantle spread prosperity throughout France or a masked harlot whose carnivalesque tricks deceived individuals, corrupted society, and threatened the order of commerce and the state. A moderate group of writers on fashion, including François de La Mothe Le Vayer in his *Opuscules* (1643), Nicolas Faret in *L'honnête homme ou l'art de plaire à la cour* (1633), Jacques Du Bosc in *L'honnête femme* (1632), and Donneau de Visé, editor of *Le Mercure galant* (1672), stressed the moral acceptability of fashionable clothing and adornment.[2] Yet, at the beginning of Louis's reign, the fierce diatribes of *frondeur* pamphlets still echoed, not only denouncing king and court, but also attacking *la mode*. M. de Fitelieu's tract, *La contre-mode* (1642), denounced fashion as "a tavern wench, the drunken invention of a tramp . . . a loose chicken-skinned whore, who hides her lowly birth by destroying the minds she captures," and went on to claim, "Lift *la mode's* masque and we will see that she is a hideous monster, a disorder without equal, and an abuse worthy of tears. It is impossible to depict her face because it is so plastered with make-up and covered with beauty marks that I cannot tell whether it is a human or a beast."[3]

For critics of fashion such as M. de Fitelieu and François de Grenaille, author of *La mode* (1642), sex and gender lay at the heart of the reign of *la mode*, with the legacy of original sin explaining why men and women followed fashions.[4] Grenaille, historian to the duc D'Orléans, explained that ever since the Fall men and women had chased after any new fashion that caught their eye. God himself had instilled this desire for novelty and restlessness in humankind, "so that he might teach us that we will never find peace outside of his Immutable Joy."[5] Thus, for Grenaille, original sin was the cause of human inconstancy and God called into being the fickle goddess *la mode* to keep men and women searching for, but never finding, perfection in the material world of the senses. For Grenaille, the effect of the Fall – the reign of *la mode* – was particularly embodied in women; just as a woman, Eve, had caused the fall of Adam, so too, women daily perpetuated humankind's vain desire for fashions through their peculiarly feminine taste for variety and novelty. As Grenaille asserted, *"La mode* for women is truly a disease, but only a simple passion for men. We may appreciate the latest vogue, but for women it becomes their idol."[6]

Like Grenaille, Fitelieu believed that women were more susceptible to the temptations of fashion than men, explaining that women "ordinarily apply themselves to nothing, and their highest achievement stops at make-up."[7] Fitelieu did not, however, attribute women's interest in adornment solely to their frivolity but, more damningly, to their evil desire to deceive.[8] Like Grenaille, Fitelieu traced the connection between women and *la mode* back to the Fall. However, Fitelieu claimed that the legacy of the Fall was women's proclivity for artifice and deception.[9] Clothing was a particularly dangerous source of artifice, a tool of Satan that could only render one's life a "perpetual disguise."[10]

The crux of the problem of fashion for Fitelieu was that people attempted to use adornment to deceive rather than imitating nature. Fitelieu was especially worried that the appearance of a fashion (*paraître*) might be mistaken for the wearer's being (*être*).[11] Fashions, he argued, not only made women look impure but also actually made them into whores. But Fitelieu was even more concerned about a slippage between appearance and essence for men. He warned that young nobles who paraded about in foppish fashions, make-up, patches and powder weakened the military.[12] For Fitelieu, elaborately dressed and powdered men were "femmes déguisées," who with "the dress of a woman on their back, are more suited to the distaff than the sword."[13] According to Fitelieu, women's love of fashion might be endured since their frivolity and susceptibility to Satan's ruses made them by nature more vulnerable to the lure of vanity; but men's virility demanded plain, stable, "natural" clothing that clearly revealed that those wearing it were men.[14]

Not only was fashion artificial and deceptive, for many early-modern writers it was utterly protean and indefinable. As Fitelieu explained, "One must go to imaginary places or to the conclave of the moon to understand what *la mode* is: she is not a material substance because her being consists only in a feeble imagination . . . and all the philosophers together don't know how to define her."[15] The discussion of *la mode* in pamphlets, verse, and treatises suggests that French men and women of the seventeenth century did not simply define fashion differently from modern dictionaries, but that they were fundamentally undecided whether fashion could be defined, or whether it was hopelessly elusive. Even those who celebrated fashion reveled in its capricious whimsy. Rather than following a predictable, patterned, cyclical, or linear change, *la mode* was seen as utterly protean, enigmatic, bizarre, ungovernable, and ultimately beyond human control.[16] Literary historian Louise Godard de Donville interprets the early-seventeenth-century discourse on fashion's preoccupation with the protean nature of fashion as part of a "baroque" fascination with change and instability. Donville claims that clothing styles during the reign of Louis XIII did not, in fact, change rapidly, but that there was a great deal of diversity in dress. Contemporaries conflated this diversity with novelty; thus, Donville writes, "contemporary descriptions teach us less about clothing fashions than about the major ideas of the époque."[17]

As Donville points out, many of the seventeenth-century pamphlets and poems on fashion were written by disaffected "anti-courtiers," and reflect the central motifs and concerns of baroque literature. Yet, the troubling vision of a protean *mode* elicited comment from a variety of observers in addition to aristocrats critical of court and elite poets caught up in "the spirit of the baroque." Common trades-men and humble merchants, who may have expected that their wives would continue to wear the bonnets, scarves and aprons which they had brought to the marriage as part of their trousseau, confronted the troubling visage of *la mode* in their wives' desires for at least a few items from the unending stream of new styles of fabric and lace appearing daily in the mercers' stalls lining the streets of Paris. Mercers, in turn, confronted with stores full of gloves, fans, and trinkets that they could not sell because fashion had suddenly changed, puzzled over the vicissitudes of *la mode*. As Fitelieu fretted, a Circe-like *mode* upset the social hierarchy and empowered "the humblest cobbler to enslave the most honest man by his caprice."[18] Steeped in the baroque discourse of instability and artifice, the discourse on fashion expressed a persistent anxiety in early-modern France, not only with court culture, but also with the impact of enigmatic and deceptive *mode* more broadly in the emerging commercial culture of Paris.

Although this deceptive goddess unsettled gender, class, and political relations and identities, even her harshest critics were clear that she could not be banished from the kingdom altogether; for *la mode* was not simply a deity, she was a French deity. And although her empire had a particularly strong hold over women, her empire extended over all the French. A poem written in 1604 described the fickle-ness of fashion as a distinctly French quality:

> *La mode* in her perfect essence
> Is the daughter of Inconstancy,
> True sister of the present time. . .
> Brusque, motley and roving,
> In France more than in any place on earth.[19]

Another early-seventeenth-century pamphlet, *Le discours nouveau sur la mode*, echoed the sentiment that *la mode* was not only feminine and whimsical, but also French:

> I am only too well known by mortals. . .
> I am (as you say) of the divine essence,

Figure 3 *Louis as Apollo, ballet "La Nuit,"* courtesy of RMN.

Mother of change, and daughter of Inconstancy.
Jupiter, Mars, Apollo, and the rest of the gods
Who have commanded from within the circle of the skies
Don't have as much power in this round earth.
Certainly I have a restless humor. . .
I make all the humans fall under my laws,

But the French above all the rest love to change.
In their common language they call me *La mode*.[20]

Although Louis XIV never fully accepted fashion's imperious drive for novelty, throughout his long reign he attempted to capitalize on both the Frenchness of fashion and its theatricality. His strategy, at least in the first two decades of his reign, was to rule with *éclat* through sartorial splendor, in explicit contrast to the sobriety of Spanish court dress. As Peter Burke has observed in his study of Louis's public image, *éclat* was one of the key words of the seventeenth century, "with meanings ranging from a 'flash' of lightning to a 'clap' of thunder, but always referring to something unexpected and impressive. Magnificence was considered to be impressive, in the literal sense of leaving an 'impression' on the viewer like a stamp on a piece of wax."[21] Whether Louis dressed as Apollo in court ballets, a Roman emperor in the Grand Carrousel of 1662, a Hungarian at a court masquerade (1666), or reviewed his troops in military uniform, costumes permitted him and his courtiers to imagine and enact their fantasies of power. Fantasies of male virility and conquest, dreams of the consumption of exotica, and visions of Versailles's hegemony as the center of the world were all enacted both by appropriating foreign styles and by exporting French court costume. Exotic consumption, imperial hegemony and the absolutist gaze all came together in the sartorial splendor of Versailles. By the 1660s Louis's sartorial vision, created with the help of royal theater costume designers Henri Gissey and Jean Berain, and disseminated through the "missionary" work of French tailors, mercers and seamstresses, had imprinted a distinctly French look on court societies across Europe and a distinctly French character on *la mode*.

Clothing the Courtier

The first obligation of any man or woman upon arriving at court was literally to be made over through clothing into a proper French courtier. In 1671, when Philippe d'Orléans (1640–1701), the king's brother, married the German princess Elisabeth Charlotte, special French clothes, including a white wedding gown, had to be made for Elisabeth Charlotte in order to transform her into a properly French member of the royal court. In her study of Elisabeth Charlotte's correspondence, Elborg Forster relates that during the princess's journey to France, her chaperone, the Princess Palatine, made a shocking discovery: the bride had only six shifts and six nightgowns. This, she informed the Palatine *chargé d'affaires* in France, must be remedied immediately, lest it become known through the bride's chambermaids or other French attendants, and Madame be made the laughing stock of the French court. Three to four thousand *livres*, she said in her urgent message, would purchase everything needed.[22]

The proper costume was not only necessary to "make" a French aristocrat, but to "mark" one as well. Thirty years later, in 1698, when her own daughter left the French court to marry the Duke of Lorraine, Elisabeth Charlotte wrote proudly to her aunt Sophie, "I don't think the Duke of Lorraine will consider my daughter ill-provided for; she has twenty thousand crowns' worth of linen, and great quantities of laces and embroidery. It is all very handsome and fills four huge chests."[23] Before leaving France, Elisabeth Charlotte's and Monsieur's daughter's trousseau was publicly displayed in Monsieur's gallery so that visitors could admire the fifteen lavishly embroidered dresses, two of which were so heavily decorated with gold that Elisabeth Charlotte worried her daughter would be unable to wear them.[24] Monsieur clearly delighted in the splendor of his daughter's trousseau as much as did her mother. At the court of Louis XIV there was no better way for a nobleman to show off than to display his daughter's trousseau. Clothing was, under Louis's regime, first and foremost a marker of privilege and social hierarchy.

Court costume and absolutist court culture came of age together during the reign of Louis XIV. In the early years of Louis's reign the court was small and itinerant; several hundred courtiers moved with the king and the royal family as they periodically traveled from the Louvre in Paris to royal chateaux at Fontaine-bleau, Marly, Saint-Germain, or Compiègne, to the Orléans family estate at Saint Cloud, or to the hunting lodge at Versailles. As Louis extended his control over the French aristocracy and the French state, the number of courtiers and bureaucrats at court increased considerably. By the time the court took up permanent residence at Versailles in 1682 it is estimated that more than 15,000 men and women lived and worked there. In addition to the royal family, the princes of the blood, the dukes and peers, foreign princes such as the dukes of Lorraine, Savoy, Mantua and Rohan, the highest military officers and great officers of the state, and hundreds of ordinary courtiers, artists, valets, lackeys, ladies-in-waiting, Swiss and French guards, and other servants also made their home at Versailles.

In the first decade of Louis's personal rule (1661–70) there was no official court costume; the fashions worn at court were merely sumptuous variations of the elite dress of the mid seventeenth century. In the 1660s the dominant style for men was full petticoat breeches or "Rhinegraves," a kilt-like culotte skirt ornamented with vast quantities of ruffles, lace and colored ribbons. Petticoat breeches extended anywhere from mid-thigh to mid-calf and were worn with *canons*, tubes of white linen with lace ruffles and bows tied around the knees. On top men wore a short doublet (similar to a modern bolero jacket) with sleeves extending to the elbow. The doublet was often left unbuttoned, revealing a full-cut silk or linen shirt beneath and ruffled sleeves. The large lace collar of the shirt was tied in front, creating the tie-like *rabat*. Some men wore a longer jacket (*cassock*) similar to the leather military cassocks of the early seventeenth century. By the 1660s men had begun to wear wigs instead of long hair and wore hats with a low crown and a wide brim edged with plumes and ribbons. Men's shoes had high heels (with red heels for all noblemen) and square toes. Boots, commonly worn in the earlier seventeenth century, were now reserved exclusively for riding and hunting.

Until the second half of the seventeenth century the main form of elite female dress was a two-piece dress ensemble that comprised a skirt and a boned bodice. The skirt (*jupe de dessus* or *manteau*) fell to the floor and ended in a train, the length of which signified the woman's social station. An underskirt (*robe du dessous*), often of taffeta, was worn beneath the skirt. This was worn without hoops, but over full petticoats. The skirt could be split and drawn back on each side of the hips better to reveal the underskirt beneath. The top part of the dress, the bodice (*le corsage*), was either sleeveless or had short sleeves that ended before the elbow in rows of lace. The bodice had a low, oval neckline and lace or muslin draped around the neckline formed a bow in the middle. A blouse (*la chemise*) often peeked out from under the dress at the neckline and sleeve. On formal occasions women's natural hair was loosely curled at the back and tightly curled around the face. At home and on informal occasions women wore small lace caps. Outdoors and while riding and traveling, women wore broad hats similar to men's. Loose hoods, kerchiefs, and hooded cloaks were worn at night and in bad weather. At court women wore heavy make-up, including foundation, rouge, and beauty patches.

Bows, ribbons, and lace were the most important ornaments for both men and women. An elegantly dressed person, whether male or female, often used as much as 300 yards of ribbon on all parts of dress, including the hair. By the 1670s and 1680s trimmings became even more ornate; *falbalas* (in English, furbelows) referred to any decorations of court costume ranging from flounces, tassels, fringe and lace, to braid and heavy embroidery. Between 1685 and 1690 greater amounts of gold and silver brocade were used to decorate costly satins and velvets for both men and women. Although both men and women in the 1650s and 1660s had favored bold colors such as yellow and shades of red, ranging from cherry to scarlet to flame (*couleur de feu*), after 1670, these gave way to darker, more subdued colors, stripes and floral prints.

A classic work of fashion history aptly describes the transformation of fashion during Louis's reign: "The long personal reign of Louis XIV opened with men dressed as beribboned birds of plumage and closed with them having the look of heavily upholstered furniture, whereas women started the reign as youthful maidens and ended it as forbidding matrons."[25] During the decade of the 1670s, the pious Madame de Maintenon, governess to Louis's illegitimate children, and later his second wife, ushered in a more solemn style of court dress. In the 1670s as court costume became more formal, elite women began to experiment with wearing a new, one-piece dress called the mantua (*mantos*) for less formal occasions in town and at court. The mantua was a simpler and more comfortable style of casual dress (*déshabillés*) than the formal two-piece skirt and bodice. Mantuas wrapped in front like a dressing gown or kimono and were fastened by a sash. Often the sides of the dress were drawn up to display the underskirt beneath. In contrast to formal court attire, mantuas were not rigidly boned and required only a small corset underneath to shape the silhouette. Some women used a stomacher to conceal the front of the corset and some wore aprons. The new printed calicoes (*indiennes*) introduced during the 1680s and 1690s were especially suited to these lighter garments, especially for summer wear. Although originally worn only at home, by the final third of the seventeenth century the mantua became popular among elite women in Paris and was worn for a variety of informal occasions. As Clare Crowston argues in her important re-evaluation of the birth of the mantua, it opened in "a new conceptual and visual terrain in which women could experiment with self-presentation in ways that challenged traditional social hierarchies."[26] And, as we will see in Chapter 2, the mantua would provoke considerable censure at court for blurring the boundaries between formal and informal attire.

During Louis's reign significant changes transformed men's as well as women's fashions. In the 1670s, men at the French court inaugurated arguably the most important change in the history of French fashion since the fourteenth century, donning the precursor of the modern three-piece suit. The adoption of the new style of male suit had as much to do with nationality as gender and was sparked by international emulation and national rivalry between the French, British and Spanish over styles of male dress. French and Spanish sartorial rivalry had proceeded hand-in-hand with French and Spanish-Hapsburg rivalry for power since at least the early seventeenth century. In an attempt to counteract French stylistic dominance at court, in 1623 the Spanish monarch Philip IV banned the French styles of huge lace collars, long hair, and slashed and embroidered clothes and imposed a more restrained male style consisting of plain doublets, narrow knee breeches, and a plain white linen collar stiffened with shellac.[27]

The English staged their own rebellion against French fashion in the 1660s. The poet Samuel Butler's *Satire upon our Ridiculous Imitation of the French* (1663) lamented English men's and women's slavish imitation of French styles, while John Evelyn protested against the tyranny of French fashions directly to King Charles II in his 1661 treatise *Tyrannus, or the Mode*: "Would the great Persons of England but owne their Nation, and assert themselves as they ought to do, by making choice of some Virile, and comely Fashion, which should incline to neither extreme, and be constant to it, 'twould prove of infinite more reputation to us, than now there is."[28] Heeding the growing complaints that French fashions imperiled both English virility and the English economy, Charles II decided in 1665 that he and his Queen would forgo French lace and silk and wear only English textiles (with the exception of imported linen and calico). By 1666 Charles II had employed two English tailors, John Allen and William Watts, to devise a more virile, anti-French and anti-

Catholic style. The narrow breeches worn in Spain replaced French petticoat breeches; and, for the sake of "Protestant" modesty, the doublet or undervest and the outer coat were both lengthened to the knee to cover the breeches.[29]

Although he railed against the effrontery of the English for banishing French fashions from their court, as early as 1667 Louis XIV donned the new English style of long vest and overcoat. In France this long jacket extending to the knees was called the *justaucorps* or *habit*, and was worn with a vest or sleeveless doublet (*veste*). The jacket was left open to reveal the doublet and shirt, which now sported a knotted tie (*cravate*). Louis and his courtiers persisted in wearing petticoat breeches, however, until around 1678. During these years the Brandenburg great-coat, adapted from the coats worn by Prussian soldiers, became the forerunner of the male overcoat of the next three centuries. The new "modesty" of men's fashions was more than offset, however, by increasingly ornate fabrics and wigs, which grew larger throughout the 1680s until they reached the waist in front and back and rose high on the head. Male courtiers continued to wear rouge and make-up and, by the end of the 1690s, sported powdered wigs.

As art and costume historian Anne Hollander has argued in her important study *Sex and Suits: The Evolution of Modern Dress*, the new male three-piece suit, with its slim, sober line that unified the body, was an important harbinger of sartorial modernity. Although the aesthetic foreshadowed by the late-seventeenth-century suit would not emerge fully in Europe until the neoclassical movement in the arts in the latter eighteenth century, by the late seventeenth century men's fashion already stood at the aesthetic forefront. "Male dress," Hollander argues, "was always essentially more advanced than female throughout fashion history, and tended to lead the way, to set the standard, to make the esthetic propositions to which female fashion responded."[30]

Although Hollander's claim regarding the more "advanced nature" of men's clothing and her contention that the adoption of the three-piece suit marked the beginning of the divergence between the "aesthetic logic" of men's and women's dress are intriguing, they leave unanswered the question of how precisely fashion was "sexed" as feminine in the wake of the adoption of the male suit: if we accept Hollander's conclusions, why was the aesthetic of feminine dress culturally constructed as "traditional" as opposed to "modern"? As I will argue in Chapter 4, we can best understand the "sexing of *la mode*" not by essentializing the logic of masculine and feminine aesthetics, but by examining the social practices and cultural discourses that gendered modern aesthetics. In addition, we should consider that the one-piece mantua adopted by French women in the 1670s shared many of "modern" aesthetic qualities of the three-piece suit. Despite the novelty of the three-piece suit and its important legacy by the nineteenth century in driving a sartorial wedge between men's and women's fashions, we also need to be attentive to the continuing overlap between men's and women's fashions and textiles well into the late eighteenth century. From the point of view of the seventeenth and eighteenth centuries, the growing distinction between fixed costume and changeable fashion, between ceremonial dress and "undress," and between court dress and town dress were as important as the incipient distinction between the aesthetic form of men's suits and women's dresses.[31]

Whether dressed in the restrained English suit or extravagant petticoat breeches, protean *la mode* remained a troubling and uncertain marker of rank and privilege in a society of orders: people might dress above their station; fashions might flagrantly sidestep the privileged absolutist gaze and contradict the king's taste; or vogues for imported fashions and fabrics might hamper the development of the French economy. Throughout the early decades of his reign Louis searched for a way to create an aristocratic sartorial culture that would better serve both his ceremonial politics and his mercantilist economy. In the early 1660s Louis envisioned creating an official court dress that could be bestowed as a reward for those who chose to take up residence at Versailles. An official ordinance of December 29, 1664 granted fifty privileged male courtiers the right to wear the *justaucorps à brevet* (warrant coats), specially tailored blue coats lined with scarlet and embroidered with gold and silver thread. The *justaucorps à brevet* entitled the wearer to a variety of privileges: those who wore the coat were permitted to follow the king on his excursions to Saint-Germain or Versailles without an invitation, and the coat could on certain occasions be substituted for mourning wear at court. Although the duc de Saint-Simon, who lived at court after 1691, claimed that he never saw Louis XIV or his brother wear the *justaucorps à brevet*, the privilege to wear the coat was still so coveted in the 1690s that when the possessor of a coat died it would be quickly transferred to another aristocrat.[32] Men who were not permitted to wear the *justaucorps à brevet* were expected to wear a suit of velvet or better quality fabric while at court. The imposition of the *justaucorps à brevet* was inspired by the desire to use royal authority both to underscore court hierarchy and to consolidate bonds among the aristocracy: court costume worked both to distinguish and to unite.

A similar desire both to create *esprit* and to perpetuate *différence* stood behind the codification of military uniform which took place under Louis (known as the "king of reviews").[33] As part of their effort to organize the French army between the 1660s and 1690s, Louis XIV's great military bureaucrats, Le Tellier and Louvois, helped him devise a more consistent French military uniform which, following the lines of men's contemporary civilian fashions, included an ample broadcloth jacket, a double-breasted vest and knee breeches. By the end of Louis's reign, uniformed soldiers had become perfect iconic embodiments of the success of royal authority and the rigorous discipline of the absolutist gaze; yet well into the eighteenth century, there was still much debate within the army over the best means for provisioning soldiers with uniforms. Although Louis imposed military uniforms, the centralization and bureaucratization of provisioning were far from complete by his death in 1715. The economic reality of clothing a professional army of 100,000 men that swelled to 400,000 in times of war was often at odds with the absolutist goal of uniformity. It was difficult to impose the absolutist vision of perfectly uniformed soldiers on a reality of muddy, frayed jackets, stubborn corporals bent on subverting royal ordinances, and the desire of some regiments to distinguish themselves from others.

If Louis found it difficult to impose order on his soldiers' dress, the clothing of aristocratic women at court proved even more difficult to control. Louis had been willing to tolerate the sartorial idiosyncrasies of his cousin, La Grande Made-moiselle, of his mistresses, and of his sister-in-law, who often wore her hunting jacket to solemn court occasions. But, after 1670, when women began to wear the new style of casual dress, the mantua, at court, Louis decided to take action by creating the *grand habit* and declaring it mandatory for all formal occasions. As the duc de Saint-Simon complained,

> Whether pregnant, ill, less than six weeks after a delivery, and whatever the ferocity of the weather, they had to be in the grand habit, dressed and laced into their corsets, to go to Flanders, or farther still, to dance, to stay up, attend festivities, eat, be gay and good company, change locations, without appearing afraid, nor incommoded by heat, cold, air, dust, and all that precisely on the days and the times directed without disturbing arrangements for so much as a minute.[34]

By the end of the seventeenth century, the *grand habit* was the norm in courts across Europe. Even the Hapsburgs and the English, who had rebelled against French men's court fashions, readily embraced this fashion for women.

Fashion Culture in Print

Louis XIV's absolutist vision of French fashion was disseminated to French elites and foreign courts through a variety of means, ranging from royal portraits to fashion engravings to mannequins dressed in court clothing.[35] Among these, *Le Mercure galant*, the first French journal to report on fashion, was the most import-ant source of information, for contemporaries as well as for modern historians, on the workings of the French "fashion system." As might be expected from a journal patronized by the king, the *Mercure* devoted many pages to describing the fashions of the king and royal family and discussing the impact of royal authority on French fashion.[36] Yet the journal also affords a glimpse of the role of Parisian commercial culture – of the involvement of artisans, merchants, and elite consumers – in the shaping of French fashion culture. In particular, the journal offers detailed informa-tion on how the fashion system operated, providing a view of the ways in which

Figure 4 *Louis XIV et les dames de la cour et de sa famille*, École française, seventeenth century, courtesy of RMN.

elite fashion was shaped by class and gender hierarchies in a culture that had not yet firmly sexed fashion as a feminine pursuit.

Established in 1672 by Jean Donneau de Visé, an author of popular farces and vaudevilles and official royal historian, *Le Mercure galant* covered a variety of light subjects and genres such as book reviews, poems, songs, and court gossip.[37] During its first six years in print the journal appeared only irregularly. Then, in 1678, the journal was renamed *Le nouveau mercure galant* and began to be published monthly. From its first volume in January 1672, the *Mercure* discussed new fashions, presented articles on fashion in the spring and fall of each year, and offered occasional supplements on fashion that included engravings.[38] These articles ranged from brief commentaries to thirty- or forty-page articles describing every detail of the new season's fashions in fabrics, clothing styles and domestic furnishings. The articles on fashion, as well as the rest of the *Mercure*, were addressed to an audience of "gens de qualité," who, as de Visé wrote, "often discuss new fashions, a topic that enters into their conversations as naturally as the cold and the heat, the rain and the fine weather."[39] De Visé presented his articles on fashion in a light, conversational style, addressing them to an imaginary provincial lady who had requested his opinion on the latest styles at Versailles and in Paris. He typically used the conceit of presenting his commentaries as conversations between himself and elite men and women at court, in Parisian salons, or while promenading in the Tuileries.[40]

Ostensibly covering the latest fashions at court, the journal tells us as much about Parisian commercial culture as about political culture at Versailles. In virtually every article on fashion, at least one, if not several, merchants are cited, including the address of their boutiques. In 1674 the journal described a new variety of button which shone as brightly as diamonds, sold only by a merchant in the Palais, "who alone possesses the secret." And October 1678 the *Mercure* informed its readers of a M. Gaultier, who owned a boutique on the rue des Bourdonnois where one could see the season's two new colors of fabric, "paille" and "Prince," along with a third, "whose name he does not yet wish to reveal."[41] These advertisements enabled readers to locate the merchant's shop when visiting Paris, or perhaps to ask friends and relatives in Paris to buy and ship the goods. On occasion the *Mercure* served as a forerunner of the mail-order catalogue, providing detailed information on how to procure the item mentioned. In the issue of August 1689, after describing the vogue for a particular kind of pearl necklace made by the brothers Berthon and Jacquin, and warning readers not to be duped into buying inferior imitations, the journal advised, "Those who do not wish to be tricked should address themselves to the brothers at la rue du Petit-Lion. One can also write to them from the countryside; it is only necessary to send two Louis d'or for each necklace, and to tell if one wishes the pearls to be round or baroque."[42] Although the *Mercure* served the interests of Parisian merchants wishing to advertise their wares, it was not a trade journal and its fashion coverage was aimed primarily at the consumer who desired to acquire specific details on the latest styles. Some provincial readers would in turn pass along this information to their local tailor or seamstress, asking him or her to make them a dress or a suit in the latest style from Paris.

The journal was especially attentive to the colors and designs of new types of fabric and lace used to decorate men and women's clothing. In the special editions focusing exclusively on fashion, the "Extraordinaire," nearly half of the text discussed fabrics and lace. These descriptions are extremely detailed; it was not unusual for a single, new style of lace to require a half-page discussion. Accessories such as gloves, fans, buttons, shoes, jewelry, wigs and hairstyles were also discussed in detail. The journal described a few specific new clothing styles, such as a new cut of skirts, the popularity of the mantua, or the lengthening of the male jacket or vest. But what is perhaps most striking to the modern reader is the paucity of information about the overall contour and shape of the major components that made up the male and female costume, in contrast to the vast amount of detail provided on fabrics and accessories. This emphasis on fabrics and accessories indicates an important characteristic of early-modern fashion culture. Despite the important innovations of the men's suit and the women's mantua dress in the latter seventeenth century, many new fashions in the early-modern period did not require major changes in the overall design of the costume such as rapidly rising or falling hemlines, or drastically widening or narrowing silhouettes. Contemporaries perceived that decoration and embellishments, such as new types of fabric, lace and accessories, were responsible for transforming yesterday's dress into today's new fashion.[43]

Beneath the *Mercure*'s chatty coverage of fashions several principles guided the journal's presentation of new fabrics, items of clothing, and accessories. Throughout the *Mercure* there were references to a host of factors such as one's weight, age, and personal preferences that influence or determine what fashions one ought to wear. In a passage describing the latest vogue for skirts with horizontal stripes the editor cautions, "These sorts of skirts are proper for delicate waists: but women who are a bit plump, must shape the sides of their skirts and decorate them with braid at the bottom."[44] For the most part the *Mercure* avoided descriptions of "particular fashions" that were seen as the idiosyncratic creations of individuals dressed to suit their own fancy and which contrasted with more noteworthy "general fashions," which greater numbers of people followed. In July 1677, the editor of the *Mercure* complained, "One has never seen in France what one sees these days; there are no longer any general fashions because there are too many particular fashions: one can scarcely find two people dressed in the same manner and everyone dresses according to their fantasies."[45]

Despite these occasional, seemingly modern references to selecting fashions that were flattering to the individual's physique, age, or personal fantasy, by far the most important determinants of what people wore were royal authority, social rank, the season or weather, and gender. De Visé reminded his readers that the fashions described were intended for the elite men and women of the aristocracy. On several occasions new styles were further distinguished from the others as belonging to "people of the highest quality" or to "people of the first rank."[46] Frequently, the fashions of the king and his family were recounted in lavish detail, the luxurious gold and silver brocades, fringe, ribbons and diamonds of the royal wardrobe casting a glittering light, by association, on the elite fashions described in the *Mercure*.[47] The *Mercure* did not, however, regularly discuss the fashions of common people of Paris, which were in theory not regarded as fashion, but as mere clothing, lying outside the domain of *la mode*. There were, nevertheless, occasional tantalizing hints at the blurred boundary between elite and common dress. In December 1681, the *Mercure* reported that not only were women of quality enamored of plush new fabrics lined with gold or silver cloth called "*pannes*," but that "One also sees *pannes* on people who are not of a distinguished quality; but these do not have any silver linings."[48] And in 1673, the journal noted the "common origin" of a new type of skirt being worn by the upper classes: "These skirts are of a common birth; and being found to be pretty and a good buy, almost all women have bought them."[49]

Louis XIV's authority over fashion also extended to official mourning costume when the court, from the highest-ranking lords and ladies to chambermaids and liveried servants, solemnly adorned itself in black. Mourning customs stood at the heart of absolutist political culture: with the sartorial distinction between "ordinary time" and "royal mourning," the death of a member of the royal family became an occasion symbolically to link the royal family to all of French history. Royal etiquette for official states of mourning precisely detailed who should wear what and for how long.[50] Purveyors of black dye and black woolen crepe doubtless profited from the sartorial etiquette required by official states of mourning, but for the most part this sacred public ritual was perceived by merchants to have a disastrous effect on fashion and business. In January 1672, the editor of the *Mercure* explained that he had been forced to postpone the publication of his article on fashion until late in the season because "The mourning attire that one has worn here for a long time . . . has stifled many fashions that have never seen the light of day, and most of them have stayed in the imaginations of those who have invented them."[51] By the end of Louis XIV's reign merchants' complaints that official states of mourning were harming commerce had become so pronounced that the crown relented and reduced mourning for the royal family to no more than six months and reduced the length of all other mourning by half. As the king's *Ordinance on Official Periods of Mourning* of June 23, 1716 proclaimed:

> His Majesty, being informed that one of the main causes of the interruption of commerce and the cessation of manufacturing, comes from the too long duration of states of mourning which often succeed one after another, and which stop during many consecutive years the sale of different types of merchandise, making the best merchants incapable of continuing the work of the workers who are constrained to abandon their profession, even to leave the kingdom; And that in addition the merchants find themselves left with a large quantity of fabrics, when mourning arises unexpectedly, they can only sell them at a considerable loss . . .[52]

By shortening the period of mourning, Louis seemingly compromised between the iconic splendor of his court and the interests of commerce and merchants; yet, this kind of compromise stood at the heart of early-modern absolutism and mercantilist practice. Just as absolutism proclaimed the omnipotence of Louis's sovereignty, mercantilist economic philosophy proclaimed that the nation was the fundamental political and economic unit and that the crown must supervise and control all aspects of the economy for the prosperity of France. Mercantilist theory and practice made increasing the overall wealth of France – whether by increasing

Figure 5 *Dame de qualité portant une lévite de deuil,* courtesy of RMN.

the stores of bullion in France, encouraging French manufactures and exports, decreasing imports, or attacking rival nations – the main concern of the king and state. Mercantilist philosophy developed hand-in-hand with absolutism and was predicated on a mixture of patriotism, centralization, and *étatisme*, the belief that all phases of economic life should be brought under royal surveillance and control for the benefit of the French nation. Mercantilist practice, however, like Louis's absolutism, which was predicated on a series of compromises and mutual agreements between classes and interest groups, was built around a series of tensions between the interests of local guilds, merchants and consumers on the one hand and the king and the nation on the other.

Sumptuary law was one of the most contested areas in which the interests of the state and individuals, the king and producers, and the imperatives of absolutism and appearance collided. In France, like other European countries, sumptuary restrictions dated to the Middle Ages and sought to shore up the boundaries of status and class hierarchies. But under Louis XIV they also existed due to mercantilist motives to increase the amount of bullion in France by discouraging imports of luxury goods. A series of sumptuary edicts enacted in the 1660s and 1670s restricted the use of ornate gold and silver fabric, braid, and lace on clothing, claiming that excessive consumption was not only personally ruinous to subjects but was "a great harm to the good order and police which must be maintained in a state" in its ability to blur class distinctions.[53] Sumptuary restrictions were aimed at both consumers and producers of illicit goods. An ordinance of 1656 granted commissioners of the Parisian police the power to search men and women on the streets of Paris for proscribed goods. Merchants caught making and selling banned goods had to pay a stiff penalty, 500 *livres* for the first offense and loss of their *maîtrise*, their privilege to work in the craft, for subsequent offenses. Yet sumptuary edicts were easily circumvented and disobeyed by consumers and producers alike. As one edict noted, the desire for gain had led many merchants and clothing workers to search for "new inventions," that is, new types of fashion that fell outside of the items mentioned in sumptuary edicts.[54]

The *Mercure* provided ample coverage of the impact, or lack of impact, of the sumptuary ordinances promulgated throughout the 1670s. In June 1677, the *Mercure*'s editor declared that recent sumptuary edicts had taken such a devastating toll on the season's fashions that there was no need to write his usual seasonal article, explaining, "The defense of gold and silver that has been published here has ruined all my plans."[55] By the following year, M. de la Reynie, head of the Parisian police, relaxed the enforcement of the new sumptuary edicts and the editor of the *Mercure* wrote, "I know very well that it is forbidden to wear gold and silver fabric, and you know it as well as I do. However, there are few persons of quality who do not possess them . . . . Time has always made these sorts of defenses be forgotten."[56]

Although Louis continued to issue sumptuary edicts throughout his reign, under the influence of finance minister Jean-Baptiste Colbert, royal legislation supplemented traditional concerns regarding luxury and ostentation with a new effort to stimulate domestic luxury production.[57] Colbert was especially determined to use sumptuary laws to aid the silk industry in Lyon, linen production in Picardy, Normandy and Brittany, and the lace-making industry in Normandy and central

France. Colbert's belief that the French could win markets by attaining a high standard of quality through careful government regulation initiated a set of French economic practices regarding luxury and quality, and sparked a new discourse on French taste and economic nationalism, which would dominate the political economy of fashion production and commerce for much of the next century.

At the same time that Colbert increased tariffs and prohibited certain European imports, he attempted to stimulate French trade overseas by helping to found the French East India Company and French West India Company in 1664. Among the most coveted goods imported from India were calico prints (*indiennes*), popular for their lively, colorfast designs. Almost immediately, merchants and artisans in France began to produce their own versions of these fabrics using woodblock printing technology. Although in the seventeenth century domestic *toiles peintes*, as they were called, had not yet achieved the artistry of later eighteenth-century fabrics based on copper-plate printing technology, they were sufficiently threatening to the Lyonnais silk industry to provoke a royal decree in 1686 prohibiting the import and manufacture of painted or printed cloth.[58] A second edict in 1692 prohibiting the wearing and use of these fabrics was largely unsuccessful, mainly because of the difficulty in enforcing it. As the duc de Saint-Simon wrote in 1716, "The mode for *toiles peintes* has prevailed over all rule and reason; the greatest ladies, and others in imitating their example, wear them publicly and everywhere with impunity, with the most scandalous public contempt for defenses against them and the penalties so often reiterated."[59] Not only the court aristocracy, but also the king's administrators responsible for enforcing these laws, openly flouted sumptuary law by wearing *indiennes* themselves. The two edicts and eighty ordinances published between 1686 and 1748 attest to the inability of kings or ministers to control *la mode*.[60]

Not only in the case of calicos, but also in many other aspects of textile and clothing production, Colbert's attempt to centralize administration and stimulate the French textile and fashion industries met with considerable resistance. Never especially popular in France, Colbert was greeted with hostility on all sides, from powerful guilds like the *six corps des marchands* of Paris, who opposed his creation of new guilds, to royal provincial courts (*parlements*) that interfered with his regulations regarding manufactures, to local elites who objected to the privileging of particular cities or regions. Ironically, Louis himself may have done the most to undermine Colbert's mercantile goals by his all-out attack on French Protestants. Seeking to make restitution for the sexual (if not sartorial) sins of his youth and to assert his sacred leadership of Catholic France, Louis began in 1679 to increase legal restrictions on Protestants in France. He subjected Protestant families to the notorious dragonnades, during which French royal troops billeted in Protestant families harassed their hosts. In 1685, when Louis revoked the Edict of Nantes, which had granted toleration to French Protestants, over a quarter million French

Protestants fled to England, the Netherlands, and Germany, taking with them their skills as textile designers, manufacturers, and weavers. In this case, Louis's iconic imperative to display his piety as "most Christian king" undermined his mercantilist goal of wooing *la mode* for the sake of French economic glory.

The *Mercure*'s publication of articles on fashion twice a year, in the spring/summer and in the fall/winter, reveals another way to organize the fashion culture. As in the case of royal mourning and sumptuary law, the attempt of the court to divide time into specific seasons also posed problems for consumers and producers. The organization of fashions based on the season and the weather may seem obvious, even "natural," in the temperate climate of Paris, which experiences distinct seasons. Yet, the association of the natural seasons with "the fashion seasons," and the organization of clothing around biannual markets and style changes was actually a relatively new phenomenon in the late seventeenth century. Although both kings and merchants promoted the idea of the "fashion season" many producers and consumers did not fully accept this mannered division of time until the late eighteenth century. The *Mercure* provided many examples of the kind of problems encountered by the attempt to organize styles around fashion seasons when the summer or winter season did not coincide with the appropriate warm or cool weather. For example, in September 1684, discussing the new winter fashions the editor wrote, "One still sees so few winter clothes that it is hard to be assured which fashions will be the most popular during this season."[61] And in another issue, the editor became so aggravated by the disjuncture between the fashion season and the weather that he suggested that the concept of the fashion season should be abandoned and that he would henceforth report on new fashions as they were invented rather than at the beginning of each season.[62] The natural seasons, like royal sumptuary ordinances, provided a problematic and uncertain way of organizing fashions because elite men and women were just as reluctant to sacrifice their bodily comfort to the season's fashions as they were to sacrifice their desire for luxury attire for the sake of the royal etiquette or the royal treasury. In contrast, a third factor determining the organization of clothing and fashion, one's sex, was presented in the *Mercure* as a less problematic mode of organizing early-modern fashion culture.

The One-sex Model of Gender and Clothing

The differentiation of clothing based on one's sex was one of many ways that fashion was implicitly organized in the pages of the *Mercure*. Tallying the number of pages devoted to the fashions of each sex in the issues of the *Mercure* published in the 1670s and 1680s, male and female fashions were typically allotted roughly equal coverage. In the lengthier articles on fashion that appeared every six months

Figure 6 "Man's Summer Dress, 1678," *Mercure galant* (July 1678), courtesy of the Bibliothèque nationale.

there was no clear privileging of men's fashions over women's and many articles did not even separate discussions of men's and women's clothing. Often, the editor moved back and forth in the course of the article between male and female fashions. In some issues an entire article might be devoted to the fashions of one sex with no mention of the fashions of the other, as in 1684, when three and one-half pages described men's fashions, followed by a brief coda on women's fashions: "As for women, imagine the most beautiful fabrics of gold and silver for their skirts and dresses, each to her taste and her purse; and there are their fashions."[63] In 1681, at the end of a seven-page article which lavishly detailed male costumes, the *Mercure* noted, "As for women, they don't have a great quantity of fashions, but they are rich."[64] Conversely, the issue of July 1677 began with nineteen pages on women's fashions and ended with only four and one-half pages on men's. In the semi-annual "Extraordinaire," devoted exclusively to fashion, the sections on men's and women's fashions were more strictly delineated and more equitably divided.

Figure 7 "Woman's Summer Dress, 1678," *Mercure galant* (July 1678), courtesy of the Bibliothèque nationale.

In both the structure and content of the articles, male and female fashions were not presented as fundamentally different from or opposed to one another but rather as variations on the same theme. The *Mercure* sometimes commented specifically on the shared features of male and female dress. In June 1699 the *Mercure* reported the appearance of two or three kinds of suits for men with ruffled flounces called *falbalas*, "a little like those that some women began to wear last year."[65] The *Mercure* also suggested that men were as subject to the empire of fashion as were women. In the issue of 1673, after devoting several pages to a description of women's fashions, the editor turned his attention to men's fashions, explaining, "I believe that men acknowledge the empire of fashion more than the most inconstant and most ridiculous coquettes of Paris."[66] De Visé went on to say that "men have in very little time changed the style of their sleeves eight or ten times, and I am assured that no one can show me an example among fashionable women of a similar inconstancy."[67]

Although the *Mercure* indicates that men's fashions were subject to the same whims as were women's, the journal particularly associated fashion with women.

All of the articles on clothing were addressed to women, to "the curiosity of our beauties from the provinces." De Visé began his article on fashions in 1673 by recounting that the previous night he was "with one of those women who only talk about skirts and frivolities."[68] He opened another article by explaining that recently two women had invited him to join them for a promenade. After an awkward silence, because "I couldn't talk to them about the war since their lovers were not in the army, the conversation turned to fashion."[69] In only one instance did de Visé explicitly mention men participating in discussions of the latest fashions, although there are indications that the social settings he describes included both sexes.[70] Considering that the *Mercure* devoted as much space to men's fashions as to women's, and made clear statements about the potential subservience of men as well as women to the "empire of fashion," its implicit presentation of fashion as a more feminine than masculine concern at first may seem puzzling. Perhaps de Visé was simply voicing the commonplace that since fashion is more frivolous than war it must be a more feminine than masculine pursuit. But more significantly, as a journalist actively engaged in creating an audience for Louis's vision of court culture, de Visé publicly recognized that fashion was one area of the public sphere in which women's participation truly made a difference: news and publicity about fashions traveled through female networks.

More explicitly, the *Mercure* claimed that men have less need for fashions than do women because men do not require clothing to enhance their appearance: "Adjustments are less necessary for men than for most women, and they do not hide their defects as much. A man is always well enough dressed when he is good looking; He looks pleasing in the costume of a cavalier without any ornaments; but women who are not well dressed rarely please, especially when they are not natural beauties."[71] This passage suggests two different ways of thinking about the relationship between gender and fashion that managed to coexist comfortably in seventeenth-century elite thought. First, de Visé suggests that stylish clothing is "less necessary" for men than for women, not that men have a qualitatively and essentially different relationship to clothing than do women. Analogous to the one-sex model of sexual difference that historian Thomas Laqueur argues was pervasive in seventeenth-century medical thought, men's and women's interest in and need for fashion were not fundamentally different, but existed on a continuum: some men might plausibly be more interested in fashion than some women, but overall, women were perceived to be more preoccupied than men with clothing and fashion.[72] Significantly, de Visé makes no moral judgments about gender identity and character based on where men and women stood on the continuum.

Yet, within the same statement about men's lesser need for adornment lurks a second more dichotomous model for understanding differences between the sexes. According to the *Mercure*, the particular imperative of fashion for women is driven by the social requirement that women be beautiful and visually pleasing. In de

Visé's model, within the aristocracy, clothing cloaks men's and women's bodies equally as an external mark of civility and social station. Yet, the female body must shoulder the additional burden of beauty; that is, for women, clothing is required to enhance their sexual attraction as well as to proclaim their noble birth. De Visé never suggested, however, that nature decrees that women be beautiful in order to please men (as Rousseau would argue in the later eighteenth century) and the context of this particular passage suggests that beauty is as much a social require-ment of elite society as a dictate of nature for women of all classes.

Interestingly, the *Mercure* never voiced the moral condemnation, so common, as we have seen, in Fitelieu's and Grenailles's religious critique of fashion; nor did de Visé make distinctions between natural and virtuous masculinity and artificial and frivolous femininity, as would many eighteenth-century moralists. Yet, by linking women's fashions to the imperative of female beauty de Visé hints at two related arguments for differentiating between men's and women's relationships to clothing and adornment which would provide the main strands of discourse on women and fashion in the eighteenth century: first, that women have a more essential and natural need for fashion and adornment; second, that there is a distinction between women's clothing, which hides physical and moral defects, and men's clothing, which transparently reveals the true (*véritable*) man beneath the clothes.

Overall, in the *Mercure*, the relationship between *la mode* and sexual difference was unproblematic and sartorial distinctions based on class in an aristocratic, court-based fashion culture continued to overshadow gender differences. As we have seen, Louis's sartorial reforms were typically motivated by the absolutist impera-tive to discipline *la mode* for the benefit of the French economy and the solemn splendor of his court rather than by the rejection of clothing, costume, and spect-acle as unmanly. Especially when one considers the *Mercure*'s portrayal of the dynamic of fashion – why fashions change and how new fashions are disseminated – distinction based on class and privilege, more than sexual difference, clearly stand at the heart of the meaning of *la mode*; and Frenchness, more than femininity, is invoked as explanation for the whims of fashion.

The discussion of *la mode* in the *Mercure* took part in the general seventeenth-century discourse on fashion as unpredictable and protean. Throughout the journal's coverage of fashions ring the refrains, "Fashions die before they are born"; "Nothing is so inconstant as *la mode*"; "Never before has there been so much change in so little time"; and "the story of fashions is inexhaustible in France."[73] The *Mercure*'s observations on the maddening fickleness of fashion are not merely literary tropes but speak to the very real anguish which the unpredictability of *la mode* caused for aristocratic men and women hoping to catch the royal gaze and trying desperately to keep one step ahead of, and above, the bourgeoisie. Several explanations were provided as to why fashions change so rapidly and unpredictably. Significantly, the trope that fashion was fickle because *la mode* was female was not invoked. Frequent recourse was made, however, to the argument that fashions change so often because the French are a peculiarly fickle people: "But as one gets bored with everything in France, one prefers to wear something much less attractive than not to change one's fashions."[74] This argument about French fickleness was too pervasive in the literature on fashion from the late sixteenth century until the Revolution (and even beyond) to be merely a self-effacing witticism. Rather, the changeability of the French character and fashion were used rhetorically to promote France's luxury and fashion trades. The above quotation on French changeability, for instance, appears in an issue of the *Mercure* in which the editor explicitly sang the praises of French fashions, stating, "everyone must agree . . . that nothing pleases more than fashions born in France, and that all that is made there has a certain look that foreigners cannot give to their goods, even when they surpass French goods in beauty."[75]

Louis XIV, the editor of the *Mercure*, and all those who profited from the French fashion trade had a keen interest in perpetuating the myth that the French people's innate sense of fashion and desire for novelties explained the rapidity of change of fashions in France. Yet, as it strove to explain the vicissitudes of *la mode*, the *Mercure* offered several more specific examples of how and why fashion changed as well. The passages in the *Mercure* which advertised specific shops often attributed the invention of a fashion to an individual merchant, praising his or her talent for creating new types of fabric or clothing designs. In October 1678, a fabric merchant, M. Charlier, was lauded as possessing a "marvelous talent" and "a distinctive inventiveness."[76] But, as the *Mercure* went on to explain regarding a new style of muff, when a merchant invents a new cloth, she or he could never foresee whether or not it will be enthusiastically embraced by the public: "One is not certain that this fashion will last, but it is certain that the merchants wish it to, and that they have made many of them."[77]

Among the many explanations for new fashions, by far the most frequently cited concerned the desire of elite men and women to distinguish themselves sartorially from the lower orders, and the desire, in turn, of the lower orders to imitate the fashions of those above them. As the *Mercure* explained, "*Gens de qualité* never fail to discard fashions which have become too common."[78] While the upper classes had to stay one step ahead of the bourgeoisie, who quickly copied their fashions, they also had to keep in step with the fashions of the *grands seigneurs* ranking above them on the social hierarchy; or, as the *Mercure* stated, "Fashions die before they are born, and all persons of quality have scarcely begun to follow a new fashion when the apes at court abort them because the grand seigneurs abandon them quickly to take up others."[79] In 1673, the *Mercure* provided a precise itinerary of how fashions passed through the social orders that encapsulated the journal's understanding of the sartorial status hierarchy:

Fashions pass from the court to the ladies of the town, from the ladies of the town to rich bourgeois women, from rich bourgeois women to the *Grisettes*, who imitate them with less costly fabrics . . . . In addition the *Grisettes*'s clothing inspires the ladies of the provinces, the ladies of the provinces the bourgeois women of the region, and from there fashions pass to foreign lands; all this happens in such a way that soon the fashions invented originally at court begin to look old.[80]

Interestingly, a passage that examines how fashions move through the Parisian class structure relies upon women's fashions to make its point. But in this example, as throughout the *Mercure*, the different relationship of men and women to clothing is not founded on a stark polarity between the sexes or profound anxiety about fashion and gender transgression.

Although the *Mercure* occasionally explored how and why particular kinds of fabric or clothing gained wide popularity, ultimately the journal seemed content to eschew explicit explanations and simply to accept that *la mode* was enigmatic.[81] The *Mercure* astutely stated that "*La mode* knows how to accustom the appetite to its caprices," but offered no commentary on how *la mode* went about doing so.[82] As we will see in the final chapter, not until the late eighteenth century would fashion journals explicitly attempt to unmask *la mode*. The *Mercure*'s disinclination to probe the workings of fashion may have arisen from the fact that for elite men and women, the changing fashions for various items of luxurious clothing may have produced some personal anxiety, but were not construed as a "social problem." The *Mercure* never rendered moral judgments about the luxurious fashions it described. The fickleness of *la mode* may have been maddening, but it was a folly in which the *Mercure*, and court society in general, willingly participated.

Furthermore, unlike moralistic writings from the seventeenth century or the women's and fashion press of the late eighteenth century, there was no indication in the *Mercure* that fashion created conflicts between the sexes. The *Mercure*'s presentation of the aristocratic fashion culture, a culture that revolved around ordering one's clothing from the most celebrated merchants of Paris, sending news of the latest fashions to one's friends and relatives in the provinces, trying to keep up with the swiftly changing fashions at court, and the playful banter among men and women about the enigma of *la mode*, did not portray fashion as an exclusively feminine realm. In the late seventeenth century, one would have to turn to groups other than the aristocratic elite who occupied *le monde*, and to other genres than the *Mercure* to find a harsh critique of fashion, to witness the sexing of *la mode*, and to hear the voices of dispute between men and women over clothing.

Conclusion

Louis XIV's attempt to costume the French and impose absolutism on appearance took place in a fashion culture that encompassed the views of both Fitelieu and de Visé and the material and cultural demands of both the craftspeople of Paris and the courtiers of Versailles. Although Fitelieu's violent attack on *la mode* was written in 1642 in the context of an aristocratic culture buffeted by the tensions leading up to the Fronde, a full quarter-century before de Visé began to write about fashion in the more settled court culture of Louis XIV's majority, the views of Fitelieu and de Visé do not mark two different historical periods but rather the range of attitudes toward fashion that circulated throughout the seventeenth century: the *Mercure* stood at one pole, celebrating fashion, and *La contre-mode* stood at the opposite pole, condemning *la mode*. Although the immediate context for Fitelieu's outbursts against fashion was the debate which had begun to rage in the 1630s with the publication of works concerning women, fashion and the proper attire for attending church, his writings took part in a larger debate on women's nature and women's sphere in the mid-seventeenth century.[83] The dozens of tracts written in the 1640s on the subject of women's proper role are sure signs of a historically specific cultural ferment of significant magnitude. However, attacks on women's fashions and women's place in *le monde* did not end with the Fronde and the establishment under Louis XIV of a new order of court culture. Carolyn Lougée argues that the violent attacks on women by writers such as Grenaille should be placed within the broader context of critiques of the role of women and salon culture in the "feminization" of the Parisian *monde* and the breakdown of social stratification in aristocratic society which persisted (at least) until the end of Louis XIV's reign.[84] Thus, many of the issues which occupied those writing on women's role in court culture and polite society in the 1630s and 1640s – luxury, fashion, and social mobility – continued to occupy moralists whose writings were contemporary with de Visé's as well.[85]

Although Louis XIV came of age in an era when many men and women in France could not decide whether fashion was a beneficent French goddess or a two-faced whore, by the end of his reign Louis had laid the foundation for the French belief that the textile and fashion industries were a vitally important national resource and that the French court stood at the center of the elite culture of fashion in Europe. But while Louis might attempt to wed absolutism to *la mode* (both economically and iconically), he could never gain full dominion over fashion, especially when his subjects played the role of individual, private consumers. Sumptuary edicts, as we have seen, were despised and disobeyed. It was, apparently, one thing to decree what people wore in the king's presence during court ceremonies and quite another to mandate what they could wear outside the king's gaze, in town and on informal occasions. Among the elite, one did not dress only to please the king; the imperative of *la mode* increasingly demanded that one dress for a wider audience of elites who gathered at salons, theaters, and chateaux far from Versailles. By the end of Louis's reign, an increasing aestheticization and commodification of both clothing and private life offered to elite men and women the seductive possibility of dressing to please, not king and court, but one's husband or wife, one's lover, or even oneself.

While elite men and women might submit to court costume to be disciplined to the absolutist vision, they relied on fashion to delight themselves personally and to distinguish themselves within the broader elite culture of *la cour* and *la ville*.[86] As much as he might wish it otherwise, when it came to fashion, Louis's sartorial script was often rejected both by individual consumers and merchants as they bowed before *la mode*, a goddess who danced to a different rhythm from that of Colbert's mercantilism or Louis's absolutism. *La mode*'s stage, French fashion culture broadly defined, was more inclusive than Louis's stage at Versailles; it included an increasingly broad spectrum of the elite Parisian population and responded to many gazes other than the king's. In this fashion culture, although clothing continued to function as costume – a fixed marker of class and station – an increasingly nuanced sartorial vocabulary playfully combined costume with *la mode*, as fashion spoke to an audience which was both "public" and "private" in a language which was at once intensely political and deeply personal.

Notes

1. This short definition of fashion is part of a much longer discussion that includes other types of objects besides clothing. See Antoine Furetière, *Le dictionnaire universel* (The Hague and Rotterdam, 1690).
2. For antecedents to these seventeenth-century works which provide a more tolerant assessment of women, fashion and adornment, see the writings of Ignatius Loyola and Francis de Sales, who accepted women's moderate use of fashionable dress and cosmetics.
3. M. de Fitelieu, *La contre-mode* (Paris: L. de Heugueville, 1642): 10, 15. On the pamphlet literature of the Fronde, see Christian Jouhard, *Mazarinades: La Fronde des mots* (Paris: Aubier, 1985).
4. In addition to *La mode* (Paris, 1642), François de Grenaille published *La bibliothèque des dames* (Paris, 1640), *L'honnête fille* (Paris, 1639–40), *L'honnête mariage* (Paris, 1640), and *Les plaisirs des dames* (Paris, 1641). For biographical information see Pierre Bayle, *Dictionnaire historique et critique*

(Lyons: Barret, 1771) t. 2: 1397–8. Ian Maclean has described Grenaille as a "feminist," but Carolyn Lougée groups him with writers such as Nicolas Boileau, who denounced women's role in salon culture and polite society as the root cause of social instability. My reading of Grenaille supports Lougée's interpretation that he was an anti-feminist writer. See Ian Maclean, *Woman Triumphant* (Oxford, 1977) 59; Carolyn Lougée, *Le paradis des femmes* (Princeton: Princeton University Press, 1976): 59–60.

5. Grenaille, *La mode*: 2.
6. Ibid.; my analysis of Grenaille is indebted to Louise Godard de Donville, *Signification de la mode sous Louis XIII* (Aix-en-Provence: EDISUD, 1978).
7. Fitelieu, *La contre-mode*: 386.
8. Ibid., 386.
9. Ibid., 20.
10. Ibid., 5.
11. Ibid., 12.
12. Ibid., 28.
13. Ibid., 357. On fears that the effeminacy of court culture saps the nobility of the robe of their virility and valor, see François de Salignac de la Mothe Fénelon, *Dialogues des morts anciens et modernes* (Paris, 1718): Chapter 62.
14. Fitelieu *La contre-mode*: 20.
15. Ibid., 9.
16. In its unpredictability, *la mode* was similar to another female personification, Fortuna. See Gerd Gigerenzer, Zeno Switjtink, et al., *The Empire of Chance: How Probability Changed Science and Everyday Life* (Cambridge: Cambridge University Press, 1989): 292. On the science of probability in the Enlightenment, see Lorraine Daston, *Classical Probability in the Enlightenment* (Princeton: Princeton University Press, 1988).
17. Godard de Donville *Signification de la mode sous Louis XIII:* 127.
18. Fitelieu *La contre-mode:* 11.
19. "La description de *la mode* qui court," quoted in Godard de Donville, *Signification de la mode sous Louis XIII:* 128.
20. Edouard Fournier, *Variétés historiques et littéraires* (Paris, 1855–63): t. 3: 241–3.
21. Peter Burke, *The Fabrication of Louis XIV:* 5.
22. *A Woman's Life in the Court of the Sun King: Letters of Liselotte von der Pfalz, 1652–1722*, translated and introduced by Elborg Forster (Baltimore: The Johns Hopkins University Press, 1984): 6.
23. *Letters from Liselotte*, translated and edited by Maria Kroll (London: Victor Gollancz, 1970): 83.
24. Kroll, *Letters from Liselotte*: 83.

25. Douglas Russell, *Costume History and Style* (Englewood Cliffs, NJ: Prentice-Hall, 1983): 269.
26. Clare Crowston, *Fabricating Women: The Seamstresses of Old Regime France, 1675–1791* (Durham, NC: Duke University Press, 2001): 41.
27. See De Marly, *Louis XIV and Versailles*: 21–5.
28. John Evelyn, *Tyrannus, or the Mode* (1661): 5.
29. On the development of the three-piece suit in England, see David Kuchta, "'Graceful, Virile, and Useful': The Origins of the Three-Piece Suit," *Dress* 17 (1990): 118–26.
30. Anne Hollander, *Sex and Suits: The Evolution of Modern Dress* (New York: Alfred Knopf, 1994): 6.
31. On these distinctions, see Roche, *The Culture of Clothing*, Chapter 2.
32. De Marly, *Louis XIV and Versailles*: 62–3. See Marquis de Sourches, *Mémoires sur le règne de Louis XIV*, ed. le Comte de Cosnac and E. Pontal, 13 vols (Paris: Hachette, 1883). See vol. 2, February 1688 and vol. 3, September 22, 1691.
33. Roche, *The Culture of Clothing*: 221, 244.
34. Louis de Rouvroy, duc de Saint-Simon, *Mémoires*, ed. Yves Coirault (Paris: Gallimard, 1984): t. 3: 112.
35. See the fashion engravings of Sébastien Le Clerc and Jean de Saint-Jean. For the most comprehensive study of early-modern French fashion engravings, see Raymond Gaudriault, *Répertoire de la gravure de mode française des origins à 1815* (Paris: Promodis, 1988).
36. By 1697 Jean Donneau de Visé earned a considerable royal pension of 15,000 *livres* for his work editing the *Mercure*. For a brief history of the *Mercure*, see Claude Bellanger, Jacques Godechot, et al. *Histoire générale de la presse française* (Paris: Presses universitaires de France, 1969): 137–43. De Visé (1638–1710) was the youngest son of a family well-connected at court. His father was marshal of the household of Monsieur, the King's brother, and his oldest bother was first valet to the Queen. Aside from his long editorship of the *Mercure galant* (from 1672 until his death in 1710) he is best known for his role in the literary quarrel over Molière's *l'Ecole des femmes* and for a series of minor comedies including *La mère coquette*, *La veuve à la mode* and *Les dames vengées*. For further bibliographic information see Pierre Mélèse, *Un homme de lettres au temps du Grand Roi: Donneau de Visé* (Paris, 1936), G. Dotoli, "Il *Mercure galant* di Donneau de Visé," *L'informazione in Francia nel Seicento Quadernni del Seicento francese* 5 (1983): 219–82, Jean Sgard, ed., *Dictionnaire des journalistes, 1600–1789* (Grenoble: Presses universitaires de Grenoble, 1976): 228–9, 371–3, and Monique Vincent, "Donneau de Visé et le *Mercure Galant*" (Lille: Atelier national réproduction des thèses, Université Lille III, 1987). On the contrast between the seventeenth- and

eighteenth-century *Mercure galant*, see Reed Benhamou, "Fashion in the *Mercure*: From Human Foible to Female Failing," *Eighteenth-Century Studies* 31, no. 1 (1997): 27–43.

37. To search for articles on clothing, see Etienne Déville, *Index du Mercure de France, 1672–1832* (Paris: J. Schemit, 1910).

38. The journal was renamed *Mercure de France* in the 1720s and was edited by Antoine de La Roque from 1726 to 1731. For an important discussion of La Roque's converage of fashion, see Benhamou, "Fashion in the *Mercure*."

39. *Mercure* (1673): t. 3: 324.

40. On the female audience of the *Mercure*, see Monique Vincent, "Le *Mercure galant*: témoin des pouvoirs de la femme du monde," *Dix-Septième Siècle* 144 (July–September, 1984): 241–6.

41. *Mercure* (1674): t. 6:77; (October 1678): 336–67.

42. Ibid. (August 1689): 315–16.

43. The *Mercure* makes several references to clothing, fabrics and accessories which lay outside of the realm of fashion. See *Mercure* (1673): t. 3: 314 and t. 4: 342.

44. Ibid. (June 1687): 323.

45. Ibid. (July 1677): 258–60.

46. Ibid. (May 1681): 378; (May 1679): 354.

47. Ibid. (May 1679): 354.

48. Ibid. (December 1681): 337.

49. *Ibid*. (1673): t. 4: 345–6.

50. On mourning etiquette, see Roche, *The Culture of Clothing*: 284–5 and the *Encyclopédie*, "Mourning," vol. 6: 910.

51. *Mercure* (January 1672): 275.

52. *Ordonnance du Roy concernant les deuils* (June 23, 1716), BN collection clair., 1053, f. 135.

53. *Ordonnance du roi, portant règlement pour les passemens, dentelles* . . . (December 29, 1664). Printed in Nicolas Delamare, *Traité de la police*, livre 3: 406. See Delamare's *Traité de la police*, BN MS FR, 21626 which contains copies of all the sumptuary edicts from the seventeenth and eighteenth centuries.

54. See ordinance of November 6, 1656, "Manuscrits français," no. 16,747, fol. 68; *Ordonnance de police* (November 29, 1673). In Delamare, livre 3: 411.

55. *Mercure* (June 1677): 264. De Visé referred to the sumptuary edict of June 5, 1677 which applied to all classes and reveals that Louis was less interested in using sumptuary laws to enforce social hierarchy than in using them as part of a mercantilist policy aimed at regulating the flow of gold and silver in the kingdom. This edict is in Delamare, *Traité de la police*, fol. 79.

56. *Mercure* (October 1678): 361–2.
57. The classic study of Colbert and mercantilism remains Charles Woolsey Cole, *Colbert and a Century of French Mercantilism*, 2 vols. (New York: Columbia University Press, 1939). On the impact of Colbert on French industry in the eighteenth century, see Philippe Minard, *La fortune du colbertisme: État et industrie dans la France des Lumières* (Paris: Fayard, 1998).
58. See Jacqueline Jacque, "Printed Textiles," in *French Textiles* (Hartford: 1985): 145. After the Edict of Nantes, printed fabric manufacture was maintained chiefly in the free ports of France and in certain privileged regions such as Chantilly. Copper-plate engraving was introduced in France by Oberkampf in 1770 at his Jouy factory near Versailles. See Stanley Chapman and Serge Chassagne, *European Textile Printers in the Eighteenth Century: A Study of Pell and Oberkampf* (London: Heineman, 1981) and Serge Chassagne, *Oberkampf, un entrepreneur capitaliste au siècle des lumières* (Paris: Aubin-Montaigne, 1980). On the vogue for cotton textiles in England in the same period, see Audrey Douglas, "Cotton Textiles in England: the East India Company's Attempt to Exploit Developments in Fashion 1660–1721," *The Journal of British Studies* vol. 8, no. 2 (May 1969): 28–43.
59. Louis de Rouvroy, duc de Saint-Simon, *Mémoires*, eds. Chéruel and Regnier (Paris: Hachette, 1887): t. 13, 34.
60. Chapman and Chassagne, *European Textile Printers*: 104. See BN MS Français, 21780, fol. 95–180 for lists of all those fined for possession of *toiles peintes*. The fine in the early eighteenth century was 300 *livres*.
61. *Mercure* (September 1684): 309–10. See also *Mercure* (June 1686): 323–4 and *Mercure* (May 1679): 352.
62. *Mercure* (October 1678): 361–2.
63. Ibid. (December 1684): 310.
64. Ibid. (December 1681): 336.
65. Ibid. (June 1699): 247.
66. Ibid. (1673): 308–9.
67. Ibid. (1673): 309.
68. Ibid. (1673): t. 4: 332.
69. Ibid. (1673): t. 3: 282–3.
70. Ibid. (1673): t. 3: 322.
71. Ibid. (July 1677): 276–7.
72. Thomas Laqueur, *Making Sex*.
73. *Mercure* (1673): t. 3: 283; (June 1687): 306; (1673): 289; (1673): t. 3: 304.
74. *Mercure* (1673): t. 3: 315.
75. Ibid., 306–7.
76. Ibid. (October 1678): 371–2.

77. Ibid. 374. Although the creators of most of the fashions described in the *Mercure* remain anonymous, there are several references to specific individuals who created new styles. In 1674, the *Mercure* reported that the newest fashion in tightly-fitted coats, "manteaux à la Sylvie," was inspired by the book *La Sylvie de Molière*.

78. Ibid. (July 1677): 272.

79. Ibid. (1673): t. 3: 282–3.

80. Ibid. (1673), 322–3.

81. In March 1678 the *Mercure* presented its readers with an extended puzzle (enigma). The following month the journal revealed that the answer to the enigma was "*La mode.*" *Mercure* (March 1678): 192; (April 1678): 391.

82. Ibid. (1673): t. 3: 319.

83. See Jean Polman's *Le Chancre* and Juvernay's *Discours particulier*. According to Polman, in 1635 the Archbishop of Arras sent a general directive to bishops concerning women's dress and ornamentation in church. Maclean, *Woman Triumphant*: 70, 76, and 126. See the anonymous tract *La femme généreuse qui montre que son sexe est plus noble*. . . .

84. Lougée, *Le paradis des femmes*: 59–60, 70–84.

85. For works contemporary with de Visé's writings which lashed out at women and their obsession with fashion, see Jacques Boileau, *De l'abus des nuditez de gorge* (Brussels, 1675; Paris, 1687); Jacques Chaussé, *Traité de l'excellence du mariage: De sa nécessité, et des moyens d'y vivre heureux* (Paris, 1685); François du Salignac de La Mothe Fénelon, *De l'éducation des filles* (Paris, 1687); Nicolas Boileau, "Satire X: Contre les femmes" (1694); and Jean Gerbais, *Lettre d'un docteur de Sorbonne à une dame de qualité touchant les dorures des habits des femmes* (Paris, 1696). See also the sermons of Suffrin and Valladier, and the anonymous *Paraenese aux filles et femmes, pour la modestie et honnêteté chrétienne*. See Florent Carton Sieur D'Ancourt's play *Les bourgeoises à la mode* (1692), and the works of Molière (1622–73).

86. See E. Auerbach, "La cour et la ville," in *Scenes from the Drama of European Literature* (New York: Meridian, 1959), 133–82 and Orest Ranum, "The Court and Capital of Louis XIV: Some Definitions and Reflections," in *Louis XIV and the Craft of Kingship*, ed. John C. Rule (Columbus: Ohio State University Press, 1969). On transformations in elite culture at the turn of the eighteenth century, see Joan DeJean, *Ancients against Moderns: Culture Wars and the Making of a Fin de Siècle* (Chicago: University of Chicago Press, 1997).

–2–

Objects of Desire, Subjects of the King

Elisabeth Charlotte, duchesse d'Orleans, confided to her German half-sister Raugräfin Luise in 1698, "It does not behoove me to look at other people's beauty or ugliness, considering that it has pleased God to make me so very ugly."[1] She was, by her own account, a stout woman who put little stock in personal beauty. Although married to a man notorious for preferring men to women, she chose not to do what his first wife, Henrietta of England (1644–70), had done; she did not take lovers at court, and she did not flirt with her brother-in-law, the king. After producing the obligatory three heirs, Elisabeth Charlotte lived out her days at court as a self-described "virgin."[2] As Louis XIV's sister in-law, she was among the most prominent women at the French court during the final five decades of Louis's reign and during the regency of her son, Philippe d'Orleans (1715–22). She staunchly upheld a court culture based on rank, privilege, and sartorial display. Yet, as an "ugly," German, Protestant princess, she always felt like an outsider at Versailles and was privately one of the most vehement critics of the role of fashion and aristocratic sexuality at court.[3]

Elisabeth Charlotte's voluminous correspondence offers an unusually rich source for exploring both aristocratic views of the meaning of clothing and female courtiers' experiences as decorative objects of desire and as powerful subjects of the king. Although widely credited with helping Louis XIV create the ceremonial *grand habit*, Elisabeth Charlotte denied any personal interest in fashion. As she defiantly wrote her to half-sister,

> It would mean nothing to me if people dressed up in pretty clothes for my birthday, for that is of no interest to me, and I never notice how people are dressed. If someone stole my own clothes and wore them in my presence, I would not even realize it, for I never pay attention to people's dress, unless it is completely ridiculous.[4]

Yet, Elisabeth Charlotte's husband, Monsieur, was a notorious fop and was described by Mme de Montespan as covered "with scents, with laces, with diamonds," and more devoted to his toilette and his mirror than even "a pretty woman."[5] While her husband delighted in dressing up for "festivals, large assemblies, and spectacular displays," Elisabeth Charlotte preferred to be unadorned and outdoors hunting with the King. As she wrote during a particularly happy period

Figure 8 *Portrait d'Elisabeth Charlotte de Bavière, princess Palatine d'Orleans*, by Hyacinthe Rigaud, courtesy of RMN.

of her life, "Every other day, and sometimes two or three days running, I hunt with the king . . . . It is a real delight for a knight-of-the-rustling-leaves like me, and there is not so much dressing up or putting on rouge as for parties."[6] Despite their largely unhappy marriage, Madame, as Elisabeth Charlotte was known at court, and Monsieur seemed to have argued relatively little over their very different practices of femininity, masculinity, and fashionable dress. (They had, as we shall see, ample other issues to fight about.) To borrow fashion historian David Kuchta's phrase regarding early-modern English clothing culture, the "old sartorial regime" in which they both played starring roles at Louis XIV's court, was flexible enough to encompass both of their sexual styles because, ultimately, it was a fashion culture fundamentally preoccupied with upholding hierarchies of class and privilege, and notably less concerned with gender transgressions.[7]

The complex connections between gender and class, between being a woman and being an aristocrat, were expressed through Elisabeth Charlotte's complicated attitudes toward fixed costume of Versailles and the new, urban culture of fashion that by the late seventeenth century was influencing court culture. Although many of her letters were filled with denunciations of contemporary fashions and the use of cosmetics, others contained long, lyrical descriptions of clothing and jewelry that she considered appropriate. Despite her protests, clothing clearly was important to her, as we see in her lavish praise for a new dress style that had just arrived at court:

> I think that fashion here will change soon, because the Queen of Spain has sent her sister, the duchesse de Bourgongne, a Spanish dress which everyone greatly admires. It is made of cherry-coloured satin with a mass of silver lace, the bodice is cut like a child's coat, the shoulders are covered, and the neckline is square . . . It suits the duchesse de Bourgongne wonderfully well.[8]

Deeply ambivalent about fashion, beauty, and women's role in court society, Elisabeth Charlotte nevertheless took a forceful position respecting fashion and costume: court costume and concern for personal adornment were appropriate for men and women when they reinforced an absolutist system based on class and hierarchy, while they were ridiculous and dangerous when driven by personal vanity, illegitimate sexuality, and the new urban rhythms and cycles of *la mode*.

Like the coverage of fashion in the *Mercure*, Elisabeth Charlotte's views on clothing and gender, were shaped by what historian Thomas Laqueur has called a "one-sex model of gender" in which the sexes were considered similar, but inverted.[9] Elisabeth Charlotte found nothing strange about admitting that, "As long as I can remember, I have always preferred swords and guns to dolls," and that "I would have dearly loved to have been a boy." As a young girl Elisabeth Charlotte found news that a woman's sexual organs had popped out after a bad fall and she literally "become a man" entirely credible. The line between male and female sexuality may have been more fluid according to the one-sex model than it would be in the two-sex model that would become widely accepted by the second half of the eighteenth century. But ultimately, Elisabeth Charlotte believed sexual boundaries served a moral purpose. She ridiculed her own desire "to be a man," relating that as a young girl she had attempted to transform herself into boy by repeatedly jumping so hard "it is quite a miracle that I did not break my neck a hundred times."[10] Her message in relaying this story is clear: only a miracle could save a foolish child who could not accept the social and cultural, if not physiological and sexual, line between being a boy and being a girl, between being a male courtier and a female courtier. While refusing to "fix" gender characteristics as would later generations of French men and women, Elisabeth Charlotte presented men and women negotiating their lives at the court of Louis XIV according to gendered rules regarding sexuality, personal propriety, and politics, even if in practice these rules were transgressed.

Although her conception of sexual identity was fluid, other types of transgressive behavior at court deeply troubled Elisabeth Charlotte. In particular, she was upset by the illegitimate political and social influence that women derived from their beauty and from sexual liaisons with the king. Late in life, when discussing two of Louis XIV's most celebrated mistresses, Elisabeth Charlotte reflected on the fleeting nature of female beauty:

> Never having had good looks, I didn't have much to lose, and I see that those who used to be beauties in the past are now as plain as I am. Not a soul could recognize Mme de la Vallière now, and Mme de Montespan's skin looks like paper which children have folded over and over, for her face is covered with minute lines, so close together that it is astonishing. Her beautiful hair is as white as snow, and her face is quite red, no longer pretty at all. I am quite content never to have had what after all passes so quickly.[11]

With hindsight Elisabeth Charlotte may have been content not to have Mme de la Vallière's or Mme de Montespan's beauty, but she was certainly not content with the illegitimate power that their beauty had enabled them and their children to attain at court.[12] Her writings are filled with reflections on the dangerous consequences for a well-ordered court society of illegitimate female sexuality.

Françoise Athénais de Mortemart, marquise de Montespan (1641–1717), widely regarded the greatest beauty of her day, reigned as Louis's mistress for twelve years beginning in the 1660s and pressured the king to legitimize for the royal family their four illegitimate children. In contrast to Elisabeth Charlotte, Montespan ruled the court, not through marriage and estate, but through her sexuality. Trading on her beauty, Mme de Montespan attained what Elisabeth Charlotte had produced legitimately, a place for her children within the royal family and lineage. When Mme de Montespan persuaded the king to permit their daughter Mlle de Blois (1677–1749) to marry Elisabeth Charlotte's son, Elisabeth Charlotte railed against "mousedroppings among the pepper" and inveighed against this child of a "double adultery" and of "the most wicked and desperate woman on earth."[13] Late in life, she was still upset enough about this marriage to complain, "I am still of the old ilk, misalliances are utterly abhorrent to me, and I have noticed that they never turn out well. My son's marriage has spoiled my whole life and has upset my cheerful disposition once and for all."[14]

Elisabeth Charlotte's and Mme de Montespan's lives were deeply entwined as they shared center stage at the court of Louis XIV, yet they were as different as were Madame and Monsieur in terms of their sartorial and sexual styles: while Elisabeth Charlotte was known for inventing the fashion for sensible, warm sable scarves, *tippets à la Palatine*, Mme de Montespan was famous for fashioning flowing robes, *à la Montespan*, to disguise illegitimate pregnancies. The writings of these two very different, and often antagonistic, women express a range of

attitudes toward costume and fashion and offer an intriguing glimpse into aristocratic women's power and experience in the court of Louis XIV. Their writings
suggest both the tensions and the interplay between not only sexuality and marriage,
and beauty and rank, but also between changeable fashions and fixed costume in
a court culture predicated on both individual consumption of luxuries and public
allegiance to the king. Together, these women's writings suggest the paradox of a
court culture based on the worship of two very demanding and antagonistic deities,
Louis and *la mode*.

The Limits of Aristocratic Women's Power

Elisabeth Charlotte was an avid correspondent, who wrote at least four letters a
day, and as many as twelve on Sundays. Her letters, which chronicle over fifty
years at the French court, reveal a feisty, opinionated, and wizened survivor of a
court system that was often far from hospitable to women or to foreigners. Physically and temperamentally incapable of playing the role of silent, decorous, beautiful courtier, Elisabeth Charlotte adopted a brash and iconoclastic style. She
preferred hunting with Louis to doing needlework with her ladies, and a rollicking
laugh at comedies to falling asleep listening to pious preachers, and would rather
be reading and writing than dancing and gambling into the night.[15] From court
doctors to French cookery, she was profoundly skeptical of much of the vaunted
culture of the French court: she complained as openly of Mme de Maintenon, "the
old trollop," and her Catholic piety as she did of her husband's penchant for
squandering money on young male favorites.

When Elisabeth Charlotte first arrived at the French court in the 1670s her
clothing and looks occasioned much ridicule. Mme de Montespan cruelly recalled
the court's initial response to Elisabeth Charlotte: "It is surely not allowable to
come into the world with such a face and form, such a voice, such eyes, such
hands, and such feet, as this singular princess displayed . . . Young pregnant
women . . . were afraid to look at the Princess Palatine, and wished to be confined
before they reappeared at Court."[16] Yet by 1676 the king had developed a special
fondness for his sister-in-law; they had become frequent hunting partners and
Louis had even taken to inviting her to the special dinner he shared with Mme de
Montespan each Saturday evening. In December 1676, when the king rushed to her
side after Elisabeth Charlotte fell from her horse while hunting, the court took note.
As Elisabeth Charlotte commented with amusement to her aunt Sophie:

> Consequently, I am now very much *à la mode*, and what ever I say or do, good or bad,
> is vastly admired by all the Court, to such an extent that when I put on my old sable wrap
> during the recent spell of cold weather everybody rushed to have one made to the same

pattern. It's the height of fashion now. It makes me laugh. The very people who now admire this style, and even wear it themselves, used to jeer at my sables, so that I didn't dare wear them. But that's how it goes here.[17]

Although she was often critical of the French court, Elisabeth Charlotte was in many respects a model female courtier, who believed firmly in the importance of a social hierarchy based on blood, birth, and allegiance to the king. Even when sick she resisted wearing the informal mantua, because it made one look "too much like a chambermaid."[18] Despite her feisty persona, at times Elisabeth Charlotte appears as a paper-doll princess, bowing before a monarch whom she clearly adored and playing her prescribed role at court, dutifully wearing her costume – the uniform of the office she held as "Madame," first lady at court.

Elisabeth Charlotte's life attests to the strength of absolutism's gaze and grip that, in the aftermath of the mid-century political rebellion known as the Fronde, were nowhere more constant and firm than within the bosom of the royal family. Not only did the court and crown possess power over the most intimate belongings and apparel of royal family members, under Louis's rule, no member of the royal court was allowed to leave court or travel without the king. Elisabeth Charlotte, who pined for her native Germany throughout a half-century of "exile" at the French court, was not even allowed to visit her beloved daughter when she married and moved to Germany. Even her correspondence with German relatives such as her Aunt Sophie, Duchess of Braunschweig-Luneburg, rendered her suspect, and she feared that her letters were intercepted and read by royal spies.

Although Elisabeth Charlotte, as Louis's sister-in-law, ranked among the very highest nobility, one of the "Sons and Daughters of France," her husband's extravagances rendered her as economically powerless as more humble French wives in the seventeenth century.[19] She complained frequently throughout her letters of her husband squandering money, particularly on his young male favorites. In one particularly poignant letter written in 1698, she laments to her Aunt Sophie,

It isn't at all surprising that Monsieur had the dressing-table things melted down, for they were his own property. But one day, although I implored him not to, he took all the silver that had come from Heidelberg, as well as all the silver things that used to decorate my rooms and look so pretty, and had them melted down too. He put the money into his own pocket. He hasn't left me so much as one poor little box for my bits and pieces.[20]

Although Monsieur possessed considerable landed wealth, over 80 percent of the couple's annual income (1,212,000 *livres*) came directly from the crown as a pension. Thus, both during her husband's life and after his death in 1701, Elisabeth Charlotte was reduced to utter dependence on the king and court for her support. She described herself as "poor rather than rich" for her rank, and attributed her financial predicament, in part, to French marriage laws by which she could not inherit her husband's appanage, the money Monsieur received each year from the king.[21] As Elisabeth Charlotte elaborated in another letter, linking female beauty to female power, her father had agreed to such an unfortunate marriage contract because of her looks, "poor dear papa had me on his hands, and he was afraid I might remain an old maid, so he got rid of me as fast as he could."[22]

Given these economic restrictions, the plight of women like Elisabeth Charlotte call into question the portrayal of powerful and autonomous Old Regime aristocratic women painted by scholars.[23] Yet, although constrained in many respects, Elisabeth Charlotte was never as powerless and decorative as Joan Kelly-Gadol has suggested women were in post-Renaissance courts, especially in Italy. Elisabeth Charlotte was keenly aware that women could wield considerable power at court, both in reality and in the popular imagination. She believed that the king was completely ruled by Mme de Montespan and that even serious matters of state such as the Revocation of the Edict of Nantes had been driven by Mme de Maintenon's wishes.[24] When her grown son became regent for the five-year-old Louis XV in 1715, Elisabeth Charlotte made a conscious decision about how she would use her power and influence as mother of the regent. Although it was clear that she could play a hand in matters of state if she chose to, she decided to refrain.[25] In her letters she cited Salic law as a reason why women could not rule; but, as was often the case with Elisabeth Charlotte, personal and familial considerations mixed with political dictates. One of the main reasons she did not want to play a role in her son's government was that she did not want to encourage her dreadful daughter-in-law and her son's oldest daughter to offer advice as well. Here was a situation ripe for breeding bickering and ill-will throughout the family.[26] As she explained to the philosopher Gottfried Wilhelm Leibniz, "What is really happening I do not know, for I am extremely concerned that it might be thought that my son is ruled by women and therefore, in order to set an example to his wife and his daughter, I have announced loudly that I will not meddle in any of his affairs."[27] Yet even with Elisabeth Charlotte's declaration to remove herself from politics the people of Paris apparently refused to believe that she had not played a part in the amelioration of economic conditions after the John Law financial fiasco in 1720.[28]

Elisabeth Charlotte had the privilege, as a woman of the highest rank, to decline illegitimate political power precisely because her station and dignity permitted her to wield power legitimately through her ceremonial position as wife and mother within the royal family, a status that neither Mme de Montespan nor Mme de Maintenon could ever attain to the same extent. Although she might complain of the sheer weight of the ornate costumes required at court, Elisabeth Charlotte bore the weight of her ceremonial power comfortably. Her feelings about the relationship between ceremonial power and the work of ruling are lucidly expressed in a letter from 1720 regarding the Queen of Sweden's decision to make her husband king:

> I feel that it is most commendable and proper that the Queen of Sweden has made her husband King. In this manner she extricates herself from a great deal of toil and worry, binds her husband to herself by a strong bond of obligation, and yet retains her royal rank and estate; in other words, she has the honor without the toil, which I think is excellent, as is the point that she reserves the right to resume her duties as reigning Queen if my nephew should die. All of this is very well thought out.[29]

The Power of Sexuality

In contrast to the Queen of Sweden or Elisabeth Charlotte, who attained their positions at court through birth and marriage, royal mistresses "toiled" ceaselessly for the king, as they strove to make themselves ever ready to please him with a sparkling wit, a charming costume, and an enticing body, with very little chance of earning any lasting honor. Mme de Montespan lamented throughout her memoirs that despite bearing eight children for the king she was still a mere marquise, not a princess: "I thought that I deserved such a distinction personally, for my own sake, and I was always wishing that my august friend would create a title specially in my favor [.] And yet, magnificently generous as any mortal well could be, he never granted my wish."[30] One of Mme de Montespan's chief grievances against the king and court was that her ceremonial rank never matched her considerable personal power at court and that the king never honored her sufficiently for her role as mother of his children: she railed against her position as "second to the queen" and even declared it "timorous and shrivelled-brained" for the French not to allow the king to honor her officially by making her his second wife.[31] Resentful of her inferior position to the queen at the French court, Mme de Montespan reported proudly that foreigner visitors, at least, acknowledged her importance: an African envoy described her as "the second queen" and an admiring Turkish ambassador burst into tears before her, declaring "that in his country I should be in the first rank whereas at Saint Germain I was only in the second."[32] Yet, as Mme de Montespan's sister, Mme de Thianges, lamented and pointedly reminded her, "The king does not treat you like a great friend, like a distinguished friend, like the mother of his son, the duc du Maine; he treats you like a province that he has conquered, on which he levies tax after tax; that is all."[33]

Although Elisabeth Charlotte played her prescribed role at court, steadfastly upholding the dignity of her estate, she remained deeply ambivalent about court ceremonial, the luxury and extravagance of the aristocracy, and the power which accrued to her as a high-ranking woman at court: she penned letter after letter with her thoughts on the relationship of fashion to court formality, the distinction between magnificence and extravagance, and the fine line between the use and abuse of power by women. She was particularly skeptical of much of the faddishness of both men and women at court and condemned fashions that she considered undignified, such as the unboned mantuas, or fashions that played on men's and women's vanity such as beauty patches, cosmetics, and "artifices," such as eyeglasses and false teeth, which surely would have benefited her in old age.[34] Mme de Montespan reports in a scathing passage in her memoirs that Elisabeth Charlotte had the bad sense even to poke fun at her:

> She singled me out as the object of her ponderous Palatine sarcasms. She exaggerated my style of dress, my ways and habits. She thought to make fun of my little spaniels by causing herself to be followed, even into the King's presence-chamber, by a large turnspit, which in mockery she called by the name of my favorite dog. When I had had my hair dressed, ornamented with quantities of little curls, diamonds and jeweled pins, she had the impertinence to appear at Court wearing a huge wig, a grotesque travesty of my coiffure. I was told of it.[35]

Of all the fashions she discussed in her letters, Elisabeth Charlotte was most critical of the fashion Mme de Montespan had set for full skirts. Writing in 1721 to her half-sister, decades after Montespan had fallen from power, she complained of the new style of full skirts worn with paniers:

> The wide skirts which are worn everywhere are my aversion, they look insolent, as though one had come straight out of bed. The manteau as I wear it is nothing new, Mme la Dauphine used to wear one. The fashion of the beastly skirts first dates from Mme de Montespan. She used to wear them when she was pregnant, so as to hide her condition.[36]

Five days later, evidently still thinking furiously about Montespan and her skirts Elisabeth Charlotte wrote again to Luise, "I told you in my last letter how the fashion of loose skirts came from Mme de Montespan, who invented it to disguise her large belly when she was pregnant. But it was little use, for everybody always knew, and whenever she appeared in this skirt it was like a signal."[37] Elisabeth Charlotte felt a deep decades-long animosity towards Mme de Montespan, yet her objection to Montespan's skirts expressed more than personal dislike. Elisabeth Charlotte's indignity at Montespans's full skirts derived from their double insolence: they set a new fashion which mocked the dignity of official court costume at the same time that their association with illegitimate sexuality undermined a regime predicated on women's legitimate reproductive capacity.[38]

Although Elisabeth Charlotte never took a lover, she was no prude and accepted that women and men at court would invariably play the part of *coquettes* and *galants*. As she wrote, "I am not given to coquetry by nature, as everyone will attest; yet I do understand what human weakness can do and pity those who fall into such calamities more than I condemn them."[39] She sympathetically advised young serving maids how to terminate pregnancies and provided counsel to her young maids and relatives regarding their love affairs.[40] She frankly acknowledged that, at least for men, infidelity was the usual state of affairs: "There is nothing unusual about a man fooling around and having mistresses; among ten thousand one barely finds one who does not love someone other than his wife. In fact, they are to be praised if they at least speak kindly to their wives and treat them right."[41] What did upset Elisabeth Charlotte, however, were the public ramifications of private affairs; non-marital sexuality became dangerous when it mixed with matters of blood and birth, crossed class lines, and marred the dignified face of court society. Elisabeth Charlotte was particularly shocked by the public immorality that exploded during the regency of her son when the court left Versailles for Paris. As she complained in 1718, "Never have there been such women as there are now. They behave as though their salvation consisted in sleeping with men."[42] Elisabeth Charlotte rejected not sexuality but impropriety: good manners and civility were more important to her than upholding a rigid moral code.

Throughout her letters she discussed what we would call today homosexual relationships. Homosexual and heterosexual extramarital liaisons were discussed in very similar moral language and social context: "Where in the world does one find a husband," she complained in one letter, "who loves only his spouse and does not have someone, be it mistresses or boys, on the side?"[43] Married to one of the most well-known homosexuals at the French court, Elisabeth Charlotte had ample opportunity to develop her thoughts on the problems associated with husbands who had "boys on the side." As she openly described her late husband:

> More different brothers than His Majesty the King and the late Monsieur cannot be imagined . . . [Monsieur's] manners were more feminine than masculine, and he was not interested in horses and hunting but only in gambling, receptions, good food, dancing, and dressing up, in a word in all the things that the ladies love. The King on the other hand loved hunting, music and the theater, but my husband was only interested in large gatherings and masquerades. The King loved gallantries with ladies; I do not believe that my husband was ever in love.[44]

Elisabeth Charlotte tried hard not to complain about her husband's "excesses" or her unhappy marriage, explaining in a particularly poignant letter to her aunt Sophie, "These things are just too tiresome and I had therefore better be quiet about them and speak of something else."[45] Although late in life she did strongly condemn homosexuality, writing in a short passage to her half-sister that sodomy "is dreadful in Paris and brings all other vices in its train,"[46] in general, she expressed little outrage about the "vice" and was willing to quip to Monsieur's male followers, "You are welcome to gobble the peas, for I don't like them." In the world of court, sexual relations between men provoked lighthearted jokes rather than outright moral condemnation. Gossiping to her aunt Sophie about King William II of England, Elisabeth Charlotte confessed, "You make me laugh by what you said about the *château de derrière*. It is true that people here think of King William as belonging to that brotherhood, but they say he is less taken up with it now."[47]

Although Monsieur was foppish and effeminate, Elisabeth Charlotte never complained about her husband's lack of virility. She was bothered neither by his high heels nor his "perfumed gloves," even when she had to smell them as he sat next to her for long hours during her confinement for pregnancies; she complained about his make-up and rouge only when he once tried to smear some white foundation (*baume blanc*) on her face to hide her wrinkles.[48] Overall, as with improper heterosexual liaisons, Elisabeth Charlotte was more concerned with the social, familial, and political consequences of homosexual liaisons than with Monsieur's "inner drives" or the nature of "the act itself." As Michel Foucault has elaborated, there was no category in early-modern Europe for "the homosexual": sodomy defined an act, not a person, a sexual orientation, or a distinctive subculture.[49]

What bothered Elisabeth Charlotte was not the act of sodomy, but the sociability that male–male sexual relations seemed to foster: she believed that homosexual relations between men made men vulgar and ill-mannered and encouraged a dangerous, homosocial bonding among men that she considered antisocial. In contrast, Elisabeth Charlotte particularly enjoyed and appreciated the thoroughly heterosocial character of court society – whether at plays, masked balls, spectacles, hunting, feasting or gambling, men and women at court mixed freely. She blamed Mme de Maintenon's repressive piety for driving a wedge between men's and women's activities at court and inadvertently encouraging homosexuality.[50] Mme de Maintenon's sanctimony, Elisabeth Charlotte charged, prevented men and women from speaking and interacting socially with each other, a practice which had previously given young gentlemen "polish."[51]

In addition to breaking down rules of civility and destroying the politesse that she considered the foundation of court culture, what troubled Elisabeth Charlotte most about homosexuality was its potential to upset the class hierarchy. As she complained, "Because they love the boys, they no longer want to please anyone but one another, and the most popular among them is the one who knows best how to be debauched, coarse, and insolent. This habit has become so ingrained that no one knows how to live properly any longer, and they are worse than peasants behind the plough."[52] Not only did same-sex liaisons potentially turn young aristocrats into "peasants," the practice of elevating male favorites by granting them commissions at court upset the rank and class hierarchy to such an extent that, in Elisabeth Charlotte's opinion, "a bunch of stable grooms and petty valets are lords and masters over just about everything."[53] In general, Elisabeth Charlotte was more worried about the illegitimate infiltration of the upper class by lower-class male favorites (and vice versa) than the penetration of male bodies *per se*; in short, gender transgressions posed problems only to the extent that they caused class transgressions.[54]

In the particular case of her own husband, Elisabeth Charlotte also worried that Monsieur's homosexual liaisons undermined her own legitimate power within her family and at court and her economic well-being. In one letter in which she explicitly complained of Monsieur's ways, she mapped out the whole constellation of economic, political and familial concerns that framed her thoughts about Monsieur's liaisons with men:

> He [Monsieur] has only one interest: his young men, with whom he spends entire nights eating and drinking. He gives them incredible amounts of money; no expense is too great for them. In the meantime, the children and I hardly have the barest necessities. When I need shifts or sheets, I have to beg for them for a year and a day, while he gives ten thousand *thalers* to La Carte [a favorite] to buy linen in Flanders. As he realizes that I know quite well where all the money is going, he is afraid that I may tell the king, who might then send the boys away. Whatever I may say or do to make him understand that I don't care what kind of life he leads, he refuses to believe me, and every day he gets me into fresh trouble with the king.[55]

Squandering 10,000 *thalers* on a male friend with a taste for fine Flanders linen was not inherently a problem. But it became a problem when it deprived one's own wife and children of their property.[56] Likewise, Madame said explicitly that she did not care what kind of life her husband led, so long as it did not harm her relationship with the king.

Whether in relation to illegitimate children, extramarital liaisons, or homosexual relationships, morality was always deeply entwined with politics at the court of Louis XIV. Both morality and immorality could be political tools, if wielded adeptly. The pious Mme de Maintenon, according to Elisabeth Charlotte, had even gone so far as to favor the appointment of the most notorious "sodomite in the whole of France" as governor of Madame's son, the duc de Chartres, as part of a deliberate plan to make him as debauched as his father so as to make her own charge, the duc du Maine (Louis XIV's son by Mme de Montespan), shine in comparison.[57] Elisabeth Charlotte also claimed that Mme de Maintenon's ostensible excuse for shutting down the theater and other forms of entertainment at Versailles may have been religious, but she was actually trying to shut down opportunities for the king to meet with a wider group of male and female courtiers, thus depriving them of access to the king to augment her own.

While the morality of extramarital liaisons at court was relative, the distinction for Elisabeth Charlotte between immoral and moral reproduction was absolute; reflections on the familial, social, and political perils of illegitimacy fill her writings, and the legacy of Mme de Montespan's and Louis's "double adultery" plagued her, in the form of their many progeny, for her entire life. This distinction between moral and immoral reproduction was echoed in Elisabeth Charlotte's discussions of fashion, as we have seen in the case of dresses *à la Montespan*. Unseemly fashions were a sign of disorderly sexuality, and, conversely, dignified costume was associated with moral reproduction. Elisabeth Charlotte, for example, chronicled her daughter's transition from virginity to reproductive married life, as she discussed in her letters the preparation of her elaborate trousseau and betrothal, the wedding night, and signs of pregnancy in the first year.[58] When her daughter traveled to her new home in Nancy arrayed in the ornate ceremonial robes that her mother and father had so proudly displayed as part of her trousseau, Elisabeth Charlotte reported that upon entering her new town "my daughter was obliged to change her clothes because her dress was so heavy that she couldn't stand up in it, and just as she had taken off her skirts, along came the duke and paid her one of his visits. She's quite used to it by now, and doesn't dislike that business as much as I did."[59] While whimsical fashion marked men's and women's individual, physical bodies, appropriate ornate costume marked not only one's rank in the body politic but, in the case of women, a body ready for legitimate reproduction of the aristocracy.

Personal Identity and the World of Goods

Both in her attitudes toward fashion and her attire, Elisabeth Charlotte represents an "old sartorial regime" and early-modern visual culture that was already drawing to a close for many members of the French aristocracy on the eve of Louis XIV's death in 1715. In this world luxurious costume was a legitimate and mandatory expression of the absolutist court and the social power of aristocracy. In such a culture, the line between signified and signifier – between princesses of the blood and jewel-encrusted gowns – was blurred. Conspicuous consumption was necessary for living the life of the courtier and clothing did indeed "make the man," or woman. Yet, the relationship between material objects, consumption, and identity was articulated differently than it would be in modern consumer societies. Although, as we have seen in the pages of the *Mercure*, court society was not immune to commercial culture, personal consumption was theoretically to be yoked to Louis's court politics: the king and aristocrats such as Elisabeth Charlotte needed to believe that they could ultimately retain control of commerce and *la mode* through the force of their iconographic power standing at the glittering apex of French society, politics, and culture.

Looking back on Elisabeth Charlotte's life from our perspective in the early twenty-first century, when our identities are constructed, in part, by the objects we consume and own, one wonders how Elisabeth Charlotte felt about the material objects surrounding her: where did she draw the line between public props and personal property, between political tools and private pleasures? How was her identity constructed through the material goods that surrounded her at Versailles and St. Cloud? How did clothing, in particular, shape her identity? Or was her identity rooted in other, less material, aspects of her life? Unlike Mme de Montespan, whose memoir chronicles her quest for country estates, furniture, and jewels, or contemporaries like Mme de Sévigné, who explicitly discussed shopping in her letters, Elisabeth Charlotte never discussed "consumption" in her letters in the modern sense of buying and procuring goods. To be sure, there were things she longed for, such as a new pair of hunting horses, but the jewelry and fashions that she specifically commented on were almost always gifts. In particular, ceremonial presents, such as the duke's wedding present to her daughter, are described at length:

> The Duke's wedding present to my daughter was delivered yesterday. It is extremely beautiful, and consists of diamond eardrops that could not be lovelier; a string of pearls, not particularly large but of excellent whiteness and perfectly round and even; two bracelets of five rows of pearls a little larger than green sugar peas; another diamond bracelet, quite perfect; and two rings. My daughter's pleasure is indescribable. Following the custom here, all her clothes are displayed in Monsieur's gallery.[60]

Elisabeth Charlotte had a clear aesthetic, as well as political, appreciation for the duke's gifts and suggests that her "daughter's pleasure in these gifts is indescribable." In general, in Elisabeth Charlotte's writings, it is only objects which had been given or received as gifts which took on a heightened emotional and aesthetic significance: she is clearly sentimental when she talks about her sadness at losing her "pretty things" when her husband has them melted down to pay his debts, and she lovingly describes an underskirt she had given to her aunt, "not bad at all: natural-looking blue flowers and gold festoons on a black background."[61]

Despite her aesthetic appreciation and sentimental attachment to particular belongings, Elisabeth Charlotte typically distanced herself from the goods surrounding her. Like costumes and props, luxurious material objects were useful, and even necessary in order to play a particular role on the stage of court, but the relationship between individuals and objects was nebulous and fleeting. Modern concepts such as "ownership" and "consumption" cannot adequately express the relationship of men and women to material objects in the Old Regime. In such a world, Elisabeth Charlotte not only ran the risk of having her personal belongings snatched away from her by her dissolute husband, but, like all courtiers, could not even claim true ownership of the goods she did possess; ultimately, her clothing belonged not to her, but to the court and its royal officers. As she explained in a letter to her aunt Sophie in 1709, "There is nothing that one can truly call one's own. Linen, nightshirts and petticoats belong to the woman of the bedchamber, and the *dame d'atour* takes possession of my clothes from one year to the next, as well as all my lace."[62]

In a world in which goods could be taken from her and she even felt herself to be in some sense "owned by the court," material goods and practices of consumption – like fleeting female beauty and illegitimate sexuality – provided an unsure foundation on which to build one's identity and a risky manner in which to fashion a self. Moreover, while accepting that magnificent objects and sumptuous dress were politically indispensable to her ceremonial position, Elisabeth Charlotte worried about the impact of magnificence and materialism on one's personal life and morality. "I appreciate the German's sincerity more than I appreciate magnificence, " she wrote. "It is easy to understand how luxury drives out good faith; one cannot be magnificent without money, and if money becomes so important, one becomes calculating, and once one has become calculating, one seeks every possible means of getting something, which opens the door to falsehood, lying, and cheating, and this in turn altogether drives out good faith, loyalty, and sincerity."[63] Elisabeth Charlotte, who abhorred gambling, refused to go into debt, feared an economy based on risk and chance, and detested a society that seemed increasingly to mistake money for true magnificence, sought a more secure basis for her identity than personal consumption.

Elisabeth Charlotte rooted her identity in what she considered more essential qualities shaped by her ethnicity, gender, generation, and class. First, she identified herself as a German, keeping her connection to Germany alive through her fond memories of her childhood and her lifelong epistolary relationship with her German relatives. As she wrote late in life, "In everything, including what I eat and drink, I am still altogether German, as I have been all my life"[64] Being "German" implied for Elisabeth Charlotte a set of qualities, including honesty, simplicity, and, perhaps most important, Protestantism. Second, her maternal relationship with her son and daughter was a primary aspect of her adult identity. Later in life her identity was clearly rooted in her age and generation and she frequently described herself as old. Finally, her identity was defined by her estate and rank as a princess of the blood. Through her birth and station she felt a deep connection to aristocrats of a similar rank – from Karoline of Wales to the Queen of Sweden – all over Europe. This was an identity that did not originate from her marriage into the ranks of the Orleans family, but one that she considered her birthright as a well-bred German princess descended from a long noble lineage.

Although Elisabeth Charlotte never explicitly distinguished between her public and private identities, her letters reveal that she acted not only according to royal dictates but also, to the extent that she could, from personal desires. While strictly following royal orders to wear the *grand habit*, she did so not only because it reflected the grave dignity of Louis's court but also because it suited her personal desire to have a uniform costume, which would permit her to maintain her own dignity in the face of the wiles of royal mistresses and the whims of *la mode*. Although Elisabeth Charlotte's entire life was wedded to the project of royal absolutism, her commitment was as much to her family and her station as to her worship of the Sun king.

While Elisabeth Charlotte endured an unhappy marriage, a forced conversion to Catholicism, and exile from her beloved Germany, one is struck by the remarkable stability over a fifty-year period of her identity as German princess, aristocratic mother, and French courtier. Her vision of a stable aristocratic hierarchy and court society, predicated on an absolutist economy of the gift and royal spectacle, provided the ballast for her identity; clothed in the heavy robes of state rather than the flimsy robes of fashion she seamlessly combined her public role with her private identity. Wedded to a belief in true noble magnificence rather than crass materialism, she managed to resolve the tension between the artifice and spectacle required by her public office and the sincerity and simplicity inspired by her private faith.

Yet, by the early eighteenth century, Elisabeth Charlotte was clearly aware that a new fashion culture was gradually replacing the sartorial hegemony of Louis XIV's Versailles, and that the aristocracy was forging a new relationship with commercial culture. She increasingly despaired at the undignified fashions being worn by her own daughter-in-law and grandchildren and lamented the explosion of commercialism in Regency Paris. Her letters from this period are filled with long descriptions of the impact on France of the financial system of the Scottish financier John Law, speculation, and fortunes suddenly made and lost.[65] The new aristocratic and commercial culture surrounding her in Paris in the last decade of her life so bewildered her that she could explain it only by resorting to the older moral language of "avarice" and "greed" and distinctions between French and German national character. As she complained in 1720,

> Except for my son and Madame de Chateauthiers, I do not know a single soul in France who is absolutely free of selfishness and greed. All the others, without exception, are greedy to the point of making fools of themselves, especially the princes and princesses of the Blood; they have gotten into brawls with the clerks at the bank and into all kinds of other ignominious scrapes. Money rules the world, that is true enough, but I do not believe that there is a place in the world where it rules people more strictly than here.[66]

Interestingly, although she cites examples of both men and women intoxicated by dreams of growing rich with John Law's schemes, she never distinguished between men's and women's greed or materialism. Class and nationality remained, as they had throughout her life, her primary categories for drawing distinctions between behavior and character. As she wrote in 1720,

It seems to me that our good, honest Germans are not quite as eager to do everything for money as the French and English; they are surely less greedy. Oh Lord, how I detest greed! It certainly is wrong to serve the god Mammon, as the Scripture says, and I believe that this is the most damnable sin, for it is the root of all evil.[67]

Old-fashioned greed and avarice fill her writing, not "frivolity," "luxury" and "taste," the new vocabulary of eighteenth-century fashion culture and a new enlightened society of taste. Nor does Elisabeth Charlotte discuss what people are buying with their wealth; she discusses only the rush to buy stocks, the grasping for money, and fortunes made and lost overnight. For a woman who never possessed any control over her own finances or any true personal property in her own clothing or jewels, urban commercial culture was not something she could clearly conceptualize. For Elisabeth Charlotte, Regency culture resembled one of Monsieur's court gambling parties to which all of Parisian society had been invited.[68] Locked in a seventeenth-century absolutist and mercantilist mentality, the ramifications of the commercial culture exploding around her were ultimately beyond her comprehension. The slippage in Elisabeth Charlotte's mind between the evils of greed and the evils of sodomy (writing in one letter during this period that sodomy was the root of all evil and claiming in another letter that greed was the root of all evil) is telling. Greed and sodomy both posed serious threats to the stable class structure and the spectacular absolutist culture, which Louis XIV and courtiers like Elisabeth Charlotte had constructed piece by piece as they clothed the private reproductive bodies of male and female courtiers with the solemn costume of the French court and absolutist state.[69]

Conclusion

Beneath the imposing edifice of Versailles and behind the glittering facade of court spectacle, Louis's absolutism had always been built on a series of tensions and contradictions: a stable economy of legitimate reproductive sexuality rubbed up against an illicit libidinal economy; an ordered aristocratic court society based on blood and birth was predicated on the services of a mobile bourgeoisie and the buying and selling of offices; a publicly masculinist state tacitly permitted the rule of the monarch by private women; and courtiers assumed multiple roles as they simultaneously played as desiring subjects and served as objects of the king's desire. The key to Louis's statecraft was the ability to harness these contradictions and the power of his iconic rule was predicated on his ability both seemingly to efface and effectively to use these tensions.[70]

Yet, in the case of women and *la mode* – whether in the position of desiring subjects or as objects of desire – Louis struggled to stabilize the contradictions of his iconic regime. Louis's first "official mistress," Mme de la Vallière, explained to her friend and rival, Mme de Montespan, in an attempt to persuade her to end her immoral relationship with Louis, that after she realized that Louis no longer loved her she began to see clearly for the first time what he really was: "I no longer saw in the father of my children anything other than a young prince, accustomed to seeing his dominating wish fulfilled in everything." It was only when she saw him thus, without the eyes of love, that Mme de la Vallière began to despise him for his lack of political and libidinal control, for his subjugation to the women who should be his subjects:

> Knowing how little in this matter he is master of himself, he who knows so well how to be master of himself in everything to do with his numerous inferiors, I deplored the facility he enjoys from his attractions, from his wealth, from his power to dazzle the heart which he desires to move and subdue.[71]

Elisabeth Charlotte understood that not only illicit sexuality, but also greed and *la mode* threatened to destabilize the edifice of power Louis had constructed at Versailles. Her letters witness that even at the height of the King's power Louis's ability to control fashion and commercial culture was called into question by men and women whose personal desires potentially undermined Louis's royal productions. What was, for example, to have been a powerful staging of absolutist magnificence at Marly in 1684 was undermined by women who spent more time courting *la mode* and their own personal desires than subjecting themselves to the requirements of Louis's political stagecraft.[72] As Elisabeth Charlotte related sadly:

> There was to have been a great fête at Marly; the king had planned to give presents to all the ladies. Soon there was so much talk about it that every lady of any quality wanted to be present, and round about the time that we were to set off for Marly such quantities of ladies arrived that one hardly knew which way to turn. Some of them had even called on the tradespeople to find out what had been bought and how much it had all cost. The King was extremely annoyed when he heard of it. He said that people seemed to have such exaggerated ideas of the magnificence of his presents that they were bound to appear insignificant by comparison. He canceled the party, made us gamble for the brocades and ribbons as well as the fans, and kept the precious stones for himself.[73]

In canceling the staging of absolutist magnificence that day at Marly, the king may have had the last word; certainly the women did not get the presents they had dreamed of (and even shopped for in Paris!). Yet, in the end, the royal economy of gift giving had been undermined by the commercial economy of Paris; for gambling was a poor substitute for the promised spectacle of royal power and abundance through gift giving.[74] In the end, his female courtiers' pursuit of *les modes* made even the king look small.

Notes

1. To Raugräfin Luise, July 4, 1698, in Forster, *A Woman's Life*: 109. Other English translations are provided by Gertrude Scott Stevenson, *The Letters of Madame*, 2 vols (New York: Appleton, 1925) and Kroll, *Letters from Liselotte*.
2. To Sophie, May 15, 1695, "If it is true that one can become a virgin again after years and years of sleeping alone, I must certainly be one now, for it is seventeen years since Monsieur and I have slept together. But I wouldn't like to fall into the hands of the Tartars to have the point proved." Kroll, *Letters from Liselotte*: 70.
3. For biographical information, see Forster, *A Woman's Life*; "From the Garden Snake to the Toad: Madame Palatine on the Ministers of the Grand Siècle," *Cahiers du Dix-Septième: Journal of the Southeast American Society for French Seventeenth-Century Studies* vol. 3, no. 1 (Spring 1989), 243–60 and "From the Patient's Point of View: Illness and Health in the Letters of Liselotte von der Pfalz (1652–1722)" *Bulletin of the History of Medicine* 60(1986): 297–320.
4. To Luise, November 19, 1716, in Forster, *A Woman's Life*: 206.
5. Montespan, *Memoirs*, vol. 1: 55.
6. To Sophie, November 4, 1677, in Kroll, *Letters from Liselotte*: 31–2.
7. On the phrase, "the old sartorial regime, see Kuchta, *The Three-Piece Suit and Modern Masculinity*.
8. To Sophie, February 19, 1702, Kroll, *Letters from Liselotte*: 105.
9. Laqueur, *Making Sex*.
10. To Karoline of Wales, August 18, 1718, in Forster, *A Woman's Life*: 216.
11. To Sophie, December 29, 1701, in Kroll, *Letters from Liselotte*: 104.
12. Louis XIV's and Mme de la Vallière's daughter, Marie-Anne de Bourbon (1666–1739), known as "the beautiful Princesse de Conti" after her marriage to Louis-Armant, Prince de Conti, was legitimated.
13. To Sophie, April 14, 1688, in Forster, *A Woman's Life*: 55–6. Descendants of this "misalliance" included Philippe Egalité and Louis Philippe of France, kings of Bulgaria and the Belgians.
14. To Luise, May 1, 1718, in Forster, *A Woman's Life*: 213.
15. Elisabeth Charlotte wrote, "Writing is my favorite occupation, because I don't like needlework; to my mind there is nothing more tedious in the world than putting in a needle and pulling it out again," in Kroll, *Letters from Liselotte*: 210. On Elisabeth Charlotte's attitudes toward the theater, see W.S. Brooks and P.J. Yarrow, *The Dramatic Criticism of Elisabeth Charlotte, Duchesse D'Orleans, with an Annotated Chronology of Performances of the Popular and Court Theaters in France* (Lewiston, NY: Mellen Press, 1995).

16. Montespan, *Memoirs*, vol. 1: 213.
17. To Sophie, December 14, 1676, in Kroll, *Letters from Liselotte*: 31.
18. To Luise, December 20, 1721, in Kroll, *Letters from Liselotte*: 238.
19. Historians have recently devoted considerable attention to women's economic power within the family during the early-modern period. Despite the legal system of coverture which denied women any legal or economic existence apart from their husbands, historians now argue that women managed to carve out some measure of economic independence. See Maxine Berg, "Women's Property and the Industrial Revolution," *Journal of Interdisciplinary History*, 34, no. 2 (Autumn 1993), Lloyd Bonfield, *Marriage Settlements, 1601–1740: The Adoption of the Strict Settlement* (Cambridge: Cambridge University Press, 1983), Amy Louis Erickson, *Women and Property in Early Modern England* (London: Routledge, 1993), Margot Finn, "Women, Consumption, and Coverture in England c. 1760–1860," (unpublished paper, Davis Center Seminar, April 1995), and Susan Staves, *Married Women's Separate Property in England, 1660–1833* (Cambridge, MA: Harvard University Press, 1990).
20. To Sophie, October 25, 1698, in Kroll, *Letters from Liselotte*: 85.
21. To Luise, January 20, 1718, in Forster, *A Woman's Life*: 210; To Luise, April 3, 1699, in Kroll, *Letters from Liselotte*: 86. See also, Letter to Sophie, October 15, 1701, in Kroll, *Letters from Liselotte*: 102.
22. Letter to Sophie, October 15, 1701, in Kroll, *Letters from Liselotte*: 102.
23. See Landes, *Women and the Public Sphere in the Age of the French Revolution*, Madelyn Gutwirth, *The Twilight of the Goddesses: Women and Representation in the French Revolutionary Era* (New Brunswick, NJ: Rutgers University Press, 1992), and Joan Kelly, "Did Women Have a Renaissance?" in *Women, History, and Theory: The Essays of Joan Kelly* (Chicago: University of Chicago Press, 1984).
24. Mme de Montespan claimed, to her chagrin, that she had not in fact been permitted by Louis to participate in matters of state. *Memoirs*, vol. 1, 128–9. In her letters Elisabeth Charlotte makes numerous complaints about the illegitimate power of Mme de Maintenon over the king. Forster, *A Woman's Life*: 98–9.
25. To Karoline of Wales, September 22, 1716, in Forster, *A Woman's Life*: 205.
26. Ibid.
27. To Gottfried Wilhelm Leibniz, November 21, 1715, in Forster, *A Woman's Life*: 203–4.
28. To Luise, June 11, 1720, in Forster, *A Woman's Life*: 250.
29. To Freiherr Von Goertz, Saint Cloud, April 25, 1720, in Forster, *A Woman's Life*: 248–9.
30. Montespan, *Memoirs*, vol. 1: 311.
31. Ibid.: 206.

32. Ibid.: 140–1. On the Turkish ambassador, see Ibid.: 134.
33. Ibid.: 311.
34. On eyeglasses, see to Luise, October 29, 1719, in Forster, *A Woman's Life*: 240.
35. Montespan, *Memoirs*, vol. 1: 213–14.
36. To Luise, December 1721, in Kroll, *Letters from Liselotte*: 238.
37. Ibid.
38. In her memoirs Mme de Montespan relates that her full skirts did at least fool the Queen, who did not suspect Montespan was pregnant. *Memoirs*, vol. 1: 149.
39. To Amalie Elizabeth, March 30, 1704, in Forster, *A Woman's Life*: 153.
40. See letter of December 3, 1705 to Amalie Elizabeth:

    > I really had a good laugh when I read that you, dear Amelise, would rather get married than commit the sin of something-or-other. In the sight of God this is indeed much more commendable, but to look at it in human terms, as many people do, marriage is more burdensome, for a husband one takes for life. But if a coquette is tired of one lover, she takes another, that is ever so much easier. (Forster, *A Woman's Life*: 162)

41. To Luise, June 30, 1718, in Forster, *A Woman's Life*: 214.
42. To Luise, March 13, 1718, in Kroll, *Letters from Liselotte*: 193.
43. To Sophie, February 13, 1695, in Forster, *A Woman's Life*: 87.
44. To Karoline of Wales, January 9, 1716, in Forster, *A Woman's Life*: 204.
45. To Sophie, May 20, 1689, in Forster, *A Woman's Life*: 63.
46. To Luise, April 21, 1720, in Forster, *A Woman's Life*: 248.
47. To Sophie, September 15, 1695, in Kroll, *Letters from Liselotte*: 70.
48. To Luise, December 15, 1716, in Forster, *A Woman's Life*: 207; to Luise, February 28, 1711, in Forster, *A Woman's Life*: 184.
49. Historians Roy Porter and Lesley Hall argue that in the late seventeenth century sex was not seen as a psychological category nor a matter of the inner self. Sex manuals were concerned with reproduction rather than problems of sexuality. Porter and Hall, *Facts of Life: The Creation of Sexual Knowledge in Britain, 1650–1950* (New Haven: Yale University Press, 1995). Michel Foucault, *The History of Sexuality, Vol. I: An Introduction*, trans. Robert Hurley (New York, 1978). The most important analyses of early modern homosexuality are offered by Alan Bray, *Renaissance Homosexuality* (London: Gay Men's Press, 1982) and Randy Trumbach *Sex and the Gender Revolution* (Chicago: The University of Chicago Press, 1998). See Jonathan Goldberg, ed., *Queering the Renaissance* (Durham, NC: Duke University Press, 1994) and Jeffrey Merrick and Bryant T. Ragan, *Homosexuality in Modern France* (Oxford: Oxford University Press, 1996).

50. Although Elisabeth Charlotte did not explicitly argue this point, a court which provided opportunities for men and women to come together socially gave women a more equal footing with men. It gave women more occasions to petition the king and high-placed officers and more chances to persuade through their charms and develop alliances. From the 1690s to Louis's death, Elisabeth Charlotte complained that the king was unavailable to her and that he was being kept "behind closed doors" by Maintenon. Elisabeth Charlotte also criticized Mme de Maintenon for wanting to shut down her beloved theater, another place where the sexes could mingle.
51. To Sophie, February 13, 1695, in Forster, *A Woman's Life*: 87.
52. Ibid.
53. To Sophie, January 18, 1697 to Sophie, in Forster, *A Woman's Life*: 98.
54. Alan Bray's work on early-modern British homosexuality suggests that the commonplace and unproblematic intimacies between male friends became worrisome and were transformed in the cultural imagination into "sodomy" when male friendship crossed class lines. Alan Bray, "Homosexuality and the Signs of Male Friendship in Elizabethan England," in Goldberg, *Queering the Renaissance*: 40–61.
55. To Sophie, March 7, 1696, in Kroll, *Letters from Liselotte*: 72.
56. Ironically, despite Madame's continual worries that her husband was squandering money, during the second half of the seventeenth century, through careful investment and management, Monsieur consolidated a vast fortune which would become the basis for the Orleans family wealth for centuries to come. See Nancy Nichols Barker, *Brother to the Sun King: Philippe, Duke of Orleans* (Baltimore: Johns Hopkins University Press, 1989), 166–98.
57. To Sophie, August 26, 1689, in Forster, *A Woman's Life*: 65.
58. To Sophie, October 25, 1698, in Kroll, *Letters from Liselotte*: 84.
59. To Sophie, November 16, 1698, in Kroll, *Letters from Liselotte*: 85.
60. To Sophie, October 1, 1698, in Kroll, *Letters from Liselotte*: 82–3.
61. To Ameliese, July 29, 1706, in Kroll, *Letters from Liselotte*: 124.
62. To Sophie, August 15, 1709, in Kroll, *Letters from Liselotte*: 137.
63. To Sophie, May 11, 1692, in Forster, *A Woman's Life*: 75–6.
64. To Raugräfin Luise, May 3, 1721, in Forster, *A Woman's Life*: 264.
65. In 1719, John Law persuaded the regent that in order to liquidate the public debt and to stimulate French overseas commerce he should create a state-owned bank which was authorized to print paper money which would be funded by the Compagnie d'Occident. The regent, the aristocracy, and a broad segment of the French population invested heavily in the company and the company's stock skyrocketed until a panic led to the collapse of the company and the bank and forced Law to flee France. See Edgar Faure, *La banqueroute de Law* (Paris: Gallimard, 1977).

66. To Luise, February 11, 1720, in Forster, *A Woman's Life*: 245.

67. To Luise, September 5, 1720, in Forster, *A Woman's Life*: 252.

68. On the culture of gambling in old regime France, see Thomas M. Kavanagh, *Enlightenment and the Shadows of Chance: The Novel and the Culture of Gambling in Eighteenth-Century France* (Baltimore: Johns Hopkins University Press, 1993).

69. Jonathan Dewald makes the important argument that although the seventeenth-century nobility's use of money seems remarkably modern (i.e. economically rational and self-interested), nobles' experiences of money were always intertwined with their experiences of hierarchy, tradition, and political power. According to Dewald, gambling, not the market economy, offered aristocrats the respite from the discomforts of traditional dependency they longed for. Jonathan Dewald, *Aristocratic Experience and the Origins of Modern Culture: France, 1570–1715* (Berkeley: University of California Press, 1993): 172 and Chapter 5.

70. On Louis XIV's negotiation of power with the nobility, see J. Russell Major, *From Renaissance Monarchy to Absolute Monarchy: French Kings, Nobles and Estates* (Baltimore: Johns Hopkins University Press, 1994).

71. Montespan, *Memoirs*, vol. 2: 99.

72. Mme de Scudéry's *Conversations nouvelles sur divers sujets* (Paris: Claude Barbin, 1684) describes what the fête at Marly should have looked like. Elisabeth Goldsmith, in her analysis of these kinds of festivities, argues that the king played the heroic role of conqueror by making himself the source of all goods at the gambling party while insuring that none of his nobles emerged feeling like losers. *Exclusive Conversations: The Art of Interaction in Seventeenth-Century France* (Philadelphia: University of Pennsylvania Press, 1988): 55–6.

73. To Sophie, September 3, 1684, in Kroll, *Letters from Liselotte*: 43.

74. On the anthropology of the gift see the pioneering work of Marcel Mauss, *The Gift: Forms and Functions of Exchange in Archaic Societies* (New York: Norton, 1967). See also Georges Bataille, *The Accursed Share: An Essay on General Economy, Vol. I Consumption* (New York: Zone Books, 1988): 63–77. On the importance of gift-giving in early-modern France, see Natalie Davis, *The Gift in Sixteenth-Century France* (Madison: The University of Wisconsin Press, 2000); on gifts and reciprocity in aristocratic culture, see Smith, *The Culture of Merit*.

Part II
La Ville: Clothing and Consumption in a Society of Taste

"Taste and Fashion – a Fable"

Fashion said one day to Taste,
You must be crazy about me,
Because I make you shine everywhere
By the forms that I vary.
"Stop kidding yourself," he responded sharply.
"You have no right to my thanks:
I mean it;
You make everything extravagantly,
And nothing with discernment.
Do you offer us agreeable forms?
Never. Everyone takes pleasure in your wildness
But I find you unbearable.
You always do everything in excess.
By you bad taste circulates . . ."
Taste would have depicted all her faults,
If Fashion hadn't departed in anger.
She declared herself his bitter enemy,
And since that time she has set all our heads a-spinning.

Almanach historique et raisonné (1777).

In the half century after Elisabeth Charlotte's death, the absolutist court and fashion culture were dealt a severe blow. During the reign of Louis XVI, court society still enacted the sacred rituals of absolutism – Marie Antoinette appeared in ceremonial court garb and Louis reviewed his troops in full dress uniform – but Versailles, as the center of the French people's cultural and political imagination, no longer held sway. Since the early eighteenth century, when the court had temporarily taken up residence in Paris during the Regency, aristocratic sociability had increasingly centered on Paris rather than Versailles. The culture of the Enlightenment flourished in social settings – academies and salons – in which nobility of the robe and nobility of the sword, aristocrats and bourgeois, rubbed shoulders. New values of domesticity and intimacy inspired even Louis XVI, and he and his family increasingly retreated from the great ceremonial halls of the palace to the privacy of the Petit Trianon. The tensions that had emerged during Louis XIV's reign regarding *la cour* and *la ville*, absolutism and mercantilism, and social rank and inner subjectivity, profoundly shaped the transformation of eighteenth-century Paris into a modern, sociable and commercial city.

By the eve of the Revolution the commercial culture of Paris witnessed a significant transformation in the production and consumption of clothing, fashion styles, and the meaning of *la mode* itself. In the seventeenth century, as we have seen, fashionable dress was restricted to a small group of elite men and women who had the resources to invest in heavy, ornate garments made from costly silks and gold and silver brocades by the privileged corporations that controlled the clothing trade. The rest of the population possessed an extremely limited wardrobe, comprising either coarse, homemade clothing or the cast-offs of the upper classes. By the late eighteenth century, fashionable dressing was no longer exclusively the privilege of the elite but something in which men and women across a broader range of stations and incomes could indulge. The wardrobes of virtually all Parisians, from manual workers to aristocrats, had increased significantly in value, in number of garments, and in varieties of clothing. Maids and shop girls sported cleaner and whiter blouses, cuffs, coifs, and stockings, while new inexpensive, lightweight calicoes transformed the gray and brown wardrobes of the populace with splashes of color. An entirely new fashion culture had emerged in which Versailles was partially eclipsed as the center of fashion and in which young fops, Parisian actresses, and *marchandes de modes* vied with the king and queen as arbiters of taste. The new commercial culture also witnessed the birth of the fashion press and new forms of publicity, including business cards and window displays, which challenged centuries-old practices of corporate and royal control of production and distribution.

Perhaps the most significant aspect of this new fashion culture was the way in which gender increasingly shaped patterns of clothing consumption. Historians now know that the perception by contemporaries that eighteenth-century Parisian women – across all classes – were more susceptible to the allure of new and luxurious fashions than were their husbands was not just the ranting of misogynists looking for yet another pretext to lash out at women. Women's consumption patterns began to diverge dramatically from men's in the eighteenth century. From the mid-eighteenth century onward the relative value of women's wardrobes across all classes increased, often five to ten times more rapidly than their husbands'. By the eve of the Revolution, whereas an artisan might possess fifteen items of clothing worth 38 *livres*, his wife might possess as many as fifty items worth 346 *livres*.[1]

Although a fashionable dress might cost more than many working women earned annually, contemporaries marveled at the colorful fabrics and pretty dresses worn by the working women of Paris. If royal mistresses such as Montespan and Pompadour embodied *la mode*, however problematically, by mid-century *la mode* was increasingly also associated with urban working women – actresses, *grisettes*, and *marchandes de modes*. Significantly, even Madame du Barry, the Bourbon monarchy's most infamous royal mistress, was publicly decried as a "mere *grisette*," an epithet that castigated her immorality, her bad taste, and her modest beginnings as an assistant in a dressmaker's workshop. For enlightened critics who reflected on the problems of commerce and urban culture, ranging from poverty and prostitution to bad taste and uppity women, these urban working women personified not only *la mode*, but also the perils of modernity more generally.

Eighteenth-century Paris was a vast, bustling city with a population that had expanded from roughly 500,000 at the time of Louis XIV's death in 1715 to close to 750,000 on the eve of the Revolution. Although revisionist historians in the past two decades have focused primarily on the political and cultural history of the *ancien régime*, social and economic historians have begun to question older views of a backward French economy mired in tradition. Jonathan Dewald has pointed to the openness of aristocrats to new economic practices. Colin Jones's portrayal of the entrepreneurial and commercial mindset of eighteenth-century French men and women argues for a vibrant commercial culture in pre-revolutionary France. Philosopher Gilles Lipovetsky has linked the new commercial practices of eighteenth-century France directly to political change, suggesting that fashion played a crucial role in ushering in a more democratic society by helping to create a culture of autonomous individuals.[2] Perhaps more than any other scholar, French historian Daniel Roche has unmasked the dynamic urban culture growing within the traditional economic structures and social rhythms of the early-modern world. For more than two decades, Roche's research has breathed life into the everyday world of Parisians, permitting us to peer into their houses, their wardrobes, and their mentalities. In his seminal work on French fashion culture, Roche argues compellingly for the role of a new culture of clothing in the birth of modern individualism, a prerequisite for liberal thought; his research on Paris directly links new practices of urban and material culture to the demise of absolutism.[3]

Although we may accept that the commercial bourgeoisie was not the driving force in the Revolution that historians once thought it to be, this new body of research does affirm the centrality of economic and material transformations to political change in the eighteenth century.[4] New representations of femininity and the newly gendered political culture that emerged during the age of Revolution were linked to developments in commercial culture. As a paradigmatic example, Jean-Jacques Rousseau's obsessive worries about the theater, female display, commerce and fashion suggest the links between commerce and politics in his critique of public women, and his model for male public authority and female domestic prerogatives was grounded on a strikingly gendered conception of both the male producer and the female consumer. Not only for Enlightenment philosophers, but for ordinary French men and women, making sense of the realm of commercial culture and the vicissitudes of *la mode* helped craft new attitudes toward the meaning of public and private, and freedom and control. The fashion culture of the Old Regime and the fashion editors, entrepreneurs, distributors, and retailers who dominated it, stood firmly within the emerging public sphere and through the fashion press, almanacs, and advice manuals, played a key role in formulating a new set of attitudes about womanhood, commerce, national prosperity, despotism and citizenship.

By examining commerce and consumption as a "middle ground," which participates both in what scholars habitually call the "public" and "private" realms of eighteenth-century culture, we may be able to see more clearly the connections between the economy and politics and to move beyond static models of state versus civil society, economic stasis versus economic modernity, Old Regime theatricality versus revolutionary representation, and public men versus private women, and to enter into the complex process by which the experiences of women and the discourses of femininity were transformed by the workshops, boutiques, and fashion magazines of eighteenth-century Paris. For eighteenth-century French men and women, who did not yet have a well-developed conceptualization of the modern economy or liberal politics, the process of "sexing *la mode*" played a crucial role in helping them make sense of the seemingly irrational economy that imbued their lives as consumers and producers and husbands and wives. Ideas about novelty, social change, fashion, and femininity were all deeply entwined. French men and women struggled and grappled with the meaning of mutability and change – those hallmarks of modernity – (and ultimately made a temporary peace with them) through the banal and everyday acts of dressing each morning, shopping in the boutiques of Paris, and reading enigmas and lighthearted poems in the pages of the fashion press. To re-read these simple, non-revolutionary acts, for a more revolutionary, if not Revolutionary, meaning, is the aim of these chapters.

Notes

1. Daniel Roche, "L'économie des garde-robes à Paris, de Louis XIV à Louis XVI," *Communications* 46 (1987): 93–118.
2. Jonathan Dewald, "The Ruling Class and the Marketplace: Nobles and Money in Early Modern France," in *The Culture of the Market*, ed. Thomas Haskell and Richard Teichgraeber III (Cambridge: Cambridge University Press, 1993): 43–65; Colin Jones, "Bourgeois Revolution Revivified: 1789 and Social Change," in *Rewriting the French Revolution*, ed. Colin Lucas (Oxford: Clarendon Press, 1991): 69–118 and "The Great Chain of Buying: Medical Advertisement, the Bourgeois Public Sphere and the Origins of the French Revolution," *American Historical Review*, 101, no. 1 (February 1996): 13–40; Gilles Lipovetsky, *The Empire of Fashion: Dressing Modern Democracy* (Princeton: Princeton University Press, 1994).
3. Roche, *The Culture of Clothing; France in the Enlightenment* (Cambridge, MA: Harvard University Press, 1998); *A History of Everyday Things: The Birth of Consumption in France*, trans. Brian Pearce (Cambridge: Cambridge University Press, 2000); *The People of Paris, an Essay in Popular Culture in the Eighteenth Century* (Berkeley: University of California Press, 1987).
4. See L.M. Cullen, "History, Economic Crisis and Revolution: Understanding Eighteenth-Century France," *Economic History Review*, 46 (1993).

–3–

A Natural Right to Dress Women

On the night of June 21, 1725, Pierre Cornu and two other bachelor tailors, accompanied by guild officials, descended on the home of Pierre Maïr in search of his wife, Marie Thérèse Sermoise, a *maîtresse couturière*. The men noisily demonstrated outside of Marie Thérèse's house, hurling all sorts of insults. Then, they stormed into her workroom, tossed several boned bodices Marie Thérèse had been working on onto the floor, and denounced her for having no right to make them. When they informed her that they were going to confiscate her garments, she threw herself between the men and the clothing. Without regard for her advanced stage of pregnancy, the men violently seized the garments. This threw Marie Thérèse into such a fit of anger that she began to vomit and bleed profusely. Her distress ultimately resulted in a miscarriage and the stillbirth of her child. Thus a legal *mémoire* (brief) written on behalf the seamstresses' corporation describes the seizure of a seamstress's goods.[1]

The seamstresses' telling of this melodramatic story served a specific end, to argue for their right to make, concurrently with male tailors, whalebone corsets (*corps*) for women and children. For the historian, however, this simple story of one *couturière's* plight encapsulates a larger story about the ways in which early-modern French men and women structured the world of clothing production around notions of gender. In the violent midnight encounter in a *couturière's* workshop between three angry tailors and a pregnant dressmaker something as seemingly abstract as a "gendered system of production" begins to assume a shape all too real. The coarse insults and heated tempers remind us how much was at stake – one's livelihood, one's work identity, one's gender identity – in enforcing the boundaries between tailors and seamstresses, between men's work and women's work. The encounter reminds us that in the early eighteenth century claims for sewing as "women's work" were not yet fully grounded in women's natural rights as women or essentialist arguments about femininity; women's work within the clothing trades was a hard-won privilege, shaped and contested by day-to-day encounters within a royally-controlled and regulated guild economy.

While highlighting the violence and physicality entailed in the construction of gender systems, Marie Thérèse's story also reveals the role of discourse and rhetoric in creating, sustaining, and contesting notions of gender. Although Marie Thérèse's *mémoire* purports to be her true story, it is just the same a story, and one that makes explicit use of her sex, with its graphic descriptions of her pregnancy and miscarriage, to argue its case. How many times must French judges have heard similar tales, following the none-too-original plot of a vulnerable, pregnant woman assaulted by male aggressors? The *mémoire* itself, then, as much as the actual seizure of goods, acts to define the relationship between men and women's work. For legal *mémoires* were not printed solely for the benefit of the royal judge hearing the case; by the eighteenth century these pamphlets were printed and distributed to the public in an attempt to shape popular sentiment.[2] As the social critic and journalist Louis-Sébastien Mercier wrote, these printed legal documents, "could serve to interest a whole nation, making it attentive to the rights of the unfortunate who has neither rank nor credit."[3] The *couturières'* guild and the *tailleurs'* guild, both of which published *mémoires* recounting this seizure, clearly hoped to convince the broader public – as well as the French state – of the appropriateness of their vision of the proper division between men's and women's work in the clothing trades.

Just as the event and the discourse surrounding it are inseparably entwined in Marie Thérèse's legal case, so they are also parts of the larger story of the gendering of the production of clothing in early-modern France. The story of how clothing production came to be understood by contemporaries as women's work cannot be understood apart from the actual history of that work, that is, from the histories of the female seamstresses, linen drapers, hairdressers, and fashion merchants. In the dynamic commercial economy of *ancien régime* Paris, new practices of clothing production constituted a particularly contested arena, provoking debates about appropriate roles for female workers, the reform of a guild economy based on privilege, and the moral dangers of an economy driven by fashion and luxury.

The seizure of Marie Thérèse's goods by journeymen tailors was just one of many such encounters between workers in the clothing trades. These disputes took place against a backdrop of perennial battles between, and within, corporations during the *ancien régime*. Police commissioners' reports and court records are filled with dozens of disputes recording rivalries between different corporations, between members of the same corporation, between masters and journeymen, between privileged and unprivileged, between those who sold new goods and those who sold second-hand, and between those who worked in Paris and those who worked or traded in the provinces.[4] Female merchants fought with other female merchants as well as with male merchants, and no group of workers escaped at least several disputes over contested territory. Although the entire system of privileged crafts was riddled with contention, conflicts among the corporations involved in the garment trades were particularly acute. With the production of an ever-increasing variety of fabrics, garments and accessories in large commercial cities like Paris, the legal privileges of particular trades often lagged behind changes in production and the demand for the dozens of new products appearing daily in the boutiques of Paris.

Although the corporate system was troubled by internal and external strife and criticism, guilds continued to play an important role in organizing production and conferred an important sense of public identity for guild masters and mistresses. Of the 35,000 master artisans working in Paris in the early eighteenth century, approximately 15,000 worked in the clothing trades.[5] By the late eighteenth century, approximately 3,000 men were master tailors; 3,000 women were mistresses in the seamstresses' guild; 2,000 women were in the linen drapers guild; and 2,000 women dressed women's hair. Hundreds more worked in the ancillary fashion trades as wigmakers, lace makers, and feather makers. While the basic elements of made-to-measure male and female attire were made by just two guilds, the *tailleurs* and the *couturières*, other components of the wardrobe and various fashion accessories were produced by a host of separate corporations.[6]

In theory, the corporate organization of the clothing trades articulated and segmented production in a highly organized manner; in actuality, complex connections linked guilds and the numerous unincorporated workers in the fashion trades. Production within a given trade was in almost continuous flux as the types and numbers of garments made, suppliers, customers, types of credit, and relations with rival corporations all were negotiated and renegotiated each week, season, and year. Labor markets were often decentralized, and as historian Michael Sonenscher has suggested, the local economies of the trades in eighteenth-century French cities had much in common with the "economy of the bazaar."[7] Sonenscher contends that corporate records themselves, with their fixed regulations and legal privileges, obscure the day-to-day practice of work in the clothing trades and "have as much (or as little) relation to the life of the trades as eighteenth-century marriage contracts have to the relationships between the men and women who signed them."[8] Sonenscher has urged historians to look beyond corporate records to the disputatious courts of law, "a world of legal argument, civil jurisprudence, claims and entitlements whose terms and propositions endowed corporate regulations with their particular form," to the world of the bazaar, "with its multiple divisions of labour, variegated products and multiform markets," and finally, relationships between "kin, members of different generations, men and women, friends, neighbours, patrons and clients."[9]

A study of women workers has much to gain from Sonenscher's approach. Women often produced "hidden work" that remains invisible if one looks only at traditional histories of corporations, but emerges when one looks at the informal "economy of the bazaar." Their work often occurs at the interstices between legal and illegal work, as part-time and/or seasonal work conducted outside the privileged craft workshop in the backrooms and bedrooms of Paris. The fashion trades especially relied on women's work: sewing, wig making, hairdressing were all practiced at home and supplemented or complemented other female work including childcare, wage-labor, and prostitution.

While women's work often took place in an informal, non-regulated labor market, and porous boundaries existed between many trades, guilds nevertheless provided their members with a powerful sense of their identity as workers as well as a public identity in an Old Regime society based on corporate identities and privileged orders. Clare Crowston's in-depth study of the seamstresses of Old Regime France challenges historians who have suggested that female guild members had a less clearly defined work identity than men by demonstrating that the seamstresses' guild provided mistresses with a powerful public identity as guild members and a strong sense of self as autonomous urban workers. A significant minority of mistress seamstresses even managed to support themselves as single women, difficult and unusual for early-modern women whose livelihood usually depended on their participation in the larger family economy. Crowston's research warns against the anachronistic projection of proletarianized, nineteenth-century female garment workers onto this proud group of women who made up the fourth-largest trade organization in early-modern Paris.[10] Even if, as was true for the majority of some 10,000 women who were busily cutting and sewing clothing in Paris by the late eighteenth century, one did not possess the *maîtrise* and thus was not an official member of a guild, one's status was still defined against the standards of the guilds: distinctions between guild and non-guild (or privileged and *sans qualité*) were as important as the distinction male and female in organizing the world of work. Moreover, as in the case of the seamstress Marie Thérèse Sermoise, the legal *mémoires* that are so useful for reconstructing attitudes toward gender and work were guild documents, arguing on behalf of particular corporate bodies.

Three of the most important rivalries in the fashion trades occurred between female seamstresses (*couturières*) and male tailors (*tailleurs*), between female linen drapers (*lingères*) and male mercers (*merciers*), and between male and female hairdressers for women (*coiffeurs de dames* and *coiffeuses de dames*) and male wigmakers (*perruquiers*). In addition, a new category of female fashion merchants, the *marchandes de modes*, challenged the monopoly of several groups of clothing workers, including seamstresses, tailors, linen drapers, and hairdressers. Exploring the sites of contestation between these groups of workers shows the variety of ways in which the production of clothing and fashion was organized by sex and gender in the eighteenth century. Seamstresses were simple artisans who did not sell cloth and usually did not have a boutique from which they sold their goods, while the linen drapers were both artisans and merchants. Male and female hairdressers occupied a different position, selling their labor rather than any particular good, and existing halfway between the world of the artisan and domestic servant. By the second half of the eighteenth century the *marchandes de modes* had emerged from the tensions generated by the various corporations of fashion workers as the preeminent merchants of *les modes*. Although both men and women could be *marchandes de modes*, the trade was overwhelmingly associated with women and played a particularly visible and problematic role in the "sexing of *la mode*."

The burgeoning numbers of seamstresses, linen drapers, female hairdressers, and fashion merchants in eighteenth-century Paris clearly marked the increasing importance of female workers in the new economy of fashion; the sheer number of these female artisans and merchants sewing and selling in the workshops and boutiques of Paris would have served as a daily visible reminder to Parisians of the connection between women and clothing production. At the same time, the seamstresses' and linen drapers' effective deployment of legal arguments that they deserved to have the "privilege" as women to make and sell clothing for women aided the construction of the new gendered ideology that linked women to clothing production and led to the assertion by the late eighteenth century that women should have an "exclusive right" to work in the clothing trades. By the second half of the eighteenth century writers such as Jean-Jacques Rousseau famously popularized this new, supposedly "natural" relationship between women and clothing production, declaring, "The needle and the sword must never be wielded by the same hands."[11]

While factors such as region and locale played an important role in shaping the conditions and politics of women's work in the fashion trades, with provincial cities following their own distinct patterns of labor segregation, by the eighteenth century the practices of gendering clothing production were so pronounced in Paris, and the debates over women's appropriate work so heated and public, that alongside the fashionable products of its booming commercial economy, Paris also exported a new and seemingly enlightened idea: no matter who has the exclusive legal privilege to sew based on royal privilege and guild authority, all women have the natural right to sew.[12] While a new naturalization of women's "right to sew" seems to have been broadly accepted by the mid-eighteenth century, concerns about women's roles in the production and commerce of clothing and fashion continued to plague French men and women. In particular, the practices of a new type of fashion retailers, the *marchandes de modes*, highlighted for many contemporaries a new set of concerns about women, production, and the urban culture of fashion. For these female fashion merchants claimed to produce something more elusive and more significant than mere garments painstakingly stitched from cloth by seamstresses working within domestic workshops. They claimed to produce not merely clothing, but *la mode* itself.

Seamstresses and Tailors

In medieval France the distinction between men's and women's clothing was relatively unimportant in structuring production, perhaps as a result of the rough similarity that existed until the fourteenth century between men's and women's long flowing robes.[13] Furthermore, despite modern cultural stereotypes of the female seamstress, making clothing for the market was not particularly associated with women in the Middle Ages. Even within the domestic economy of the family, in which early-modern women were certainly associated with spinning and needle-work, women were not, for the most part, responsible for making clothing. As historian Nicole Pellegrin has revealed, many families in France purchased their clothing from male tailors.[14] During the later seventeenth and eighteenth centuries, however, legal battles between male tailors and female seamstresses played a key role in shaping women's particular claim to dressmaking, laying the foundation for what historian Judith Coffin has called "the feminization of sewing" in the nine-teenth century.[15]

At the beginning of Louis XIV's reign, male tailors were the preeminent corporation in the clothing trades, possessing the exclusive legal privilege to make and sell new clothing for men and women. Whether one wanted a man's vest, a boy's breeches, a girl's dress, or a woman's cape, one had only to purchase the appropriate fabric through a mercer or draper and convey it to one's tailor, who would make the desired item to measure. *Tailleurs de robes* specialized in making women's garments, including the skirts and bodices that were the main elements of female dress in the seventeenth century. Tailors were also allowed to sell a few items, such as tights, shoes, and accessories, that they had no legal privilege to make. The widows of master tailors were permitted to practice dressmaking and tailoring as long as they did not remarry outside of the profession.[16]

In the mid-seventeenth century, a group of female seamstresses in Paris working independently from the tailors' guild challenged the tailors' monopoly of the production of clothing for women, men, and children and called for a new division of production.[17] Employing an altogether novel argument, they contended that production should be organized not only according to the sex of the producer, but also the sex of the consumer: that is, female seamstresses should make clothing for women and children because, they argued, it was consonant with female modesty to be dressed, if one preferred, by a woman.[18] Two of the most celebrated seam-stresses of Paris, Mme Charpentier of the rue Montorgueil and Mme Billard of the rue Saint-Avoie, enlisted their clientele of marquises and duchesses to plead their case with the crown.[19] Finally, in 1675, the seamstresses of Paris, benefiting from Colbert's mercantilist initiative to incorporate workers, succeeded in gaining legal privileges to make and sell a wide variety of clothing for women and children.[20]

The roughly 1,700 seamstresses practicing in Paris were now *maîtresses cou-turières*, part of a legal corporation that provided them with the authority to govern their own trade. They attained the privilege to make a variety of items of clothing for women and children, including dressing gowns, skirts, informal dresses, overcoats, and camisoles. In addition, they were permitted to use whalebone ribbing (*baleine*) and other materials necessary to make and perfect their clothing (this right, as we saw in the raid on seamstress Marie Thérèse Sermoise, would be contested). Making clothing for men, however, with the exception of boys under the age of eight, was strictly prohibited. Perhaps even more important, seamstresses were forbidden from making two items required for women's formal dress at court, bodices and formal skirts with trains. Male tailors retained the exclusive privilege to make these items as well as the privilege to make all the items of clothing that seamstresses could make. The seamstresses were further restricted in that they were required to decorate clothing with the same fabric from which the garments were made. This was a serious restriction, given the importance of ribbons, lace, and braid to the decoration of women's dress.

The most significant item seamstresses were allowed to make was the new informal dress called the mantua, a style abundantly recorded, as we have seen in chapters 1 and 2, in the fashion coverage of the *Mercure galant* and in Elisabeth Charlotte's letters. The mantua would set the pattern for the dresses, often called *robes négligés*, worn by elite and bourgeois women for most of the eighteenth century. A one-piece construction with a kimono-like cut, the mantuas was relatively easy to make, comfortable to wear, and less expensive to buy than the formal two-piece dresses mandated by court etiquette. Clare Crowston's research links the emergence of the seamstresses' guild directly to the beginnings of the widespread wearing of the mantua. Crowston argues that,

> Producing thousands of these gowns in workshops across Paris, the seamstresses propagated a novel form of dressing for women, using it to establish a niche in the high-end of the garment trades and to spread the new taste to other social groups. Like Coco Chanel in her day, seamstresses prospered by rending casual, comfortable garments into a new style for elite women and their social inferiors.[21]

By the 1720s the mantua had been transformed into the flowing *robes volantes* made famous in Watteau's paintings; adopting a more fitted form, by the mid-eighteenth century these dresses gave rise to the *robe à la française*, the most common form of dress until the 1770s for humble working women and elite women alike. By the 1770s, the vogue for the *robe à l'anglaise* introduced the English version of the mantua to France. Although male tailors as well as female seamstresses could make the mantua and its successors for women, Crowston's research suggests that the dress became the special province of the seamstresses.[22]

The seamstresses' guild's founding statutes made it clear that tailors and seamstresses were to cease their internecine squabbling, but tailors and seamstresses continued to battle. In both 1678 and 1693 legal battles arising from seizures of seamstresses' goods by tailors embroiled the tailors and seamstresses. And in the 1720s tensions between the two groups erupted over who had the right to make *paniers* (elliptical hoopskirts), a dispute preserved in a set of legal briefs written by lawyers for each side. The tailors argued, with telling logic, that they should have the exclusive privilege to make the hoopskirts and other garments that required whalebone to be embedded within cloth, because they alone possessed the skill (*art*) to perform this difficult work. In addition they claimed that their superior skill was demanded by the important public responsibility involved in working with whale-boned garments, explaining that surgeons used whale-boned corsets to correct a whole variety of bodily imperfections such as malformed spines. Thus, they claimed to seek the exclusive privilege, not for self-serving reasons, but only for "the great utility of the public."[23] The seamstresses countered that their founding statutes in 1675 had included the privilege to work with whalebone and thus to make *paniers*. They reiterated the argument of this founding document that it was in keeping with "propriety, decency, and modesty" for women to have the option of being clothed by members of their own sex.[24]

While the tailors demanded the exclusive privilege to make hoopskirts, the seamstresses argued that they were not trying to deprive the tailors of their rights but merely sought to be able to make hoopskirts along with them. The seamstresses' other arguments rested on the plea that the courts take into consideration that they were female workers. They stressed repeatedly that they were a community "of women and girls" and that "their daily work was the sole honest means which is reserved for their sex for subsistence and the sustenance of life."[25] The seamstresses' pleas were rejected and it was not until the reorganization of the trades after 1776 that they were permitted to make *paniers*. But the terms of the debate between male and female workers had been set: male workers would base their arguments on the new Enlightenment language of specialized skills and public utility while female workers would stress the need to protect the modesty of female consumers and the vulnerability of female workers.[26]

While the seamstresses did not possess as elevated a public stature as the elite group of mercers and dry goods corporations known as the Six Corps, they took considerable pride in their public status: 1675 became a significant date in their craft's history and for their collective identity.[27] In 1776, having just celebrated their centennial, mistress seamstresses were hardly pleased to learn of controller general Jacques Turgot's plans to abolish their corporation and reform the arts and crafts. The mistress *couturières* were among the most vehement opponents of Turgot's plans to eliminate the guilds. Their defense of their corporate privilege combined older arguments about female protection and vulnerability with a new rhetoric about women's rights:

> In society there are certain tasks that call for only gentleness, intelligence, and justice; there are honors that could reward peaceful heroism and charity; there are labors that require only a quick and sparkling imagination, only grace and finesse in the execution.

Women have had the right to claim these; man has snatched them away because he is stronger.[28]

Although the seamstresses clearly feared that Turgot's vision of a liberal economy of free trade would rob them of their privileges, they couched their arguments in the language of female vulnerability and protection.

Although the seamstresses' language in this *mémoire* deploys a thoroughly gendered understanding of the difference between male and female workers' talents and rights, the reality of the division of labor between men and women was even more complicated.[29] From one point of view, female seamstresses had made significant inroads in the dressmaking trades by the later eighteenth century. With the reorganization of the guilds in 1776, women over the age of eighteen were permitted to become members of the tailors' guild, although they were still denied positions in guild government. In 1781 the seamstresses finally gained the privilege to make, concurrently with tailors, boned bodices, corsets, and hoopskirts. They even gained the privilege to make two items for men, capes and dressing gowns. But male tailors also gained ground. In 1776, with the reorganization of the trades and the joining of the tailors with their age-old rivals the *fripiers* (sellers of second-hand clothes) the tailors' dominion over women's clothing increased to include the refurbishing and re-tailoring of used women's clothing.[30]

The seamstresses had certainly made great gains since their incorporation in 1675 in selling the idea that female consumers were best served by female dressmakers. Yet, the seamstresses' discourse of female entitlement to the clothing trades did not perfectly match a reality filled with roughly equal numbers of male and female workers and a persistent blurring of boundaries between tailoring and dressmaking, between "men's work" and "women's work." As we will see in the next chapter, as French working men and women slowly adopted their mentality and practices toward an emerging economy of free trade and production outside the confines of the traditional guild system, the seamstresses' language of female particularity and entitlement helped to create the conceptual justification (in a very different way than the male tailors' language of skill and utility) for a new division and hierarchy of labor based on gender.

Although the tailors' and seamstresses' legal arguments employed strikingly different language (male skill and public utility versus female modesty and vulnerability), both male tailors and female seamstresses were equally concerned to uphold their privileged position as honest, skilled, and respected artisans; both guilds were threatened by the new economic clout of retail merchants like linen drapers, mercers, and *marchandes de modes* who worked both within and without the corporate structure.[31] Celebrity tailors and seamstresses worked for some of the wealthiest members of Parisian and court society, but most of the nearly 10,000 tailors and seamstresses worked for a more modest clientele. Despite a few exceptions, tailoring and dressmaking were small-scale operations in the eighteenth century. The tailors' statutes forbade masters to employ more than six workers. In the 1760s the abbé Expilly estimated that, on average, each master tailor in Paris employed fewer than two workers.[32] None of the mistress seamstresses working in Paris in 1791 researched by F. Braesch employed more than ten workers.[33] In keeping with the small scale of their operations tailors and seamstresses did not possess their own stocks of cloth, and scissors, needles and thimbles were the only tools required.[34] Without large investments of capital, both tailors and seamstresses relied exclusively on their skill and painstaking labor to turn bolts of cloth into clothing. Although both mistress seamstresses and master tailors did not always clearly perceive it, enlightened proponents of a "free" economy and new kinds of fashion merchants threatened them more than they did each other.

Linen Drapers and Mercers

For centuries Parisians had used linen cloth to make underclothing and accessories (*lingerie*). Yet Daniel Roche has argued that a revolutionary "invention du linge" occurred in the seventeenth and eighteenth centuries as linens acquired new meanings and gained new functions in social and bodily comportment as clean, white markers of propriety and civility.[35] Roche's research documents the marked increase in the amount of linen worn in Paris: the streets were seemingly awash in clean white collars, scarves, shirts, cuffs, stockings, aprons, and handkerchiefs. Benefiting from, and helping to instigate this commerce in linen goods, were the women and men who made and sold these garments, the *lingères* and *lingers* of Paris.[36]

Female and male linen drapers made a variety of items of clothing both for men and women. They were merchants as well as artisans and were permitted to set up shop to sell their wares. In addition to selling the items they made, they also sold lace and other items needed for layettes and trousseaux.[37] Both men and women could be linen drapers, but the trade was nevertheless organized into a two separate corporations according to sex. The men who practiced the linen drapers trade belonged to a subgroup of the large, diverse corporation of the mercers.[38] Although a few female mercers specialized in selling linen goods, most of the women who made and sold linen goods belonged to the all-female corporation of the *lingères*. Female linen drapers participated in a larger commercial world than did the seamstresses; as retailers and owners of boutiques they participated in the larger market of buying and selling. As part of their trade they were permitted to travel throughout Paris and its environs to buy cloth.[39] In large part because they were merchants as well as craftswomen, the linen drapers enjoyed a higher social and economic status than did the seamstresses.

Although no official statutes for the linen drapers are known to have existed before Charles VIII's *lettres patentes* in 1485, both male and female linen drapers had plied their trade in Paris since the thirteenth century.[40] Saint Louis had reputedly granted the poorest *lingères* permission to display their wares near the cemetery of the Innocents, on a street that subsequently became known as the rue de la Lingerie. By 1418 they had founded their confraternity at the église Saint-Sauveur on the rue Saint-Denis. In 1572 the linen drapers united with two other corporations engaged in the commerce of fabric, the *toilières*, who sold hemp fabric (*toile de chanvre*), and the *canevassières*, who sold linen fabric, to form the corporation of the *Toilières–Lingères–Canevassières*.[41] With the formal establishment of the guild in 1595, male *lingers* and male *toiliers* joined the corporation of the mercers, and except for husbands and widowers the corporation of the *Toilières–Lingères–Canevassières* remained exclusively female.[42] By 1723, according to Savary des Bruslons, there were 659 mistress linen drapers in Paris.[43] Many more female linen drapers probably worked as the wives of mercers within the mercers' guild, the chief rival of the *lingères*.[44]

The principal tension that arose between the female linen drapers and the mercers concerned the central Parisian fabric market, the *halle aux toiles*. In order to regulate the buying and selling of cloth, all commerce was strictly limited to this centralized market where it could be overseen by officials known as *halliers* and *auneurs*. Since the time of Saint Louis, the *lingères* had possessed the exclusive privilege to make their purchases at the *halle*, the privilege having been granted, according to traditional accounts, to protect the *lingères* from the dangers that women might encounter if they were forced to travel long distances to purchase fabric. Saint Louis reputedly argued that "the delicacy of their temperament and their fear of harm would turn them away from the trade, and it is to remedy these inconveniences that the *halle aux toiles* has been established in the female linen drapers's favor."[45] On May 20, 1634 Parlement confirmed this privilege, and specifically forbade the mercers from buying linen within a radius of twenty leagues of the *halle*.[46]

By the early eighteenth century the mercers, one of the largest and most powerful corporations in early-modern Paris, were challenging the *lingères*' exclusive right to buy cloth at the *halle*. Tensions between the two guilds came to a head in 1738 when the *merciers* proposed a new set of regulations for the linen market which would give them a larger share of control over the market for linen cloth. The proposal also would have permitted cloth merchants from outside of Paris to buy at the market. The *lingères* were particularly incensed by the proposal that all cloth purchased at the market be stamped with an official mark. They objected not only that this would ruin the fine linens with which they worked, but also that the stamp would be stored in an cabinet which could be opened with any one of three keys, one of which would be kept by the *merciers*. In one legal brief, the *lingères*

argued that the *halle* belonged exclusively to them "since the guild is only composed of women and girls, it is natural to assume that they are often in a condition
in which they cannot undertake long voyages to furnish their boutiques."[47]

Like the seamstresses, female linen drapers staked gendered claims for their
right to work in the clothing trades: they contended that women were particularly
skilled at sewing and that this productive work would keep women from falling
into poverty and vice. Moreover, during the 1776 crisis over finance minister
Jacques Turgot's suppression of the guilds, they deployed the emerging eighteenth-
century discourse concerning femininity, aristocracy and corruption to argue for
women's right to ply the *lingères'* trade. As Judith Coffin has perceptively noted,
"Turning physiocratic arguments against Turgot, the linen drapers cast their guild
as a bulwark against the decadence of aristocratic display and consumption."[48]
Like the seamstresses, the *lingères* strove to create a sympathetic bond with their
female clientele *as women* by claiming that the rapacious male mercers threatened
both female garment workers and their female customers. As the *lingères* argued
in their petition against the suppression of the guilds: "For a long time the vulgar
hands of men have held the delicate waist of a woman in order to measure it, and
to cover her with elaborate clothing; for a long time modesty has been compelled
to suffer the prying gaze that prolongs its regard under the pretext of a greater
exactitude."[49] In urging that female modesty required that women's made-to-
measure clothing be made by women, the linen drapers, like the seamstresses,
argued that it was unchecked, lascivious masculinity, not modest and restrained
female sensibility, that corrupted the culture of fashion.

Hairdressers for Women and Wigmakers

In early-modern France, maintaining an attractive hairstyle was a costly and time-
consuming part of elite women's fashionable dress. From the reign of Louis XIII,
when religious authorities denounced the immorality of women's display of their
luxurious locks, to the reign of Louis XVI, when enlightened social critics denounced
the frivolity of women's elaborate, towering hairstyles, women's hair provoked
commentary and concern. In early-modern Paris four groups of workers, comprising approximately 2,600 workers, were involved in hairdressing: barbers (*barbiers*),
wigmakers (*perruquiers*), male hairdressers (*coiffeurs*) and female hairdressers
(*coiffeuses*).[50] Unlike the occupations of seamstresses, tailors, linen drapers and
mercers, male and female hairdressing for women was originally a non-guild, free
trade.[51] In the Middle Ages men's hair was cut by barbers or occasionally by
wigmakers. Women of means had their hair coifed by their chambermaids (*cham-
brières*). On grand occasions such as balls or weddings, women called *atourner-
esses* styled women's hair. Because the church strictly forbade men to dress

women's hair, male barbers and wigmakers were not allowed to style women's hair.

By the mid-seventeenth century, however, it had become fashionable for women to have their hair styled by someone other than their own chambermaids. The *Livre commode* mentions several female *coiffeuses*, Mlle Canilliat near the Palais-Royal, Mlle Poitier near Quinze-Vingts, Mlle Le Brun at the Palais, Mlle De Gomberville at the rue des Bons-Enfans, and Mlle D'Angerville behind the Palais-Royal.[52] In 1700, more than 500 women were working as hairdressers in Paris.[53] Despite opposition by the church, in the seventeenth century male hairdressers also began to style women's hair. During the early years of the reign of Louis XIV the vogue for having one's hair styled by a man was established by a *coiffeur* named Champagne who was patronized by the ladies at court.[54] His reputation spread abroad and so did he, ultimately traveling to Poland to dress the hair of Marie de Gonzaga and to Sweden to style the Queen's hair. During the reign of Louis XV, as women's hairstyles became an increasingly elaborate and important component of fashionable dress, male hairdressers continued to gain in numbers and prestige. By the 1760s there were an estimated 1,200 male hairdressers for women in Paris.[55]

In the 1760s the wigmakers launched a series of legal attacks against the male hairdressers, claiming that they were harming their trade and violating their privileges to work with hair. The wigmakers' fears of encroachment on their trade were marked by both rank and gender anxieties. They felt threatened by their *garçons*, journeymen who would learn their trade from the wigmakers and then set themselves up in hairdressing which, as noted above, was a free, non-guild trade. A police ordinance of May 23, 1753 officially forbade journeymen wigmakers to work as women's hairdressers. But a decade later, in 1763, the wigmakers complained that hairdressers had found a new way of sidestepping existing prohibitions against their work: women and girls were now learning the art of hairdressing (in essence, apprenticing) right under the roofs of wigmakers by pretending to be learning to be chambermaids to wigmakers' wives. They were then taking their newly learned skills and styling hair, to the great injury of the master wigmakers, and circumventing existing prohibitions on their work.[56]

The male hairdressers countered these charges with a celebrated legal brief, *Mémoire pour les Coiffeurs de dames de Paris contre la communauté des maîtres Barbiers–Perruquiers–Baigneurs–Etuvistes*, in which they argued that they were artists, not artisans, and that their trade should remain free.[57] As their lawyer explained, "The wigmaker works with hair, the hairdresser works on hair . . . . The wigmaker is a merchant who sells his products; the hairdresser sells only his services; the material on which he works does not belong to him."[58] The rhetoric attempted to lift the hairdressers out of the guild world of privilege and territorial disputes over production, by claiming a higher calling as artists. As we shall see in

Figure 9 *Anonymous engraving with multiple hairstyles*, courtesy of RMN.

the next chapter, this was not an uncommon strategy in the eighteenth century and was similarly used by other workers in the fashion trades. Despite the ingenuity of the *coiffeurs de dames*' arguments and the eloquence of their legal brief, in 1768 the *coiffeurs* were ordered to join the corporation of the barbers.[59] By 1777, 600 male hairdressers had paid the required fee to join the *barbier–perruquiers* corporation, but it is likely that many more hairdressers continued to work outside the guild.

It is difficult to estimate the respective numbers of men and women who dressed women's hair. Because hairdressers often had no fixed address (all they needed was a comb and pair of scissors), it was practically impossible to regulate or to document them effectively. Male hairdressers for women do seem to have gained

Figure 10 "Marchande de Mode's boutique," *Encyclopédie*, courtesy of Rutgers University Library.

in popularity throughout the eighteenth century. But despite the condescending tone of the male hairdressers to their "sisters" in the trades, claiming that they alone were the great artists, a significant number of female hairdressers practiced as well.[60] The 1777 *Almanach Dauphin* cites as the most celebrated female hairdressers the widow of Legros, on the rue Saint-Honoré facing the rue de l'Arbre-Sec, and Mme Desmares, located on the corner of rue Saint-Louis du Louvre, who dressed hair "with much taste and a light touch."[61] The peculiar ability of hairdressers to slip through the cracks in the corporate system aided both male and female hairdressers. This same ability to work around the edges of the rigid corporate system was mirrored in the rise of a new profession in the fashion trades, the *marchandes de modes*.

Marchandes de Modes

By the late eighteenth century a group of predominantly female merchants had emerged in France as the pre-eminent merchants of fashion. They were primarily known as *marchandes de modes*, but were also known as *mercières en modes*, *marchandes de frivolités*, *faiseuses de modes*, or *enjoliveuses*.[62] *Marchandes de modes* performed a variety of the tasks that were also performed by seamstresses, linen workers and hairdressers, such as finishing garments, decorating hats with feathers and artificial flowers, selling lace and ribbons, designing hairstyles, and making simple ready-made items such as capes and neckerchiefs.[63] The *Encyclopédie méthodique* defined the *marchandes de modes* as

> Those who arrange and sell all the little objects that aid the dress, particularly, of women. Taffetas, gauze, linen, lace, decorations, ribbons of all types, flowers, feathers, and so on are the items they employ. They arrange, diversify, and mix these materials according to their purpose, their fantasy, and the manner that the taste and caprice of the moment inspires and necessitates. Their art is not to make anything; it consists in ingeniously furnishing a new look with all the varied and gracious ornaments of other arts, particularly that of braid and trimmings. Women's hairstyles, except for the arrangement of the hair, is the realm of the *marchande de modes*, and that which they practice the most, just as much as the adornment of the neck, arms and the trimmings of clothing and all that can be considered embellishment and properly brings out the beauty and elegance of the dress. But the decoration of the head, and finally the bust, is their object, is their talent *par excellence* and the triumph of their art.[64]

Although before 1781 *marchandes de modes* only decorated women's dresses and skirts, leaving the work of cutting and sewing to seamstresses and tailors, by the mid-eighteenth century *marchandes de modes* were already beginning to eclipse seamstresses and tailors in creating fashion. In an age in which there were reportedly 150 different ways to decorate a dress, the *marchandes de modes* claimed that they were the true creators of *la mode*.[65] As Louis-Sébastien Mercier explained, while seamstresses and tailors might be compared to masons who build the edifices of buildings, the *marchande de modes*, "in creating the accessories, in imparting the grace, in giving the perfect pleat, is the architect and decorator *par excellence*."[66] In theory the *marchandes de modes*, like the mercers, sold and embellished rather than produced goods; in fact the *marchandes de modes* made several items of apparel, including outerwear cloaks and capes and a variety of scarves, shawls, and mantles.[67] By the 1770s they also made the special attire required for formal presentation at court and court ceremonies, known as the *habit de cour* or *grand habit*, which was characterized by a boned corset, train, and voluminous dress draped over huge *paniers*.[68] Prior to the reorganization of the trades in 1776 the *marchandes de modes* had been responsible only for the elaborate decoration of formal court costumes. Tailors made the boned bodices (*corps*) and long trains (*bas de robes*) and seamstresses the skirt (*jupon*). But under the terms of their incorporation, *marchandes de modes* gained the right to make the entire outfit. When the baronne d'Oberkirch was presented at court in 1784, she related that her dress was made by the male *marchand de modes* Baulard:

> I was required to wear the grand habit with an enormous hoopskirt, according to etiquette, and a train that could be detached. I bought the cloth and had the costume made by Baulard, because mademoiselle Bertin made me wait too long. The cloth was gold

Cœffure à l'Indépendance ou le Triomphe de la liberté.

Figure 11 *Coiffure à l'Indépendance ou le Triomphe de la Liberté*, anonymous, eighteenth century, courtesy of *RMN*.

brocade with natural-looking flowers that were remarkably beautiful; I received a million compliments. It was not less than 23 *aunes* of fabric; it was enormously heavy.[69]

While the construction of an elaborate court costume would keep a *marchande de modes* and her employees busy for days, there were only a limited number of aristocrats who needed formal court dress. There was a much larger market, however, among bourgeois and aristocratic women, for a third category of apparel made by the *marchandes de modes*, hairstyles, bonnets, and hats. Beginning in the later 1770s, following the accession of Louis XVI and the increasingly prominent role of Marie Antoinette in setting fashions, hairstyles and bonnets became ever more elaborate. The *poufs* and *bonnets montés* created in the 1770s and 1780s were a far cry from the simple bonnets and modest caps worn by bourgeois women at home. Each year the *marchandes de modes* of Paris invented dozens of new hairstyles and head adornments called *poufs* and *bonnets montés* with names such as "à la Bonne-maman," "à la Caisse d'escompte," and "à la Belle Poule." *Poufs au sentiment* included pictures of loved ones and associated symbols and trinkets; and the *pouf au parc anglais* included windmills, sheep, shepherds and even a hunter. According to the *marchandes de modes*, these often fantastic compositions of hair wound around wool, cotton, false hair, and gauze, piled atop the head, supported by wire mesh, and adorned with feathers, lace and ribbons, exhibited their highest artistry; to contemporary critics, they revealed the heights (often literally) of their frivolity.[70] By the early 1780s, women's hairstyles had returned to a lower and flatter silhouette, but still required nearly constant updates in ribbons, feathers, and arrangements to stay *à la mode*. By the mid-1780s *marchandes de modes* began to make and sell hats for women made from straw or fabric, laying the foundation for their nineteenth-century evolution into milliners and *modistes*.

For both historians and eighteenth-century observers, the origins of the *marchandes de modes* are obscure.[71] Parisians knew that by the second half of the eighteenth century the *marchandes de modes'* shops had sprouted throughout their city; but they did not always understand from where the *marchandes de modes* had arisen. As the abbé Jaubert contended in his *Dictionnaire raisonné et universel des arts et métiers*,

> It is not possible to give a fixed point of origin for this art. All that one can say is that since *la mode*, being the custom or manner to clothe and adorn oneself in everything that regards appearance and luxury, the desire to please, accompanied by wealth, gave birth to this frivolity of spirit, from which has arisen many branches of commerce.[72]

Some people believed that the *marchandes de modes* began as *lingères* before becoming a separate trade in the late seventeenth century.[73] Others, such as the author of the *Encyclopédie* entry on "Modes," claimed that they had always been part of the *merciers'* corporation: "The *marchandes de modes* come from the mercer's guild, which can sell everything they can; but since the mercers are so diverse, the *marchandes de modes* are committed to sell everything concerning the accessories and dress of men and women, and what one calls ornaments and embellishments."[74]

By the mid-eighteenth century, although there was a great deal of ambiguity to the definition of a *marchande de modes*, with female linen drapers, mercers, and non-corporate women styling themselves *marchandes de modes*, most observers linked the *marchandes de modes* to the mercers' guild. Garsault, in his *L'art du tailleur*, explained, "They do not have any guild and only work in the shadow of their husbands, who to give them this right, must belong to the guild of the Marchands Merciers."[75] The abbé Jaubert supported Garsault's view, claiming that although the *marchandes de modes* were not officially incorporated, they could style themselves *marchandes de modes* if their husbands were mercers.[76] Jaubert also suggests that even if women were not married to mercers they could rent the privilege to be *marchandes de modes* from a mercer: "Although the *marchandes de modes* are not precisely guild members, and they give the name 'talent' to what they do, they can nevertheless only work if they borrow the privilege from someone who is in the mercers' guild, or by having their husbands received as a *marchand de modes*."[77] After 1776 one no longer had to speculate as to the precise legal status of the *marchandes de modes*, for in August of that year they were formally incorporated as a guild with the feather makers (*plumassières*) and artificial flower makers (*fleuristes*).

The confusion over the origins of the *marchandes de modes* is telling. These women, who became the principal fashion merchants of their day, had risen, so to speak, from within the cracks in the corporate system, originally eking a small trade from privileges granted to them as wives of *merciers* or *lingers*. Many historians have suggested that the *marchandes de modes* did not emerge as a distinct group until the second half of the eighteenth century. But there is evidence that a group of women who defined themselves as *marchandes de modes* existed in Paris as early as the second half of the seventeenth century. In 1692, Dancourt's play, *Les bourgeoises à la mode*, identified a character named Madame Amelin as a "*marchande de modes*."[78] By the second half of the eighteenth century, although both men and women declared themselves *marchandes de modes*, the occupation became particularly associated with women. Of the bankruptcy cases for *marchandes de modes* in the Archive de Seine for the period 1748–89 (most bankruptcies occurred in the 1780s), seventy-nine are for women, twenty-one for men, and nine for married couples.[79] Although no precise figures are available for the numbers of *marchandes de modes* practicing in Paris, let alone the number of workers they employed, one must assume that because the *marchandes de modes* occupied a high status in the fashion trades and produced for an elite clientele, their numbers were considerably smaller than those of the linen workers or seamstresses.[80] What is certain is that contemporaries perceived that Paris was awash with *marchandes de modes*' boutiques. As Desessarts exclaimed, "The capital has seen the number of *Marchandes de Modes* multiply to an incredible extent."[81]

The central role of *marchandes de modes* in the production of fashions is perhaps evoked most colorfully, if not most representatively, by the most celebrated *marchande de modes* in the eighteenth century, Rose Bertin.[82] She numbered among her clients the most elegantly attired women in France, from Marie Antoinette to the actresses of the Comédie-Française, and shipped her creations to aristocratic women throughout Europe. The collaborative frivolities of Rose Bertin and Marie Antoinette made both the object of ridicule, and Bertin's perceived influence over the queen earned her the epithet, "first minister of *modes*."[83] Unlike previous queens, who had left the ordering and construction of their wardrobes to their mistresses of the robes (*dames d'atours*), Marie Antoinette met directly with Bertin twice a week to order her clothing. As their friendship and business relations grew, Bertin was invited to private court events such as the theater at Marly and even rented an apartment near Versailles in order to be closer to the queen.[84] The queen's intimate friendship with her clothing merchant was perhaps as shocking to the aristocrats at court as the prodigious amount of money that she owed (but rarely paid) for her dresses was to the public.[85] As Mme Campan, the queen's Woman of the Bedchamber, complained, "It is fair to say that the admission of a dressmaker into the queen's apartments had unfortunate results for Her Majesty. The skill of the shopkeeper, received in private despite the custom that kept out all people of her class, without exception, made it easier for her to advocate a new fashion every day."[86]

The Feminization of the Fashion Trades

From seamstresses and linen drapers to female hairdressers and *marchandes de modes*, women played an important role in the Parisian fashion trades. In addition, women's work as semi-skilled laborers and piece workers was essential to a host of fashion-related trades such as wigmaking, tailoring, hatmaking and second-hand clothes selling. Economic conditions both pulled and pushed women into the fashion trades. On the one hand, women were lured into these trades by the demand for cheap, flexible labor in an expanding and often unpredictable market. It is difficult to calculate wages, but women's wages, even when they had corporate status, as did the linen drapers and seamstresses, were certainly lower than those of their male counterparts. On the other hand, they were pushed to accept these low-paying jobs by the ever-present specter of economic misery. Women in the cities of early-modern France made up the majority of the working poor. There were few opportunities to become mistress artisans or merchants and most were forced to endure the economy of makeshift, finding work by the day or re-selling small amounts of food or clothing in the markets and on the street. Prostitution was often the only alternative to starvation.[87]

The sheer number of women involved in the fashion trades does not in and of itself usher in the "feminization" of fashion production; but in conjunction with the movement of large numbers of women into the fashion trades, contemporaries came to believe that the production of clothing was particularly appropriate work for women. The cultural factors which pulled and pushed women into the clothing trades are perhaps more difficult to explain than the economic factors, involving as they do important redefinitions of masculinity and femininity and the meaning of men's and women's work. The original statutes in 1675 regulating the seamstresses had claimed that women should be allowed to practice dressmaking because female modesty demanded the option of being dressed by a member of one's own sex. This rationale remained an important element in the seamstresses' rhetoric in the eighteenth century and was used by the linen drapers, as we have seen, in their petition against the suppression of the guilds in 1776. But increasingly in the eighteenth century the principal argument for women's access to the clothing trades, made by both guild members and commentators outside the guilds, was that sewing would provide women with an honorable way to earn their livelihood. In Beaumarchais's *The Marriage of Figaro* (first performed in 1784), Marceline delivers an impassioned speech arguing for women's "natural right" to work in the clothing trades:

> *Marceline (excitedly):* Men, more than ungrateful, who stigmatize by contempt the playthings of your passions, your victims! It is you who should be punished for the errors of our youth; you and your magistrates, so vain in believing they have a right to judge us, and who deprive us, by their blameworthy negligence, of all honest means of subsistence. Is there a single occupation for these poor girls? They should have a natural right concerning all of women's clothing; [instead] one gives the training to thousands of workers of the other sex.[88]

Beaumarchais's sentiments were echoed by a number of eighteenth-century authors. Rousseau's assertion that "the needle and the sword should never be wielded by the same hands,"[89] was taken up by Mercier, who argued throughout his *Tableau de Paris* that women could be ensured a decent living by reserving for them the work of clothing trades:

> Since no one is more interested than me in the happiness of working women, I believe it is necessary to reserve for them all the crafts that belong to them. Is it not ridiculous to see male hairdressers for women, men who hold the needle, ply the shuttle, who are merchants of linen and fashions and who usurp the quiet life of women while women are dispossessed of the arts they should exercise to sustain their lives and are instead obliged to succumb to arduous work or abandon themselves to prostitution? Yes, I blush for

humanity when everywhere I see, to the shame of the name of man, strong and robust men cowardly invading a state which nature has particularly destined for women . . . . One should condemn all men who forget their estate, all the hairdressers, the male fashion merchants, the tailors who make women's clothes and spinners of wool . . . to wear women's clothing.[90]

By the second half of the eighteenth century writers such as Mercier, Rousseau and Beaumarchais, all advocates of the most enlightened ideas of their day, held that women had a natural right to work in the clothing trades.[91] Moreover, giving women exclusive rights to these trades would spare them from poverty and prostitution. Several authors, including Mercier, suggested that not only should the clothing trades be transferred from men to women but that these trades should be thoroughly reformed by abolishing the *maîtrise* and its attendant fees to enable as many women as possible to enter them. Joachim Faiguet de Villeneuve in his *L'économie politique* (1763) proposed that

To increase the resources of modest households, and additionally to remove women from the corrupting softness of luxury, it is necessary to train them from a young age in occupations that have been practiced only by men; to do so, women must not be bothered by the *maîtrise*, and should have complete freedom to do their work making shoes, stockings, clothing outfits, wigs, all sorts of fabrics, and other products that are not fatiguing.[92]

Authors such as Mercier not only argued that sewing and clothing are naturally feminine, but also that they are inappropriate for men. Similarly, Rousseau wrote, "Give a man work which is appropriate to his sex, and a young man a job which is appropriate to his age: all sedentary and stay-at-home jobs, which effeminate and soften the body, don't please men and don't suit them. A young working man would never aspire to be a tailor."[93] To ground his argument about appropriate men's work in classical notions of manly virtue, Rousseau concluded this passage with the bold declaration that in the ancient world men were never tailors and their clothing was always made at home by their wives. Mercier, quoting Rousseau on the effeminacy of tailors, wrote, "You will find at least two thousand individuals cutting, adjusting and sewing; 'women's work,' as J.J. Rousseau said."[94] During the late eighteenth century male *marchandes de modes* and male hairdressers became a common target of ridicule. The author of the *Toilette des dames* asserted that the male *marchand de modes* was no less a freak of nature than a female soldier and that "a male *marchand de modes* should wear women's clothing so that the metamorphosis can be complete and the feathers of this bird will respond to his pretty song."[95]

The apparent effeminacy of male fashion merchants, tailors, and hairdressers for women was not only a product of the equation made in the eighteenth century between women and the production of fashions, but also of the new equation between women and the consumption of fashions. But more was at stake as well. The problem was not just that men were involved in an activity that produced goods for women, but that sewing and selling clothes were increasingly regarded as altogether unmanly activities. While the sedentary activity of sewing was believed to suit and even morally benefit women, it was considered degenerating to men. As novelist and social critic Restif de la Bretonne commented in *Les nuits*:

> How does it happen that men degenerate faster in Paris than do women . . . ? This is because a sedentary life is less harmful to a woman, whose fiber is softer. But there is another reason. It is that the moral education of Paris is less harmful to the second sex, than to the first. Everything is craft, trade, and homework in Paris – which is what degrades men, but is particularly suitable for women.[96]

Just as the fashion trades were increasingly considered inappropriate for men, writers throughout the second half of the eighteenth century such as Rousseau and Mercier contended that "men's work" was inappropriate for women. While it might horrify Mercier to see men working as *marchandes de modes*, decorating with linen, gauze, mousseline, and artificial flowers, he was scandalized to see women out in the streets vending beef and pork, pulling wagons and hauling jugs of water: "A woman lugging water on the hard pavement of Paris! Nothing is more shocking."[97] The exclusive privilege to work in the fashion trades may have been welcomed by many women, but the price of this privilege was high. Women would have to concede that this "natural right" derived from their "nature," in Mercier's words, as that half of humankind "to whom nature has only granted weakness and charm."[98]

Underlying the belief that the fashion trades were particularly suited – even naturally suited – to women was the belief in the difference between what consti-tuted virtuous work for women and for men. Perhaps in a Rousseauean idyll the wives and daughters of artisans might have no need to work, and could devote all their energy to raising their little Émiles and Sophies; but most enlightened thinkers of the late eighteenth century realized that work was a necessity for many women and that virtuous mothers were working mothers. The task, then, was to find jobs appropriate for women, consonant with their nature, and morally uplifting. For many men and women, the clothing trades seemed to fit this bill perfectly.

According to many enlightened thinkers work was a positive source of virtue for men, a realm in which hard-working men could express their skill in public; but for these same social critics, women's work had a fundamentally different mean-ing. Ignoring the considerable public presence and professional skills of the mistress seamstresses and linen drapers of Paris who governed their own guilds, trained apprentices, and contributed to the royal coffers with entry fees and yearly

Figure 12 *Jeune fille brodant*, Jean-Etienne Liutard, courtesy of *RMN*.

taxes, these authors only saw the potential of women's work in negative terms: work kept women from falling into ruin. The women of Paris, as seen through the eyes of social critics like Mercier and Rousseau, were perched on a cliff with one foot ready to slip over the edge into the abyss of destitution and prostitution, of physical want and moral depravity. Work in the needle trades, they hoped, would provide women not only with a way to earn their livelihood but also with the much-needed moral discipline to save them from ruin.

The cultural connection between needlework, discipline and morality was not merely a new invention of enlightened observers like Rousseau and Mercier, but can be traced back to medieval and classical culture. The *lingères'* earliest formal statutes in 1485 devoted a great deal of attention to the issue of morality, with the first four of six articles regulating the sanctions to be imposed on "any guilty or scandalous women or girls."[99] The preamble to Charles VIII's statutes observed that even the most elevated and notable judges and bourgeois of Paris placed their daughters in the care of the *lingères* so that in addition to learning how to sew they might "learn honest deportment."[100] The *lingères*' statute of 1645 reaffirmed this commitment to the "moralizing" of the trade, declaring in its opening article that no one would be received as a mistress linen draper in Paris unless she led a good life, had good morals, and upheld the Catholic faith.[101] The Catholic Reformation in the seventeenth century institutionalized the connection between needlework, devotion and discipline in the hundreds of convent and charity schools founded in and around Paris. In these schools, both the wealthy daughters of the bourgeois or the poorer daughters of the laboring class would learn proper discipline as they perfected their stitching. So many of the poor girls and orphans who attended these charity schools later worked in the fashion trades that charity schools became de facto trade schools, teaching "all work appropriate to their sex and their estate."[102]

Conclusion

While the legal conflicts in the clothing trades we have explored in this chapter took place in the context of many of the same legal and economic transformations that provoked disputes among corporations outside the fashion trades, the rhetoric of these disputes reveals the ways in which common understandings regarding the connection between women's work and the fashion trades were transformed from the mid-seventeenth century, when women first made their entry into the public sphere of clothing production as seamstresses, to the Revolution, when female garment workers boldly demanded, "We ask that men not be allowed, under any pretext, to exercise trades that are the prerogative of women – such as seamstresses, embroiderers, *marchande de modes*, and so on . . . . If we are left at least with the needle and the spindle, we promise never to handle the compass and the square.[103] A world of difference separated the seamstresses' petition for corporate status in 1675, a request for the privilege to share the making of women's clothing with male tailors, and the request by female garment workers in 1789 for the exclusive right for women to produce clothing. In 1675, the seamstresses based their arguments for women's entitlement to make clothing on the argument that the customer's modesty required a choice of female as well as male workers. By 1789, the arguments centered instead on the workers' nature as women rather than on the female customer's modesty. This shift reveals some of the ways in which the production of clothing and fashion in the Old Regime was "gendered," and how certain roles in production were assigned exclusively to women, and claimed specifically by women, because of their "nature" as women.

The eighteenth-century commonplace that women were particularly suited for the work of the fashion trades and that this work was too effeminate for men was slowly constructed through the experiences of new groups of female producers, including seamstresses, linen drapers, hairdressers, and fashion retailers, as well as new styles of women's dress and the increasing divergence between male and female clothing consumption across all classes. But, like all ideologies – even the most effectively naturalized – this one had its areas of contradiction and instability. Just as male mercers and male tailors had challenged the female linen workers' and seamstresses' right to participate in the fashion trades, so too the ideology which posited women's suitability for the fashion trades was itself contested. Although it might have been in the interest of certain sectors of French society for women to gain the exclusive privilege to make and sell fashions, it was clearly in the interest of male tailors and hairdressers to defend men's pre-eminence in making women's fashions. In the book *Toilette des dames, ou encyclopédie de la beauté*, written in the Napoleonic period, the author asserted men's superiority over women in creating fashions:

> Can a man give women tasteful advice regarding their toilette? Yes, without a doubt. Is it not men that women prefer to call upon either to give their dress the most skillful cut and the most gracious form, or to artfully adjust the most important part of their costume, that it is to say, the hairstyle? Women are no longer called "tailleurs," and the word "coiffeur" is no longer a feminine noun in the French language. Only the hand of a man can cut with success a beautiful head of hair, and arrange and distribute with taste the different tresses and make the shining locks ripple, combining them with gold, pearls, and diamonds or simple wild flowers . . . The fact that women choose masculine artists would sufficiently decide the question in my favor is there was not another reason, perhaps even more important, that comes to my rescue: Women dress in part, they say, with the intention of pleasing us: who better than men, then, can know how to make women pleasing to us? We are then, the naturally born judges of the toilette of women; it is we who make the pronouncements from the highest court without appeal.[104]

Although many contemporaries readily agreed that sewing was "women's work," the connection between women and the production of fashion remained problematic. Work that was supposed to uplift them morally was in fact exposing women directly to that most dangerous of vices, luxury. The young clothing workers and shopgirls of Paris – the *grisettes* – ran the constant risk of succumbing to luxury's morally corrupting sway. Although *grisettes* had traditionally worked both in the workshop sewing and behind the counter selling, increasingly in the later part of the eighteenth century, as the *lingères* and *marchandes de modes* of Paris became more commercially expert, in the larger establishments some girls now worked exclusively in the front of the boutique as sales girls. Contemporaries worried that, divorced from the disciplining labor of stitching, they would become even more vulnerable to the corrupting influence of *les modes*.[105]

But whichever position one argued – that the creation of fashion should be the prerogative of men or of women or that the clothing trades morally benefited or imperiled female workers – by the end of the eighteenth century the terms of the debate had been set in such a way that gender was an integral factor in all arguments on the subject: suppositions about masculinity, femininity and fashion, structured the debate over who should produce fashions. It became virtually impossible to discuss clothing production without invoking masculinity and femininity as important categories. Even before the formal abolition of the guilds in 1791, distinctions that had once structured the production of clothing such as privileged versus *sans qualité*, Parisian versus provincial, and master versus journeyman began to lose some of their importance, placing an even greater burden on the distinction between male and female as an organizing principle of clothing production.[106]

An accommodation between those who argued that sewing was women's work, those who defended male superiority in the fashion trades, and those who worried about immoral *grisettes* and presumptuous *marchandes de modes* would be reached in the nineteenth century by placing the grueling manual work of stitching in women's hands and reserving the artistry of designing fashions for a select group of male tailors and hairdressers.[107] If for a brief moment in the eighteenth century it was possible for a woman like Rose Bertin to climb up from her humble origins to reign as queen of fashion, new gendered hierarchies of skill and genius would crown men like Charles-Frédéric Worth emperor of *la mode* in the nineteenth century.

Notes

1. *Mémoire signifié pour la communauté des marchandes maîtresses Couturières . . . contre les maîtres Tailleurs d'Habits* (Paris, 1727), BN, Joly de Fleury, 2000.
2. For an introduction to the function of legal *mémoire*, see Sarah Maza, "Le tribunal de la nation: Les mémoires judiciaires et l'opinion publique à la fin de l'ancien régime," *Annales E.S.C.* 42 (January 1987): 75–90. See also Sarah Maza, *Private Lives and Public Affaires: the Causes Célèbres of Prerevolutionary France* (Berkeley: University of California Press, 1993).
3. Louis-Sébastien Mercier, *Le tableau de Paris*, 12 vols (Amsterdam, 1783–88), t. 6: 319. See Cynthia Truant's analysis of Parisian guildswomen's use of print culture in "Parisian Guildswomen and the (Sexual) Politics of Privilege: Defending their Patrimonies in Print," in *Going Public: Women and Publishing in Early Modern France*, ed. Dena Goodman and Elisabeth C. Goldsmith (Ithaca: Cornell University Press, 1995).

4. See Steven Kaplan, "The Character and Implication of Strife among the Masters Inside the Guilds of Eighteenth-Century Paris," *Journal of Social History*, 19 (1986): 631–47 and "Réflexion sur la police du monde de travail, 1700–1815," *Revue historique*, 261 (1979): 17–77.

5. Jacques Savary des Bruslons, *Dictionnaire universel du commerce* (Paris: J. Estienne, 1723). Crowston, *Fabricating Women*, 75–76.

6. Daniel Roche estimates that at the beginning of the eighteenth century the clothing trades, broadly defined to include workers ranging from wigmakers and laundresses to seamstresses and tailors, employed between 15,000 and 20,000 masters and mistresses, or close to 60 percent of all masters and mistresses working in Paris. *The Culture of Clothing*: 279.

7. Michael Sonenscher, *Work and Wages: Natural Law, Politics and the Eighteenth Century French Trades* (Cambridge: Cambridge University Press, 1989): 137–8.

8. Ibid., 4.

9. Ibid., 30.

10. Although I researched and wrote this chapter before I read Crowston's *Fabricating Women* or her 1996 Cornell University dissertation, as I have revised the final version of this chapter I have benefited immeasurably from her careful scholarship and sophisticated understanding of the connection between the material history of fashion, guild culture, and new ideologies of womanhood.

11. Jean-Jacques Rousseau, *Émile, ou de l'éducation* (Paris: Garnier Frères, 1961), 3: 232.

12. On women's participation in the seamstresses' guild outside of Paris, see Crowston, *Fabricating Women*, Chapter 4, and Daryl M. Hafter, "The Spinners of Rouen Confront English Technology," *Proceedings of the International Conference on the Role of Women in the History of Science, Technology, and Medicine* 1 (Budapest, 1983): 70–5.

13. On the medieval organization and origins of the clothing trades in Paris, see Etienne Boileau, *Le livre des métiers d'Etienne Boileau*, ed. René de Lespinasse and Françoise Bonnardot (Paris: Imprimerie nationale, 1879).

14. Nicole Pellegrin, "Techniques et production du vêtement en Poitou, 1880–1950," in *L'aiguille et le sabaron: Techniques et production du vêtement en Poitou, 1880–1950*, ed. Nicole Pellegrin, Jacques Chauvin and Marie-Christine Planchard, (Potiers: Musée de la Ville de Poitiers et de la Société des antiquaires de l'ouest, 1983).

15. For the most important study of the feminization of the clothing trades in the nineteenth century see Judith Coffin, *The Politics of Women's Work: The Paris Garment Trades, 1750–1915* (Princeton: Princeton University Press, 1996).

16. *Lettres patentes de Henri III confirmant les statuts des tailleurs d'habits, en 30 articles* (Paris, 1583), AN, X1a 8637, fol. 62. René de Lespinasse, *Les métiers et les corporations de la ville de Paris* (Paris: Imprimerie Nationale, 1897), t. 3: 190.

17. The most comprehensive study of the seamstresses is Crowston, *Fabricating Women.* See also, D. Badiou, "Les couturières parisiennes" (Maîtrise Paris I, 1981). For an important study of modern French seamstresses see, Yvonne Verdier, *Façons de dire, façons de faire: La laveuse, la couturière, la cuisinière* (Paris: Gallimard, 1979).

18. See *Edits de création de maîtrise pour les couturières de la ville de Paris* (March 30, 1675). Most of the edicts pertaining to the incorporation of the seamstresses are found in AN, AD XI, 16.

19. For information on Mme Charpentier and Mme Billard see G. Levasnier, *Syndicat de l'aiguille: Papiers de famille professionnelle* (Paris, 1906): 4. Daryl Hafter claims that a *couturière* named Catherine Gallopine played an important role in gaining rights for the seamstresses by securing the right to clothe the royal children. Daryl M. Hafter, "Artisans, Drudges, and the Problem of Gender in Pre-Industrial France," in *Science and Technology in Medieval Society*, ed. Pamela O. Long (New York: New York Academy of Sciences, 1985). See also, G. Fagniez, *La femme et la societé française dans la première moitié du XVIIe siècle* (Paris, 1929): 108–9.

20. The *couturières* were one of only four exclusively female corporations in early-modern Paris, along with *filassières*, *lingères*, and *bouquetières*. On female corporations in Paris, see Cynthia Truant, "La maîtrise d'une identité? Corporations féminines à Paris aux XVIIe et XVIIIe siècles," *Clio, Historie, Femmes et Sociétés* 3 (1996).

21. Crowston, *Fabricating Women*: 40.

22. Crowston claims that seamstresses quickly monopolized the production of mantua dresses. Her principal evidence for this is that the mantua began to be widely worn in the 1670s, the same decade the seamstresses were incorporated. Crowston, *Fabricating Women*: 25.

23. *Arrêt de la Cour de Parlement portant règlement entre les Tailleurs et des Couturières*, 88. For a description of the ways in which whalebone corsets and paniers were thought to correct and prevent skeletal defect, see Bailly, *Avis aux mères qui aiment leurs enfants* (Paris, 1786). See also Nicole Pellegrin, "L'uniforme de la santé: Les médecins et la réforme du costume," *Dix huitième siècle* 23 (1991): 129–40.

24. *Mémoire signifié*, 94v.

25. *Mémoire signifié*, 91v. Tailors also stressed their financial need. *Mémoire pour les Maîtres Tailleurs contre les Maîtresses Couturières*, BN, Joly de Fleury, 2000, 84.

26. *Arrêt de la Cour de Parlement, portant règlement entre les Tailleurs et des Couturières* (August 7, 1727), AN, AD XI, 26.

27. Levasnier, *Papiers de famille professionnelle*: 12.

28. *Supplément au mémoire . . . des couturières*, BN, Joly de Fleury, vol. 462, fol. 117, 1–2. Quoted in Coffin, *The Politics of Women's Work*: 36.

29. According to Jacques Savary des Bruslons' figures, there were 1,882 master tailors and 1,700 mistress seamstresses in Paris in 1723. Although these figures remained the same in all subsequent editions of Savary des Bruslons's work, the number of tailors and seamstresses grew considerably by the second half of the century. In 1780 Louis-Sébastien Mercier estimated that there were 2,800 master tailors, and 5,000 journeymen tailors in Paris. Mercier, *Tableau de Paris*, t. 10: 266.

30. The *tailleurs-fripiers* conceded that *couturières* were permitted to refurbish and resell old garments for women and children, but only for those who specifically ordered them and not as part of their general commerce. See article 1 of *Lettres patentes du Roi, portant homologation des statutes et règlemens de la communauté des Tailleurs–Fripiers de Paris* (March 22, 1785), AN, AD XI, 26.

31. The mercers levied a serious blow against the tailors in 1670 when they attained the right to finish and sell a number of items made by tailors, such as camisoles, dressing gowns, and vests. Roche, *The Culture of Clothing*: 300.

32. Jean Joseph d'Expilly, *Dictionnaire géographique, historique et politique des Gaules et de la France* (Paris: Desaint et Saillant, 1762–70).

33. F. Braesch, "Essai de statistique de la population ouvrières de Paris vers 1791," *La Révolution Française* (July–December 1912): 294.

34. Although tailors did not typically sell fabric, some tailors did set themselves up as *tailleurs et marchands de tissus*. See the papers of a tailor named Sauvage who worked in Paris between 1719 and 1759. Archive de Seine, D5B6, 2325.

35. Roche, "L'invention du linge au xviiie siècle," in *The Culture of Clothing*: 227–38.

36. On the linen drapers, see A. Franklin's *La vie privée d'autrefois* (Paris: Plon, Nouritt et Cie, 1887–1902) and Jeanne Bouvier, *La lingerie et les lingères* (Paris: Gaston Doin et Cie, 1928).

37. See Franklin, "L'enfant," t. 2: 16, and "Les magasins de nouveautés," t. 4: 125, in *La vie privée*. See also "Etat d'un trousseau," in Garsault, *L'art de la lingerie* (Paris, 1780).

38. The mercers included both wholesalers and retailers. See Jacques Savary's description of retail mercers in *Le parfait négociant* (Paris: L. Billaine, 1675): 46.

39. Savary des Bruslons, *Dictionnaire universel*, t. 3: 590.

40. *Lettres patentes de Charles VIII confirmant les premier statuts des lingères, en 6 articles* (August 20, 1485), AN, Bannières, vol. 1, Y7, fol. 283. Reprinted in Lespinasse, *Le métiers et les corporations*: 69.

41. *Lettres patentes de Henri IV confirmant les statuts des toilières, lingères, canevassières, en 23 articles*, BN, Coll. Delamare, fr. 21796, fol. 1. In 1645 the *lingères'* corporation was granted new statutes, which were reaffirmed in 1782. See *Lettres patentes de Louis XIV confirmant les statuts des lingères-canevassières, en 25 articles* (March 1645), AN, S1a 8656, fol. 399. *Lettres patentes de Louis XVI portant homologation des statuts des lingères de Paris*, AN, Coll. Rondonneau, AD XI, 20.

42. Husbands could continue their wife's trade after her death as long as they did not remarry. They were not, however, permitted to attain the *maîtrise* or to participate in the government of the trade. In this, their status was similar to that of widows in male trades.

43. Savary des Bruslons, *Dictionnaire universel*, t. 2: 424. This figure remains the same in editions published in 1773 and 1779.

44. An estimate of the number of male and female linen drapers can be obtained from the Y series in the Archives Nationales, which lists the number of people achieving the *maîtrise*. See AN, Y9395. According to Jeanne Bouvier, between 1783 and 1790, 119 women became mistress *lingères* and forty men became master *lingers*. Bouvier, *La lingerie et*: 203.

45. Bernadette Roux Oriol, "Maîtresses marchandes lingères maîtresses couturières, ouvriers en linge aux alentours de 1751" (Maîtrise: Paris I, 1981): 11.

46. AN, Collection Lamoignon, t. 11, fol. 607.

47. *Mémoire pour les marchands Lingères sur le projet de règlement pour la visite et la marque des toiles* (Paris, 1738), 2. BHVP, 92260, in-folio.

48. Coffin, *The Politics of Women's Work*: 38.

49. "Réflexions des marchands et marchandes lingères," Joly de Fleury, vol. 462, fols 128–9. Quoted in Coffin, *The Politics of Women's Work*: 36.

50. See Chart 24, "The number of masters in the clothing trade 1700–25," Roche, *The Culture of Clothing*: 280.

51. For a classic work on the history of hairdressing in France, see Charles Desplanques, *Barbiers, Perruquiers, Coiffeurs* (Paris: Gaston Doin et Cie, 1927).

52. Abraham Du Pradel, *Le livre commode des adresses de Paris* (Paris: Veuve de D. Nion, 1692) t. 2: 41.

53. Desplanques, *Barbiers, Perruquiers, Coiffeurs*: 93.

54. Ibid., 93.

55. *Mémoire pour les Coiffeurs de dames de Paris contre la womanauté des maîtres Barbiers–Perruquiers–Baigneurs–Etuvistes* (Paris, 1769): 19. This

source, signed "Bigot de la Bossière Procureur," was probably written by the lawyer for the hairdressers, François-Michel Vermeil, who had a vested interest in exaggerating their numbers and importance vis-à-vis the wig-makers.

56. *Arrêt de Parlement qui homologue la délibération de la communauté des maîtres Barbiers-Perruquiers* (Paris, 1763), AN, AD, XI 25.
57. See also the poem, "Les coiffeurs de dames contre ceux des messieurs" (Paris, 1769) BN, Ye 18719.
58. *Mémoire pour les Coëffeurs de dames*: 12.
59. The stiff entrance fee of 2,000 *livres* may have led the hairdressers to resist joining until the fee was lowered in 1777.
60. A pointed poem written at the height of tensions between wigmakers and hairdressers in the late 1760s, "L'art des coiffeurs de dames contre le méchan-isme des perruquiers," asserts the superiority of male hairdressers over barbers and wigmakers in cutting and styling hair. The author concedes that female hairdressers have the right to style hair, but insists that they are much less talented then men.
61. *Almanach Dauphin* (Paris, 1777), supplément, 15.
62. The term "marchandes de modes" did not appear in the *Dictionnaire de l'Académie* until 1815. In the eighteenth century, *marchandes de modes* were not yet called "modistes." The *Dictionnaire de l'Académie* defined "modiste" for the first time in 1835 as, "Ouvrier, ouvrière en modes, marchande de modes."
63. The hatmakers' guild retained the monopoly on making and selling felt hats.
64. *Encyclopédie méthodique: manufactures, arts et métiers* (Paris, 1785), t. 1: 133.
65. Franklin, "Les magasins de nouveautés," in *La vie privée*: 236. For an exam-ple of the elaborate decorations invented by the *marchandes de modes* see Olivier Bernier's description, based on one of Rose Bertin's invoices, of a dress ordered by Mme de Chatenay in 1786 and costing 1,235 *livres*. Olivier Bernier, *The Eighteenth-Century Woman* (New York: Doubleday, 1982): 119. Originally quoted in Pierre de Nouvion and Emile Liez, *Un ministre des modes sous Louis XVI, Mademoiselle Bertin* (Paris: Leclerc, 1911).
66. Mercier, *Tableau de Paris*, t. 11: 218.
67. See the Abbé Jaubert's description of these three types of cloaks. Jaubert, *Dictionnaire raisonné et universel* (Paris, 1773), t. 3: 91–2. For pictures of six items made by the marchandes de modes, see the plates in *Encyclopédie méthodique* (Paris, 1785), t. 1: 136.
68. On ceremonial court dress, see Mme de Genlis, *Dictionnaire critique et raisonné des étiquettes de la cour* (Paris, 1818), t. 1: 254, and Jaubert, *Diction-naire raisonné et universel*, t. 3: 91.

69. Henriette-Louise Waldner de Freundstein, baronne d'Oberkirch, *Mémoires de la Baronne d'Oberkirch* (Paris: Charpentier, 1869), 91. Mercier describes the rivalry between Baulard and Rose Bertin as "like that between two great poets." Mercier, *Tableau de Paris*, t. 6: 313.

70. See the baronne d'Oberkirch's description of *poufs au sentiment. Mémoires de la baronne d'Oberkirch*: 51. See also the description of a *coiffure en bonnet monté* in Jaubert, *Dictionnaire raisonné et universel*, t. 3: 92.

71. For documents pertaining to *marchandes de modes* and *plumassiers* in the period 1599–1692, see AN, AD XI25. For background on the *marchandes de modes*, see Roche, *The Culture of Clothing* and A. Varron, "Créateurs de modes parisiens au XVIIe siècle," *Les Cahiers Ciba* 2, no. 16 (December 1947): 542–75. Jean Allilaire contended that the *marchandes de modes'* lineage should be traced back to the twelfth and thirteenth centuries, and that they were descendants of the hatmakers (*chapeliers*). Jean Allilaire, *Les industries de l'habillement* (Paris: Société d'éditions française et internationale, 1947): 248.

72. Jaubert, *Dictionnaire raisonné et universel*: 90.

73. "L'art de coiffures des dames," 3, fn. 1, claims that the *marchandes de modes* split from the *lingères* in 1669.

74. *Encyclopédie, ou dictionnaire raisonné* (Paris, 1751–72), 10: 598. The *Almanach général des marchands* for the year 1772 also claimed that the *marchandes de modes* were members of the mercers' guild.

75. Garsault, *L'art du tailleur* (Paris, 1769): 54–6.

76. In a detailed study of *marchandes de modes'* boutiques in eighteenth century Anvers, Marguerite Coppens has found that the majority of shops were run by married couples and that equal numbers of men and women plied the trade. The men worked as mercers and the women as *faiseuses de modes*. Marguerite Coppens, "'Au magasin de Paris' Une boutique de modes à Anvers," *Revue belge d'archéologie et d'historie d'art* 12 (1983): 85.

77. Jaubert, *Dictionnaire raisonné et universel*, t. 3: 93. In the bankruptcy records in the Archive de la Seine most of the *marchandes de modes* whose husband's occupations were listed were married to *merciers*.

78. A poem by Alexandre-Jaques Chevalier Du Coudray written in 1773 refers to a certain Madame Duchap as "a famous *marchande de modes* of the last century." Du Coudray, *Le luxe, poème en six chants* (Paris, 1773): 153.

79. The series D5B6 at the Archives de Paris et de l'ancien département de la Seine contains over one hundred bankruptcy documents for *marchandes de modes*.

80. Roslin's *L'esprit du commerce, almanach pour 1754* lists thirteen *marchandes de modes* and the *Almanach des arts et métiers* (Paris, 1774) lists twenty. A more detailed list, is found in the *Tablettes de renommé, ou almanach général*

(Paris, 1773). Additional sources for piecing together the numbers of *marchandes de modes* are found in the Archive de la Seine D43Z, "Publicité commerciale à Paris," which contains business cards for *marchandes de modes* and advertisements in the fashion press. One must, however, keep in mind that only the most prosperous shops would have been listed in almanacs and had business cards and advertisements.

81. Nicolas-Toussaint Desessarts, *Dictionnaire universel de police* (Paris, 1785–87): 625.

82. Contemporary accounts of Rose Bertin include Auguste François Fauveau Frénilly (1768–1848), *Souvenirs du baron de Frénilly*, new edition (Paris, 1909), Oberkirch, *Mémoires de la baronne d'Oberkirch*, 52, Louis Petit de Bachaumont, *Mémoires secrets pour servir à l'histoire de la république de lettres en France* (London: John Adamson, 1780–1789), t. 13: 299, and Mercier, *Tableau de Paris*, t. 6: 308. Her reputed memoir which appeared in 1824 was false and was probably written by the royalist Jacques Peuchet. In the early twentieth century Jacques Doucet collected many documents pertaining to Bertin, which are preserved in five cartons in the collection Jacques Doucet at the Institute d'art et d'archéologie in Paris. In addition, two biographies of Bertin were written in the early twentieth century, Emile Langlade, *La marchande de modes de Marie Antoinette, Rose Bertin* (Paris, 1911) and De Nouvion and Liez, *Un ministre des modes sous Louis XVI* (Paris, 1911). A concise portrait of Rose Bertin is sketched by Olivier Bernier in *The Eighteenth-Century Woman*: 117–27. See also Clare Crowston, "The Queen and her 'Minister of Fashion': Gender, Credit and Politics in Pre-Revolutionary France," *Gender and History* 14, no. 1 (April 2003): 92–116.

83. The *Correspondance secrète* of April 11, 1778 first referred to Bertin as "le ministre des modes." See also, *Encyclopédie méthodique* t. 1: 135.

84. On the friendship between Bertin and the queen see Mercier, *Tableau de Paris*, t. 6: 314 .

85. In 1785 Marie Antoinette spent 258,352 *livres* on clothes, 91,947 of which was owed to Bertin. Bernier, *The Eighteenth-Century Woman*: 119.

86. Campan, *Mémoires sur la vie de Marie-Antoinette*, quoted in Bernier, *The Eighteenth-Century Woman*: 122.

87. See Olwen Hufton, "Women and the Family Economy in Eighteenth-Century France," *French Historical Studies* 9, no. 1 (Spring 1975): 1–22. For the most important study of eighteenth-century prostitution, see Erica-Marie Benabou, *La Prostitution et la police des moeurs au xviiie siècle* (Paris: Librarie Académique Perrin, 1987).

88. Pierre Augustin Caron de Beaumarchais, *Le mariage de Figaro* (1784), act 3, scene 16.

89. Rousseau, *Émile* 3: 232.

90. Mercier, *Tableau de Paris*, t. 9: 177–8. For another strong statement on the need to preserve the needle trades for women, see "Filles publiques à l'Hôpital," in *Tableau de Paris*, t. 11: 53.

91. For an introduction to scholarly disputes over how to characterize Beaumarchais's politics, see Maza, *Private Lives and Public Affairs*: 290.

92. Joachim Faiguet de Villeneuve, *L'economie politique, projet pour enricher et pour perfectioner l'espèce humain* (Paris, 1763), 144–5. The second edition of this work was titled *L'ami des pauvres*.

93. Rousseau, *Émile*: 232.

94. Mercier, *Tableau de Paris*, t. 10: 266.

95. Auguste Caron, *Toilette des dames, on encyclopédie de la beauté* (Paris: A.-G. Debray, 1806): 202.

96. Restif de la Bretonne, *Les nuits*, 2: 246–7, quoted in Jeffrey Kaplow, *The Names of Kings: The Parisian Poor in the Eighteenth Century* (New York: Basic Books, 1972): 85. Kaplow suggests that for a similar observation one see Maille Dussausoy, *Le Citoyen desintéressé* (Paris, 1767), 2: 128.

97. Mercier, *Tableau de Paris*, t. 10: 173.

98. Mercier, t. 9: 179.

99. *Lettres patentes de Charles VIII.*

100. Ibid.

101. *Lettres patentes de Louis XIV confirmant les statuts des lingères-canevassières, en 25 articles* (March 1645), AN, AD XI, 20. The *couturières*' statutes of 1675, although less explicitly concerned with proper moral discipline than the lingères', did call for the creation of a religious confraternity.

102. "Règlemens de la communauté des Filles de Sainte-Anne," (1698), Bibliothèque Mazarine, ms 3309. Quoted in Martine Sonnet, *L'éducation des filles au temps des Lumières* (Paris: Cerf, 1987): 251. See also Crowston, *Fabricating Women*: 323.

103. "Pétition des femmes du tiers état au roi" (January 1, 1789), trans. and cited in *Women in Revolutionary Paris* ed. Harriet Applewhite, Darlene Levy and Mary Johnson (Urbana, IL: University of Illinois Press, 1979): 19–20.

104. Caron, *Toilette des dames,* 22–5.

105. On nineteenth-century concerns about shop girls, see Jules Simon, *L'Ouvrière* (Paris, 1861): 200.

106. On the continuing resonance of the Old Regime language of labor into the nineteenth century, see William Sewell, *Work and Revolution in France: The Language of Labor from the Old Regime to 1848* (Cambridge: Cambridge University Press, 1980).

107. Sewing machines did not begin to be used for making clothing commercially
until the 1850s. Thus, well into the nineteenth century hand sewing filled
many hours in a dressmaker's day. On the commonplace that women were
more naturally suited to the manual skill of sewing, see Simon, *L'Ouvrière*:
184, 207.

–4–

The Problem of French Taste

On June 3, 1776, the so-called Boniface Prêt-à-Boire delivered a mock funeral oration titled, *Funeral Oration and history of the very short, very fat, and highly skilled citizen Monsieur Master Nicodême Pantalèon TIRE-POINT, Bourgeois de Paris, Master and merchant Tailor.*[1] Nicodême Tire-Point's eulogy begins, "He is dead, this miracle of intelligence, this wellspring of science, this phoenix of industry, this marvel of the city, this prodigy of the court, this star of the universe, this guardian angel of the great, this holy protector of fools and poets . . . . Tire-Point, a born *artiste*, Tire-Point, the most sublime artist." Tire-Point's genius rested, according to his eulogist, on his ability to transform sartorially, with little expense, "the puniest little plebian into a brilliant lord." Tire-Point's skill imbued him with even more power than even the most absolute monarch. For while a king could ennoble men, "Tire-Point creates men, great men, whose minds are revered like oracles, geniuses more praised than the Montesquieus, d'Alemberts, Diderots and Buffons of the world."[2]

Tire-Point's eulogy is only one of several extant eighteenth-century orations celebrating "the sublime genius" of workers in the clothing trades. Another oration hails the genius of the tailor Christophe Scheling: Quite different from boring Geometricians, Metaphysicians who only discuss imaginary beings, or Philosophers who want to destroy this world to create one more to their taste, he will imagine a way of dressing that neither the Greeks, Romans, or even the most clairvoyant French person has been able to discover.[3] The author claims that when Scheling assesses samples of fabric, "he dissects color like Fontenelle analyzed the mind; he perceives in the smallest piece of velour or satin nuances and shadings that even the most skilled scientific eye of a Reaumur could not see in tulips and insects." Just in case the satirical intent of comparing tailors to scientists, *philosophes*, and artists was not apparent from the outset, the satire concludes with the following punch line:

> That is how it goes, Messieurs, in a century when the agreeable arts are held in such honor, in a century when one is considered a great man if one has the talent to appreciate carriages, furniture, and clothing, in a century when a lady singer is a divine person, where the most insignificant concert gives rise to a deliberation by the Academy of

Sciences, . . . finally, in a century when the foolishness of fashionable authors appears superior to all the reasoning of the ancients and the moderns.[4]

We do not know the precise audience for Tire-Point's and Scheling's orations: they may have been written as part of a festive, confraternal ritual within the tailors' guild or possibly for a Masonic gathering.[5] Certainly the publication of Tire-Point's speech in 1776 suggests that it was delivered against the backdrop of debates over Turgot's plan to free the trades. Yet, regardless of the specific context, Tire-Point's and Scheling's funeral orations reveal the extent to which French culture by the second half of the eighteenth century was consumed by discussions of taste, genius, and fashion. Not only did philosophers such as Montesquieu and Rousseau debate whether or not the taste for luxury and fashion had weakened and rendered French culture effeminate, but also ordinary artisans and craftsmen were so deeply immersed in these contemporary debates that they could readily tap into them with wicked satirical intent.

In his *Tableau de Paris*, the late-eighteenth-century social critic Louis-Sébastien Mercier claimed his contemporaries would never boast, "I have genius," but might without hesitation proclaim, "I have taste." Mercier suggested that one did not boast of one's genius because, "Everyone in the world knows what genius is because it is easy to recognize." But, Mercier went on to explain, since it is difficult to contest whether or not one is an "homme de goût," one might without hesitation appropriate this title.[6] Poking gentle fun at the "man of taste," Mercier suggests how uncertain his contemporaries were about the meaning of the increasingly important attribute; in many respects, *le goût* appeared as elusive as *la mode*. As Mercier concluded in another passage, "The word *goût* is perhaps the most difficult word in our language to understand," echoing Jean-Jacques Rousseau's paradoxical definition of taste: "of all the natural gifts, taste is the one which is felt the most and which can be explained the least: it wouldn't be what it is if one could define it."[7]

As French society, which had been constructed based on privileged orders, rank, and the luxurious display of costume, was slowly transformed in the course of the later seventeenth and eighteenth centuries by the new commercial culture of fashion, a mysterious quality, the *je ne sais quoi* of taste, helped to create a new social hierarchy. Although Rousseau and other Enlightenment philosophers joked that taste eluded definition, the emerging science of aesthetics was predicated on the assumption that the influence of *le beau* on an observer could be precisely examined and measured. But many theorists threw up their hands in despair and refused to analyze taste for commodities such as clothing that they defined as material objects rather than fine arts.

In the past decade, cultural historians have begun to explore the ways in which an emerging "society of taste" played a central role in eighteenth-century culture, shaping new codes of aristocratic refinement and providing a new vocabulary of manners that legitimized an emerging middle class and a reformed aristocracy.[8] But much remains to be learned about the ways in which the new category of taste and the elevation of the artist's genius were understood by more humble members of the social hierarchy, such as artisans working in the clothing trades. Moreover, although scholars such as Tjitske Akkerman have revealed how women and gender ideology stood at the heart of eighteenth-century philosophers' construction of their vision of a civilized, commercial society, much remains unknown about the ways in which women, across a range of classes, responded to the enlightened discussions about femininity and taste.[9]

The half century that preceded the French Revolution witnessed men and women from almost every level of French society questioning and redefining the meaning of taste, genius, and imagination. From technical trade manuals to the female press, as well as in formal treatises on the *beaux arts* and aesthetics, discussions of taste appeared in a wide variety of contexts, which are not usually thought of as sites for aesthetic theorizing. This was not merely the result of a "trickling down" of "high" intellectual discussions of aesthetics by men like Du Bos, Hutcheson, Hume and Kant; the discussions of the meaning of taste and genius in both "high" and "low" literature were products of a shared economic, social and cultural development – the process of sorting out and defining the meaning of the new commodities that saturated eighteenth-century Paris, and of the relationship of men and women to material goods in a society which, while not yet industrialized, was marked by a lively and growing commercial culture. Not only the upper classes – the people one usually associates with the eighteenth-century society of taste – but shop girls, merchants, and artisans also had a stake in the perfection of the *arts agréables*, in French taste and genius, and in the elevation of Paris as the commercial and artistic capital of Europe. And they too, although in a way very different from the aristocracy, were forced to cultivate their senses of sight and discrimination as they picked and chose objects in the market-place, to define their relationship to the new goods which surrounded them, and to find a place for these objects in their homes, on their bodies, and in their systems of moral and aesthetic values.

In the midst of this incipient culture of the marketplace, the relationship between "the agreeable arts of clothing" and objects of "high art" posed a particularly vexing problem for philosophers, humble artisans, and female consumers alike. Understanding the relationship of hats and fans to history paintings and sculptures ultimately required the construction of a new hierarchy of the arts and crafts – and of high culture and commercial culture – which assigned a different worth to the *beaux arts* and the *arts agréables*. Women and workers were clearly at the bottom of the new hierarchy of the arts that emerged by the later eighteenth century. In this new hierarchy, an aristocratic woman living in the Faubourg Saint-Germain was perceived to have much in common with a male or female artisan from the Faubourg Saint-Antoine: both lacked genius and the taste of both was particularly susceptible to corruption by the whims of fashions and novelties. In a culture that did not yet have, as Sarah Maza has argued, a clearly articulated language of class, gender ideology played a particularly important role in the construction of the new hierarchy of the arts and crafts and distinctions between elite and commercial culture.[10]

But to start with the denouement and to narrate the story of the construction of society of taste through the writings of Hume, Kant, and the other "founding fathers" of the modern study of aesthetics (even with a sensitivity to the ways in which gender ideology played a role in shaping eighteenth-century philosophers' theories) would be to prematurely write women and workers out of that story. Taste was an emerging and still malleable discourse throughout much of the eighteenth century and artisans and female consumers, as well as philosophers and artists, attempted to grasp and shape its meaning. Moreover, to rely on the late-eighteenth-century neoclassical conception of the difference between female taste and male genius – and between hats and history paintings – as the final word on the new economy of aesthetic value which emerged in the eighteenth century leaves little room for the problematic role of taste in French national character: were the French a particularly frivolous people? And, how could frivolity and the taste for *les nouveautés* be harnessed to French national glory? Momentarily turning the hierarchy of the arts "upside down" and focusing on artisans, female consumers, and the agreeable art of fashions will reveal a more nuanced picture of the ways in which gender and class worked together, throughout multiple levels of French society, to naturalize the frivolity of fashion and to problematize the frivolity of the French.

Taste and Genius

Historians have noted that eighteenth-century aesthetic theory characterized taste as one of the few qualities, in a society otherwise structured by a belief in the hereditary basis of rank and distinction, which potentially spread throughout society: although contemporaries disagreed over exactly what taste was, and most eighteenth-century commentators assumed that the culture of the upper class was particularly conducive to the refinement of taste, few suggested that taste was the exclusive, innate property of a particular class.[11] The aesthetic theories of both Hume and Kant were explicitly founded on the universality of "the common sentiments of human nature."[12] Contemporary satires were as quick to lampoon the poor taste of the aristocrat as that of the bourgeois or the artisan. And, the fashion press continually insisted that taste would enable even a poor woman to dress with grace and style.

Yet, lurking beneath the new science of aesthetics' claim to universality was a persistent belief in the social dimension of taste and genius.[13] The belief that taste was determined by one's class position reinscribed older notions of the importance of blood and birth onto an emerging liberal culture based on merit and individualism. However, a crucial component of the reassertion of "aesthetic inequality" in the midst of the culture of the Enlightenment was the naturalization of inequality through gender difference: according to eighteenth-century thought, taste and sentiment might potentially cross class lines, but they were nevertheless resolutely gendered. The categories of class and gender worked together to undermine the theoretically universal basis of taste.

From satires on women's ballooning hoopskirts in the 1720s to parodies of their fantastic poufs in the 1770s, eighteenth-century social critics poked fun at women's taste. Writing shortly after the Revolution, Julien Joseph Virey summarized the pernicious effect of women on the arts in his *De l'influence des femmes sur le goût dans la littérature et les beaux arts*. Under Louis XIV, according to Virey, women were firmly governed by men and the arts had flourished. In contrast, during the reign of Louis XV, who allowed himself to be enslaved to his mistresses Pompadour and Du Barry, men similarly let themselves be governed by women to the detriment of arts and letters. The fine arts declined, according to Virey, because of "the natural taste of women for tinsel and baubles"; only with the Revolution and men's reconquest of the public realm and the relegation of women to the domestic sphere did "the beaux arts reclothe themselves in an austere costume" as the masculine taste for classical forms drove out the "incompetent and bizarre taste" of women.[14]

Virey was one in a long line of critics who denounced the effects of women's taste on the arts. Lord Shaftesbury, whose philosophical writings had a considerable impact on the development of French aesthetics, equated "effeminate" with debased taste: "While we look on paintings with the same eyes as we view commonly the rich stuffs and colored silks worn by our Ladies, and admired in Dress, Equipage or Furniture, we must of necessity be effeminate in our Taste and utterly set wrong as to all Judgment and Knowledge in the kind."[15] Writing for a more popular readership, Boudier de Villemert, the editor of the *Courrier de la mode ou journal du goût* and the author of *L'ami des femmes*, was equally disparaging of women's taste. He lamented that, "Women's imaginations continually nourish themselves on the details of jewels, clothing, etc; these so fill up their heads with colors that there does not remain any attention for objects which might merit it more . . . . The mind of woman glides over essential qualities and only attaches itself to the drapery."[16] Similarly, the anonymous author of *Sur la peinture*, denounced women, "these female automatons who from the seat of their easy chair talk about everything and in making up their minds influence their friends and give the command; women could make or break a painter's career, for no other reason than their capricious fantasy."[17]

The denunciation of women's taste and influence on the arts was directly tied to worries about the effeminacy of French art and the weakening of French culture more generally. The same author of *Sur la peinture* who denounced women's influence quickly turned his attention to the impact of badly trained artisans on the arts, drawing a firm distinction between elevated artists and mere artisans:

> Who is not struck by the difference between an artisan and an artist in the attention they give to human happiness and the good of the State. The artisan is absolutely dependent for his comfort on the rich and is assured his existence by consumers: the artist is only motivated by public esteem: he works for the good by a total abnegation of himself and the sacrifice of his life . . . Properly speaking, one is the body of the state while the other is its spirit.[18]

The distinction that the author of *Sur la peinture* made between the high moral seriousness and spirituality of the artist and the more base goals of the artisan, was echoed in the second half of the eighteenth century in the emerging distinction made between the fine arts and the agreeable arts. During the seventeenth and early eighteenth centuries, although a hierarchy of the visual arts had already been articulated which placed history painting at the summit, all arts – whether clock-making, embroidery, silver plating or painting and sculpture – shared one important quality: they were all considered *agréable*. According to the most widely respected art critic of the first half of the eighteenth century, the abbé Du Bos, all arts shared a common end, pleasure: "Does the work please or not please? Is the work good or bad? It is all the same thing." From brocaded cloth to history paintings, objects affected their viewers by operating on their senses, capturing the viewer by sensual delight, and arousing either the sentiment of pleasure or distaste. As Du Bos explained, the purpose of painting is "to touch and please, just as the end of eloquence is to persuade."[19]

But at the heart of the neoclassical ideology of the arts that developed in the second half of the eighteenth century lay a new distinction between those arts that were consumed for sensual pleasure and those arts that were not to be consumed because they did not and could not act on the base level of the senses. In positing this radical disjuncture between the fine arts and the agreeable arts, neoclassical aesthetic theory marked an end to the unified, although hierarchical, conception of the visual arts which had existed prior to the mid eighteenth century. No matter how strenuously fabric designers, wigmakers, or even portrait painters might proclaim their aesthetic talents and genius, according to the neoclassical vision, their products were essentially different from the pure arts of history painting and sculpture because they were meant to give pleasure through consumption by the senses rather than to elevate the soul.

By the mid-eighteenth century, as part of the neoclassical reaction against the sensuous lines and decorative curves of rococo art, critics began to question whether the "beautiful," the "pleasing" and the "artistic" were really synonymous. A new conception of art emerged which denigrated works of art that captured the viewer through sensual delight – works of art that were merely agreeable – and elevated works that demanded a higher appreciation by the intellect. The base passions and desires piqued in the viewer by the agreeable arts were now antithetical to true aesthetic contemplation. As one critic of rococo art phrased it, "The history painter alone paints for the soul, other artists only paint for the eyes." According to this perspective, those who painted for the eyes rather than the soul would always be hostage to "trifling subjects of the current time and fashion."[20] Artists were elevated above artisans as the exclusive processors of genius. Their genius alone could express truly noble sentiments that embodied the highest values of the French.

At the heart of this re-evaluation of the relationship between art and the beholder was a profound re-evaluation of what it meant for art to be consumed. One way in which critics distinguished the high arts from the crafts was by creating a theory of the arts according to which the painting did not, or should not, act sensually on the beholder. As art historian Michael Fried has elegantly argued, critics such as Diderot were interested in the "de-theatricalization of the relationship between painting and beholder." That is, in Fried's view, they sought to "find a way to neutralize or negate the beholder's presence, to establish the fiction that no one is standing before the canvas."[21] Among the arts that lost prestige according to this new conception of art was portraiture, a genre that was, according to Fried, "singularly ill-equipped to comply with the demand that a painter negate or neutralize the presence of the beholder."[22] Like the other agreeable arts, portraiture could not negate the presence of the beholder precisely because its entire *raison d'être* was to be consumed by the beholder. Portraits were, according to a contemporary tract, commissioned for one reason only, to flatter their subjects: "Self love, whose empire is even more powerful than that of *la mode*, creates the art of presenting to the eyes, especially of women, reflections of themselves that are the more enchanting the more they are untrue."[23] Fashion, of course, as much as portraiture, was designed to make women even more enchanting than they really were. And no matter how much women by the late eighteenth century had de-theatricalized their fashions and adopted a simple and more "natural" costume, fashion, like portraiture, could never be completely de-theatricalized: it was always predicated, even in the private realm of domesticity, on the presence of a spectator.

Although the neoclassical discourse on the arts was the dominant public discourse in the second half of the eighteenth century, artisans' creative attempts to elevate their crafts reveal the profound tension in French society between conflicting views of what was an art and what was a craft. In the case of the fashion trades, these debates over the distinctions between art and craft, and taste and genius reveal both the ways in which male and female artisans resisted the feminization of "the agreeable art of clothing" and the ways in which critics used class and gender in tandem to problematize the skills of the artisan and consumer.

Arts and Crafts

There was still a great deal of fluidity between the visual arts and the crafts in the eighteenth century, especially in the realm of luxury goods such as jewelry, brocaded dresses and elaborately painted fans, where artisans could claim that they, like artists, produced goods that transcended the rudimentary needs of human life. Despite the fact that Diderot and other art critics had embraced the modern conception of the artist as a creative genius, many French painters, sculptors and engravers continued to practice anonymously within the guild structure. Furthermore, many activities that we now define as crafts, such as embroidery, continued to be exhibited next to paintings at the Royal Academy's art salon. In 1766, the *Dictionnaire portatif des arts et métiers* included among the "arts dépendants au Dessin," the arts of the *brodeur, ciseleur, damasquineur, découpeur, fabriquant de dentelle, ébeniste, eventailliste, ferandinier* and *fabriquant d'étoffes*. And as late as 1777, an advertisement for the salon solicited "works of painting, sculpture, engravings, models of architecture, mechanical models, and even embroideries imitating painting."[24] In a passage which simultaneously reveals the persistence of a social and cultural overlap between the world of the visual arts and the world of crafts, and suggests the rift that had by the late eighteenth century rendered the artist and the artisan members of two distinct and separate castes, the artist Jacques-Louis David complained that even the seemingly rarefied world of the Royal Academy reeked of the sweat of the craft workshop:

> The Academy is like a wigmaker's shop; you cannot get out of the door without getting its powder on your clothes. What time you will lose in forgetting those poses, those conventional movements, into which the professors force the model's torso, as if it were the carcass of a chicken. Even the latter, with all their tricks, is not safe from their mannerisms. They will doubtless teach you to do your torso, teach you your *métier* in the end, because they make a trade out of painting. As for me, I think as little of that *métier* as I think of filth.[25]

The birth of the modern system of the arts, marked by the elevation of the artist as genius and the distinction between the arts and the crafts was neither swift nor easy. Transformations in the relative status of the fine arts and of the crafts developed unevenly, by fits and starts, occasioning much pain for those, whether wigmakers or salon painters, whose work and status in society was at stake. The agreeable art of clothing occupied a particularly troubled status: linked since the seventeenth century to French cultural prestige, *la mode* could not easily be dismissed, or divorced, from a vexing set of issues concerning the taste, genius, and public morality of the French nation. Many artisans – whether tailors, dress-makers, silversmiths or furniture painters – felt that their work was being devalued as the gulf between the artist and the artisans and between the fine arts and the agreeable arts, widened in the course of the eighteenth century. As "artisans," they not only were denied the chance to attain the fame that painters enjoyed, but were also denied participation in the high moral world of "Art," and relegated to the inferior world of the *arts utiles* and the *arts agréables*.

There were two very different responses to craftspeople's complaints that their aesthetic skills had been devalued. One was the response of the *philosophes* and *encyclopédistes*, who asserted the "nobility" and honorable nature of crafts as crafts. But in doing so, they drove an even larger wedge between the world of art and the world of craft. The *Encyclopédie* celebrated hatmaking, dressmaking and wigmaking, but esteemed these crafts for the mechanical skills of the human hand rather than any involvement of the heart or mind. In large part the *encyclopédists'* celebration of the artisan derived from the perceived social utility of his or her work: the crafts and luxury trades not only contributed to the health of the French economy, but also helped instill habits of discipline, and hence morality, among the artisan class. Still, crafts provided none of the transcendent values or power to express the human condition, which was the role of the arts. Moreover, the *Encyclopédie* celebrated the craftsperson's work, rather than the individual crafts-person. Nowhere is the *Encyclopédie*'s primary interest in work as a mechanical, rather than as a human, activity more evident than in its descriptions of specific crafts and in the detailed engravings which accompanied these descriptions: human workers are reduced to small, sketchy figures, mere background for the tools, implements and minutely rendered stages of production which are the *Encyclopédie*'s real focus.[26]

A second type of response to artisans' fears that their aesthetic skills had been devalued was the response by artisans themselves: they attempted to raise the status of their various crafts by claiming either that they were as worthy of being consid-ered arts as were painting or sculpture, or that they were sciences, and so deserved to be placed on an equal footing with the liberal arts. Responses in this vein, which ranged from attempts to have tailors certified by the Academy of Sciences or by the Academy of Painting to treatises which boasted of the "artistry" of wigmaking, will be examined in the final section of this chapter.[27]

Reorganizing the Trades

Part of the problem in neatly dividing the world of production between the fine arts and the mechanical crafts was that, as we have seen in Chapter 3, so many divisions and distinctions traversed the world of eighteenth-century work. Although Diderot could neatly summarize the difference between the arts and the crafts with his statement that the arts belonged to the realm of the heart and the crafts to the realm of the hand, the terminology used in the eighteenth century to distinguish between different kinds of productive and artistic labor was varied and often confusing. The world of work was divided by a number of shifting boundaries: between privileged and "free" trades, *arts* and *métiers*, boutiques and ateliers, workshops and academies, liberal arts and mechanical arts, fine arts and agreeable arts, and between the *utile* and the *frivole*. To add to the confusion, eighteenth-century terminology was often quite different from our own; for example, in 1735, the most widely read theorist of the arts, the abbé Du Bos, was still referring to painters as *artisans*.

During the three decades that preceded the Revolution, the French public turned its attention to this vast, murky world of the arts and crafts and tried to make sense of its confusing divisions, boundaries, and practices which were criss-crossed and obscured by privilege and tradition. The public's interest in examining the world of the arts, crafts and luxury trades was prompted by a growing fear that French superiority in the arts was being rapidly eclipsed by the economic boom across the English Channel. The French might stand by passively while the English outstripped them in coal or iron production, but when it came to goods such as clocks, porcelains, cloth and *les modes*, France's traditional pride in its luxury manufactures and exquisite national taste demanded a swift response.

The public's interest in reinvigorating crafts and commerce was translated into a growing desire to learn more about the world of the *arts* and *métiers*. In the pursuit of knowledge about the trades, one needed to look no further than the local *librairie*; for by the second half of the eighteenth century dozens of treatises, dictionaries and encyclopedias were published which discussed the actual technical processes of the arts and crafts and the skills involved in various kinds of labor. These books ranged from the pocketbook *Dictionnaire portatif des arts et métiers* (1766) to the multiple volume, folio editions of the *Encyclopédie, ou dictionnaire raisonné* and Panckoucke's *Encyclopédie méthodique: manufactures, arts et métiers* (1785). Works such as the *Encyclopédie* and the *Encyclopédie méthodique* treated a variety of trades, whereas others, such as Watin's *L'art du peintre, doreur, vernisseur* (1773), delineated the skills and talents necessary for particular arts and crafts. The audience for these works was diverse as well. Certainly the grand, folio volumes of the *Encyclopédie*, complete with dozens of engravings, were affordable only to elite bibliophiles. Appearing in excerpt form, however, individual articles from the *Encyclopédie* might be read by any entrepreneur who wished to study the processes of a particular craft in order to run a workshop more efficiently. Moreover, many of these works were explicitly aimed at a broader audience. The author of the *Dictionnaire portatif* stated that he hoped that his dictionary would reach a wider audience. And in the preface to his *L'art du peintre*, Watin explained that his work was inspired by the question, "Why not offer at the same time to workers and artists, elementary books that are portable, handy and inexpensive?"[28]

In addition to works that discussed the specific tools and processes of each trade, the reading public was also saturated with a variety of treatises and proposals that examined how the crafts were organized, policed and privileged: the public was as interested in the politics and economics of production as in the aesthetic judgments and technical processes involved. Whether one was a defender of the traditional privileges of the corporations or a proponent of freeing the arts and crafts from the guild system, most French people conceded that the corporate system was in need of some kind of reform. A wide variety of proposals were published, ranging from radical plans to dismantle the centuries-old system of corporations and to open the production of the arts and crafts to a free market, to plans to strengthen and consolidate the privileges of the elite core of craftspeople and merchants who made up the Six Corps. Among the most innovative plans were numerous proposals to open schools of design, which would teach artisans and craftspeople the skills that many French people feared were not being adequately taught in the course of gaining the *maîtrise*.

The most famous proposal for reform was, of course, Louis XVI's enlightened controller general, Jacques Turgot's aborted attempt in 1776 to abolish the corporations and free the world of arts and crafts productions to the "natural" forces of the market. Although many tailors and dressmakers who were fortunate enough to have gained admittance to the *maîtrise* may have remained satisfied with the corporate system, with both its limitations and privileges, many of the artisans and merchants involved in the fashion trades were profoundly dissatisfied with the restrictions which the corporate system placed on their skills, production, and social status.[29] Moreover, a growing number of clothing workers were unable to attain the *maîtrise* and were stranded at the lowly level of journeyman or simple *ouvrière*. For many talented and ambitious men and women the corporate system must have seemed a dead end; and in February 1776, upon hearing that Turgot had abolished the corporate system, countless journeymen retired to the cabarets to celebrate. As the *Mémoires secrets* reported in March 1776, "The bars overflowed with workers who had abandoned their masters."[30]

Historians have characterized the debate over the corporate organization of the arts and crafts, which raged from the mid-eighteenth century until the abolition of the corporate system in 1791, as a debate between the upholders of tradition and privilege on the one hand and the liberal harbingers of a free-market economy on the other. Historian Steven Kaplan has incisively described the debate as an "epic battle between . . . the marketplace and the market principle."[31] Elaborating on this distinction, Kaplan observes,

> Marketplace meant surveillance and control for the sake of public order . . . . The market principle was utterly corrosive of the marketplace as physical location and as regulatory apparatus. It meant laissez-faire: freedom from control and surveillance. It stemmed from natural laws that were said to be anterior to all forms of social organization. It frankly vaunted self-interest as its calculus, without regard to moral or political factors, and it postulated an underlying harmony of interests through infinite self-adjustment. Defined as a principle, the market was elusive, everywhere and nowhere at once, unclassifiable and mobile.[32]

According to Kaplan, the furor over the suppression of the corporate system was fueled by deep-seated anxieties about the economy that would emerge when the traditional social taxonomy of the corporate world was abolished. For proponents of the corporate system, permitting anyone to engage in any profession would turn the economy topsy-turvy, permitting Jews, outsiders, and incompetent artisans to gain control of the crafts and commerce. Even for those who welcomed Turgot's reforms, the natural inequality that Turgot claimed would accompany the liberty of commerce might have given some cause for pause. For Turgot stated explicitly that the price of liberty was inequality: the freeing of commerce would result in the creation of two types of people, those entrepreneurs who possessed the capital to set up businesses, and those simple workers who would be forced by their circumstances to work for the entrepreneurs.

The craftsmen and women of France did not, however, view the choice as lying between liberty and equality, between a free market and corporate traditionalism, as starkly as Kaplan has seen it with hindsight. In the interest of narrating the important "epic struggle between marketplace and market principle," one may lose sight of the host of other issues such as boundaries between the liberal arts and the crafts, the *frivole* and the *utile*, and masculinity and femininity, which were also entwined with the battle between freedom and privilege. Furthermore, not all workers rigidly conceptualized the choice as either absolute freedom for the market or absolute control of the market.

Several alternative models existed for workers to draw on for imaginatively recreating the world of work in addition to the corporate model or free trade.[33] One of the most appealing models for artisans who hoped to restructure the world of the *arts* and *métiers* was that provided by the elite institution of the Academy. Yet, at the same time, proposals to found academies of fashion also served the satiric interests of those who hoped to ridicule artisans' pretensions and the triviality of women and fashion and to underscore the very real gulf between the free pursuit of ideas in an enlightened academy and the enslavement to *la mode* of the commercial classes.

The Academic Model

The allure of the academic model was manifold. First, and perhaps foremost, academies had traditionally been elite institutions comprising the most learned and talented men (and occasionally women) of the aristocracy and upper bourgeoisie. What could be more ideal for the wigmaker or dressmaker who wished to elevate his or her craft than to situate it within the hallowed confines of an academy? Freed from the commerce of the street and market, perhaps the craftsperson's talents and skills might be appreciated by French society in a new light. Second, whereas the whole system of the corporation and *compagnonnage* was based on secret knowledge, the academic setting was far more compatible with the desire for openness and enlightenment that had become generally *à la mode* by the later eighteenth century.[34] Like the masters of the corporations, the academicians were experts, but their goal was to disseminate knowledge for the benefit of French society rather than to protect and guard it for private or corporate gain. Thus, academies played an important educational role in society. In doing so, they provided an attractive alternative to the corporation, in which the apprenticeship and completion of the *chef-d'oeuvre* often did little to educate apprentices in the fundamentals of design necessary to excel in one's craft. Furthermore, the Academy offered a more democratic principle of organization than had the corporation. Although the Academy's governing structure was hierarchical, the basis for this hierarchy was talent and merit, whereas in many corporations, wealth and privilege, rather than talent, separated masters from the journeymen and workers *sans qualité*. Finally, the great academies of France, The Royal Academy of Painting and Sculpture and the Academy of Sciences, were founded at the height of French absolutism by Colbert, and thus were imbued with the prestige of that peerless invigorator of the French arts: what better way to usher in a second renaissance of French arts and crafts than to associate one's craft with one of Colbert's greatest legacies to France, the Academy?[35]

Reformers deployed the model of the Academy in four different ways. Some artisans suggested that established Academies such as the Academy of Sciences or the Royal Academy of Painting should certify them. Others proposed setting up their own academies to be made up exclusively of members of their particular trade. A third type of proposal suggested founding academies – free schools of design – which would instruct a wide variety of artisans in the elements of mathematics and design necessary to succeed in their trade and restore taste and genius to the French arts and crafts. Finally, the academic model was used satirically to mock the ridiculousness of artisans' claims for the elevation of their crafts, and to reinforce the boundary between the high moral seriousness of the fine arts and the realm of craft and commerce.

In the "arts et métiers" section of the November 1776 issue of the women's journal *Journal dédié à Monsieur*, there appeared a review of a book by M. Sarrasin, *tailleur costumier* to the comte d'Artois. In this book, *L'Art du tailleur costumier*, Sarrasin argued that the distinction between the liberal and the mechanical arts was predicated on "accident," since both derived from the same "vulgar origins." Sarrasin's primary concern, however, was not to elevate all of the mechanical arts, but to "pull this art [of the *tailleur costumier*] from the crowd of crafts, and place it at the rank of the liberal arts." Sarrasin's case for including the art of tailoring among the liberal arts rested on his contention that the tailor possessed specialized skill and knowledge. For example, the tailor "knows both ancient and modern costumes and can make clothes for all necessary occasions, all time and for all nations and all estates." According to Sarrasin, the tailor's detailed knowledge of historical costume was indispensable to painters and actors, who were often ignorant of the sartorial details necessary to represent historical characters authentically on canvas and on stage. Sarrasin went on to suggest that the inclusion of *tailleurs costumiers* in the Royal Academy of Painting would greatly benefit the arts, and that because of the tailor's utility and taste, he "must be regarded as an erudite artist, in his way, and not as a simple artisan, who only knows how to take measurements and cut out an outfit."[36]

Like Sarrasin's *L'Art du tailleur costumier*, Bailly's *Avis aux mères qui aiment leurs enfants* (1786) also pleaded that because of its usefulness for society the profession of tailoring should be elevated to the realm of the liberal arts. Bailly argued, however, that the utility of tailors rested on their scientific knowledge rather than their artistic taste: instead of aspiring to be artists, tailors ought to assert their right to be called scientists and practitioners. Bailly, a *tailleur de corps pour femmes*, exhorted young workers who were learning the art of making corsets to raise their ambitions and "no longer be simple artisans. Become enlightened practitioners."[37] Bailly explained that a profession such as that of the *tailleurs de corps*, which "interests all of humanity, must be subjected to supervision, and to proofs which enable the public to be assured of the capacity of workers." Thus, according to Bailly, the ideal place for the *tailleurs de corps* to learn their trade was in the Académie royale de chirurgie, where they could take courses in human skeletal structure taught by learned anatomists. To prove their mastery of the rigorous theory on which their work rested, the tailors, like bandage makers, dentists and midwives, would be required to pass a public examination administered by the Royal Academy of Surgery. Thus certified, and in order to animate the tailors' zeal for their profession and to distinguish them from ordinary tailors, they would be permitted to title themselves, "Tailleurs Baleinists approved by the College of Surgery."[38]

In the case of Sarrasin and Bailly, linking one's craft to learned academies that could train and certify tailors was an important step not only to freeing one's trade from corporate control and elevating one's work, but also to re-masculinizing the clothing trades. All three ends were tightly linked. Moreover, these were not merely two artisan's quirky, utopian visions for elevating their craft. Louis-Sébastien Mercier indicates that the practice of using the prestige of academies was well established by the 1780s. In his *Tableau de Paris* he complains "The least significant artisan equips himself today with the approbation of this illustrious Academy, which stoops, it seems to me, to concern itself with objects which are sometimes unworthy of it." Mercier cites as an example the stamp of approval that the Academy of Sciences granted to a particular black shoe polish called "coquettish wax."[39] The Academy of Sciences was also active in testing and approving cosmetics. In February 1777 the *Journal de Paris* reported that the Academy of Sciences had examined the zinc-based rouge manufactured by M. Doucet of Normandy to assess its health risks.

A second way in which artisans used the prestige of the academy to elevate and re-masculinize their trade is outlined in the hairdresser Legros's *L'art de la coiffure des dames*: artisans might set up their own academies.[40] Legros's book, in addition to dispensing advice to women on how to care for their hair and providing engravings of different hairstyles, describes his Académie de l'art de la coiffure des dames.[41] This Academy of Coiffure was divided into three courses. In the first, which cost a tuition of six *louis*, the student *coiffeurs* and *coiffeuses* (unlike other eighteenth-century trade schools, Legros's academy was open to both men and women) learned how to copy Legros's thirty-eight original hairstyles. If one wanted to learn to be a men's *valet-de-chambre*, one could for a fee of four *louis*, attend a second course where one learned to copy an additional twenty-eight hairstyles. Those wishing to become *femmes-de-chambre* attended a third class which cost only two *louis*, but which taught one only how to style, not cut, hair. When the students had finished all three courses, they were officially sworn in as "Master Professors and Academicians of the Art of Women's Hairdressing."

Unlike barbers and wigmakers, hairdressers practiced freely in Paris; yet, Legros felt the need to justify and explain his elevation of hairstyling to an art, and his placement of training in an academy:

> There are perhaps some people who find it wrong that my book is titled *l'art de la coiffure des dames*, and my classes are called an Academy. Here is the explanation: dressing women's hair has become an art for me because I've created and drawn up plans for all my hairstyles . . . . I've created 52 different hairstyles for all different tastes . . . . My school is called an Academy because I teach the foundation of the art of hairdressing and how to create designs for all types of hair, flowers, feathers and I award my students a printed certificate when they have demonstrated their skill in styling according to 38 different designs. [42]

Touting his own talents as much as the artistry of his profession, Legros went on to declare, "Because I am the only one in the world who has pushed the dressing of women's hair to this highest level . . . I believe that I am truly permitted to call myself the first Artist of *la Coiffure des Dames*."[43]

Legros is a colorful example of an eighteenth-century artisan who had broken with corporate structures and traditions and boldly charted new ground in the virgin territory of "free trade."[44] Through a hodge-podge of ventures and a striking talent for self-promotion, he achieved considerable renown among the women who made up the society of taste of eighteenth-century Paris: two editions of his *L'art de la coiffure* were reviewed in the *Journal des dames*, and Legros claimed that his engravings earned "the applause of French women and of all the women of the foreign courts of Europe."[45] Legros had first tried his hand as a cook, but had soon embarked on a new career when he could not find a publisher for his *Livre de cuisine*. His career change from cooking to coifing was fortuitous, for his *L'art de la coiffure* proved a relatively profitable venture, selling for two *louis* a copy and being reprinted in four editions between 1765 and 1778. In addition to his publications and his Academy, he also ran a mail-order wig business. Customers had only to select their desired wig style from his book and send a sample of their hair color and their head measurement.[46]

Among Legros's considerable talents, perhaps his greatest gift was in the realm of public relations. When the wigmakers challenged his competence to make wigs in 1763, Legros promptly set up a display at the fashionable Foire Saint-Ovide on the place Vendôme at which he styled the hair of thirty mannequins to the enthusiastic applause of the ladies who stood watching. And in 1766, when people began to question whether Legros's elaborate hairstyles could work for natural hair, he had his students style the hair of thirty-three models in thirty-three different styles and then paraded them along the ramparts of Paris.[47] In the cut-throat world of eighteenth-century commerce, Legros employed some of the strategies – associating one's craft with the prestige of the academy, publishing a book to advertise one's wares, and enlisting the approbation of the public – necessary for success. Legros's tactics were emulated by many, from Marie Antoinette's celebrated hairdresser, "Le Grand Léonard," who appropriated the title "académicien de coiffures et de modes," to humble neighborhood hairdressers who displayed the word "Académie" in their shop windows. Legros's use of mannequins to display hairstyles was also widely copied, and by the reign of Louis XVI plaster (and later wax) busts displayed hairstyles in the store windows of hairdressers throughout Paris.[48]

Although an artisan/artist such as Legros doubtless had boundless confidence in his aesthetic judgment and talents, many observers of the world of arts and crafts were dismayed at the lack of taste and artistry exhibited by many artisans. Commenting on the state of the arts and crafts, Jean-Baptiste Descamps lamented in

1767: "How many examples of bizarre works! Workers without principles, without taste, taking the designs of our best artists and piling on them a multitude of decorations without taste, without realism: one sees a cabbage larger than a human figure, a feather supporting the heavy weight of seashells, imaginary forms.[49] The lack of aesthetic judgment, ignorance of the rudiments of design, and the inability to copy after nature were believed to have taken a devastating toll on French trade and commerce. Whereas other nations might attribute their economic gains to hard work, thrift, or natural resources, the French widely believed that sheer quality of design was the basis for French success in commerce; as Descamps wrote, "It is to the taste of our designs, it is to this single taste of the Nation, to this genius at continually creating and varying" that the French owe their superiority in the arts and crafts.[50]

Beginning in the mid-eighteenth century, academies of design began teaching artisans the aesthetic skills, which they apparently were not learning within the apprenticeship and corporate system.[51] The first of these *écoles de dessin* was founded in 1741 in Rouen, and by the 1780s, most major cities in northern and northwestern France had established schools to train male artisans. Locally run, each of these schools had different structures and programs. Some were open to all who wished to enroll, while others were open only to youths who planned to become artisans. While some were free, others charged a small tuition. Most of these schools offered lessons two days a week in geometry, architecture, and the drawing of the human figure, animals, flowers and other ornaments. Emphasis was placed on teaching artisans, whether locksmiths or fabric designers, the rudiments of design; for in the eighteenth century design (*dessin*) was the foundation of all the mechanical and agreeable arts. As one reformer wrote, "design is the basis of all machine-made works (*les ouvrages mécaniques*) and workers are only superior to others to the extent that they are more or less expert in this art . . . . Without the study of design, not only won't they become good artists, but even the most talented will degenerate into vulgar workers."[52]

Although design schools sought to raise the taste and aesthetic sensibility of artisans by teaching them the principles of good design, they in no way advocated the elevation of the artisan's status vis-à-vis the artist, as had proposals such as Sarrasin's *L'art du tailleur costumier* or Legros's Academy of Hairdressing. Bachelier, the director of the Paris school of design referred to his school as "the *Encyclopédie* put into action," and in many ways these schools, like the *Encyclopédie*, were utilitarian attempts to reform the crafts by reinforcing the distinction between mechanical craftspeople and artists.[53] In these schools, artisans were trained so that they could help artists in executing – but not creating – works of art. As DeRozoi phrased it in his *Essai philosophique sur l'établissement des écoles gratuites*, the free schools would help the "artisan, with his own skills, guided by the genius of the artist; if the one merits to be called the creator, then the other surely merits to be shaped by him, or to work on the artist's creations."[54] The founders of these schools did not encourage artisans to stimulate their imaginations and apply their creativity; for, as the founders believed, left to their own devices artisans would create objects of poor and childish taste, "twisted forms, without smoothness, solidity, intelligence, or realism."[55]

Descamps, in his *Sur l'utilité des établissements des écoles gratuites de dessin*, did hold out the hope, however, that design schools might be an ideal place for the natural artistic geniuses among the artisan class to prove themselves. Descamps suggested that with the discovery of their talent, the doors of the Royal Academy of Painting would be opened to them and great artists would invite them into their ateliers and share the wonders of the *beaux arts* with them.[56] Yet even in this hopeful vision of artistic glory, the distinction between the mechanical arts and the *beaux-arts* held fast; the design schools may have offered a route for a small number of artisans to escape from the *utile* and *agréable* world of the crafts to the lofty world of the arts, but these schools denied the crafts the right to shake off their reputation as lowly, manual work and join the *beaux-arts*: the *écoles de dessin* could teach their students taste but they could not instill them with *génie*.

In their attempt to reform the arts and crafts, the founders of free schools of design insisted that in addition to learning the skills of design workers also needed to be instilled with "a spirit of order and good morals." The founders of these schools hoped to correct the "petit libertinage" and the "dangerous idleness" which they believed characterized the children of the artisan class.[57] Even the most cursory glance at the rules of these schools reveals their emphasis on maintaining order: all students will present themselves for classes with "decency and propriety;" no student will be admitted to class without showing the teacher his identifying badge; strict silence will be observed during the class; no one may leave the room before the end of the exercise; no one is permitted to miss class without an authorized excuse; on leaving the class one will give each student a token stamped with the date as a proof to one's parent or master that one has attended class.[58]

This emphasis on discipline was a further way of enforcing strict class hierarchies and effeminizing male workers – the disciplined world imagined by the schools of design was a far cry from the rowdy, male world of camaraderie in the eighteenth-century craft workshop and more closely resembled the kind of discipline that girls had long endured as they learned to do needlework under the watchful eye of their mothers at home or of nuns in convent schools. In addition to the inculcation of discipline and morality, design schools attempted to encourage a competitive spirit among their students by holding frequent competitions among the students for prizes and distinctions. At the end of each year there would be a championship to determine the first prize for each class. DeRozoi explained that these "public prizes elevate the soul, making honor a personal sentiment, illuminating in hearts a sacred fire."[59] Perhaps most important, these competitions would prepare young male students to succeed in a reformed economy in which talent and merit, rather than privilege, would determine who succeeded or failed in a trade.

With their stress on instilling discipline, a competitive spirit, and a sense of good taste, design schools hoped to prepare students for a new economic order. In some cases those who urged the creation of schools of design sided with economic reformers such as Turgot and proponents of a free market for labor. But in other cases, the schools of design were intended to reform rather than to abolish the corporate structure. As DeRozoi explained, "it is less a matter of daring innovation, than of intelligently correcting." He denied any desire to deprive guild masters of their traditional rights, wishing only that they would choose their members from those who had excelled as students in design schools rather than selecting them according to wealth or privilege.[60]

A number of late-eighteenth-century proposals to found academies of fashion mixed satire with a serious desire to rethink the organization of the clothing trades. The first of these proposals, "Projet d'une académie de modes," appeared in *La feuille sans titre* in February 1777. A similar proposal, "Etablissement d'une académie de modes," appeared at the end of J.H. Marchand's satire *Les panaches ou les coiffures à la mode* in 1778. And a third variant, titled "Projet utile," appeared a decade later in the January 20, 1787 edition of the *Magasin des modes nouvelles*. The organization of each of these proposed academies was roughly similar. The proposal that appeared in the 1777 *La feuille sans titre* suggested that the academy would comprise sixty *académiciennes* selected from the most distinguished women of France. The academy was no democracy, and the president, elected for life, wielded supreme powers over the other *académiciennes*. When any of the *académiciennes* died or retired ("because they will have attained the age when fashionable dress is no longer useful") an open competition between all the "petites maîtresses" would determine her successor. The winner would be obliged to present to the assembly a description of all of the fashions she had personally invented. In addition to the sixty *académiciennes*, the academy would include twelve mistresses selected from among the most famous and talented *marchandes ou faiseuses de modes*, each of whom would be paid 4,000 *livres* per year for directing the production of all of the fashions invented or ordered by the ladies of the academy. The actual work of making these fashions would be placed in the hands of thirty-two "young ladies whose taste and dexterity will be well known among hatmakers." Six other mistresses would be selected to teach free lessons in design, painting and engraving to the students of the academy, and also to engrave or paint pictures of all of the fashions invented by the *académiciennes*. The academy would pay its expenses from the revenue raised by operating a store in which it sold a wide variety of fashionable goods and accessories. The shop would be furnished with lavish woodwork and dozens of mirrors. Through eight huge windows the public would be able to view the *faiseuses de modes* and "the serious academicians" as they worked and deliberated. In addition, the academy would raise money by publishing a *Gazette des modes* that would contain transcripts of the papers on fashion presented at the sessions of the academy, the names and addresses of the academicians, mistresses, students, and associates of the academy, the names and addresses of all of the most celebrated *modistes* of the capitals of Europe, descriptions of all new fashions complete with engravings and a list of prices, histories of various fashions, and "interesting and romantic anecdotes."

The institutional structure of the academy of fashion proposed by Marchand varied slightly from *La feuille sans titre*'s proposal.[61] His academy would comprise twenty-five men and twenty-five women who were "singled out by their good taste and chosen among the people of the court and Paris who distinguished themselves by their studied elegance." The men and the women would meet separately each week to discuss the fashions for their own sex, then jointly each month to discuss "the most appealing form of decorations that can be applied to both men's and women's clothing." One of the main purposes of the academy would be to accredit merchants and craftspeople who had invented new fashions. In addition, the academy would have two professors of fashions, one male and one female, who would give weekly lessons on "the art of inventing and perfecting objects of taste, coquetry, and generally all things connected to the arts of pleasing." Finally, the academy would distribute two medals each year to distinguish the most accomplished inventors of new fashions and avid pursuers of novelty.

The satire in these proposals cut two ways. On the one hand the humor rested on the laughable proposition that creating fashions was as important and noble as the work of the great academies of France. The association of commerce and fashion with all of the trappings of the learned culture of elite males, such as assemblies, prizes and medals, ultimately highlighted the utter frivolity of women and their fashions. Moreover, the inclusion of men in Marchand's proposal, mocked the men who participated – as consumers or producers – in the culture of fashion, feminizing them by association.[62]

Yet, while these proposals ridiculed female consumers and male artisans' pretensions to elevate fashion to the realm of science and art, they also simultaneously mocked learned culture. In stressing the utility of the academies of fashion these proposals commented on the potential frivolity of learned societies such as the Académie française and the Académie des belles-lettres. As Marchand explained in his proposal,

> France has for many years been honored with the Academy Française. But this Academy is only a tribunal to decide which words are fashionable and to proscribe those that are no longer fashionable . . . . Certainly the harmony of clothing is as interesting as the rules of grammar. More people make their living on a yard of ribbons than a fathom of words.

The symmetry of ornaments agreeably pleases the eye, while the arrangement of sentences only creates a momentary oral sensation.[63]

The proposal for an academy of fashion found in the *Magasin des modes* similarly mocked the ways in which the Académie des belles-lettres was swayed by fashions and novelty in language, and argued that an academy of fashion would be more beneficial to the public good:

The Académie des belles-lettres also creates systems of what is fashionable, by destroy-ing ancient usages; but all its operations are pure speculation and are often subject to controversy: it produces little for the good of the public; while on the other hand, a new discovery in fashions opens up the banks, enriches the provinces, ... A fact about science only interests about five hundred citizens, while an agreeable fashion affects four million subjects.[64]

These proposals' explicit comparison of elite academies and imaginary academ-ies of fashion dimly echoes the very real debate that raged in the late seventeenth and early eighteenth centuries between the ancients and the moderns, revealing the doubts that still lingered in the late eighteenth century concerning the compatibility of French national cultural glory and the empire of frivolous fashion. Moreover, the satires poke gentle fun at faddishness of the late-eighteenth-century culture of the Enlightenment: academies, encyclopedias, projects and prizes, had become generally *à la mode* in France.[65] These institutions became targets of ridicule for those who felt that the once serious and politically subversive nature of the Enlightenment had been eroded by banality and trendiness. From this perspective, an academy of fashion seemed hardly more ludicrous than the learned academies that did exist. Unlike most elite academies, academies of fashion could at least claim a publicly useful purpose aiding French commerce and providing jobs for Parisian garment workers. Paradoxically, these proposals affirmed that fashion was both frivolous and useful. As the "Projet utile" proclaimed, "In vain our alleged wise men have bitterly ranted against the frivolity of our fashions: it is precisely in the bosom of our inconstancy that flows our abundance and the circulation of goods that are our national glory."[66]

Clearly these proposals were aimed at the frivolity of women and fashion and at the trendiness of elite learned culture and were part of a bantering literature on women and on the Enlightenment that flourished in the later eighteenth century. But these proposals may also reveal an earnest desire to reform the fashion in-dustry.[67] Although reformers such as Descamps and DeRozoi found the corporate system's inability to train artisans competent in the principles of design, good taste and work discipline a serious impediment to French commerce, for many com-mentators the corporate system was most glaringly inadequate for the production of that most treasured of French commodities, *les modes*. As Marchand paradoxically phrased it, "It is of universal interest to establish a fixed order concerning a area whose foundation will never require fixed and determined rules."[68] Or, as the "Projet utile" claimed, "It is then of the greatest importance for the state that one establish honors and distinctions and compensation for these profound geniuses who through their good taste have furnished the public with models of the finest ornamentations."[69]

Fashion demanded the participation of producers in a wider culture than that of the closed craft workshop. The producers of fashion, as opposed to clothing, were not beholden to the mastery of traditional craft skills; fashion thrived on constant innovation and interaction with a wider culture that encompassed operas, actresses, novels, events at court, military battles, and scientific discoveries. In addition, more than workers in other industries, the producers of fashions had to react to and manipulate ever-changing consumer tastes. Whereas the fashion trades of Old Regime France encompassed a patchwork of competing corporate and non-corporate bodies, the proposals for academies of fashion suggest a yearning for a vast enterprise, encompassing both consumers and producers, which would unify "under one roof" a series of subsidiary industries, including not only the manufacture of clothing, but the marketing of fashions, publicity, and the dissemination of information about fashion through a specialized fashion press. Like Sarrasin's plan to include tailors in the Academy of Painting and Legros's attempt to set up an academy of hairdressing, the academies of fashion reveal an attempt to conceptualize (if not to realize) a new way of organizing production and a new way of harnessing fashion to the needs of a society of taste and the cultural and economic glory of France.

Women and Taste

Proposals to found academies of fashion poked fun at women's taste for fashion as much as the taste of workers in the fashion trades. Just as some artisans creatively resisted the relegation of their work and skills to the world of the base crafts, several eighteenth-century authors challenged the idea that fashions and trinkets wholly occupied women's minds and praised not only women's taste, but also even their genius. Dom Philippe-Joseph Caffiaux, in his *Défense du beau sexe* (1753), contended that when it came to the *beaux-arts*, "one sees everywhere that women are no less distinguished than men." Caffiaux praised female artists such as Anne-Marie Schurman, Sophonisba Anguisola, Diane de Volterre and Elisabeth Chéron and even went as far as to suggest that the art of painting had originally been discovered by a woman.[70] Caffiaux's spirited defense of women clearly engaged the longstanding and often elevated tradition of the *querelle des femmes*. But women's aesthetic skills were valorized in a more popular and less rhetorical literature as well. Joubert de l'Hiberderie, for example, the author of a treatise on fabric design, praised women's artistic skills and deplored their exclusion from careers in the arts and sciences, stating that "the injustice that one has made to this delicate sex, adroit and full of taste, is too common." [71]

At the forefront of efforts to praise women's taste and genius were the female editors of the female press. The editor of the *Bibliothèque des femmes* declared in 1759, "Women possess good taste instinctively; however, people pretend that they do not love any arts and that they do not know any. What could be more inconsistent?"[72] Madame de Beaumur, editor of the *Journal des dames* from 1762 to 1763, publicized in the "Arts et Modes" section of her journal the artistic achievements of the many unknown craftswomen of Paris.[73] Beaumur's successors at the *Journal des dames*, Mme de Maisonneuve, Mathon de la Cour, and Mme de Montaclos, continued to praise the taste and genius of the female artists of Paris.[74] The editor of the journal suggested that if women's taste and genius appeared restricted to the realm of fashions and trinkets, social and educational practices, rather than women's nature, were to blame.

In October 1774 Mme de Montaclos used the opportunity of a review of a novel by M. de Bastide in which the protagonist was a talented female artist to lament, "For a long time people have injured our sex by believing that it cannot distinguish itself by *chefs-d'oeuvre* in artistic careers, nor even arrive at an understanding of artistic processes." She went on to claim that although it was true that "no famous monuments, either in sculpture or architecture, have yet been produced by the creative genius of a woman," this was not a sign of lack of talent and genius, but the unfortunate effect of the denial of a proper education to women. Because of the absence of training or encouragement in the arts as children, women are limited by the "prejudices and enslaving usages for the remainder of our lives."[75] Montanclos's review of Bastide's interpretation in novel form of a treatise on aesthetic theory and art education, *L'Homme du monde éclairé par les arts*, by Jacques François Blondel, architect to the king and premier art educator of his day, indicates the serious interest that female readers and editors of the *Journal des dames* took in aesthetic issues. The editor complained that Bastide's attempt to popularize Blondel's work, and his explicit attempt to tailor it for a female audience by recasting it in novel form, was unsuccessful and suggested that her readers would be better served by reading the original documents of aesthetic theory, such as the abbé Du Bos's highly respected *Réflexions critiques sur la poèsie et sur la peinture*, rather than facile attempts at popularization.

Whether disparaging women's taste and artistic talents, as did Boudier de Villemert, or praising them, as did Beaumur and Montaclos, what united both sides of this eighteenth-century version of the *querelle des femmes* was the agreement that women had an avid taste for fashions and novelties. At issue, however, was not whether women possessed the ability to discern the beauty in objects, but whether they had the ability to channel their taste toward morally-edifying and socially-productive ends: was women's taste limited to the realm of fashions and *les modes*, or did it extend to the more "elevated" realm of fine arts? Were women slaves to *la mode*, or were they fashion's graceful and disciplined mistresses? Most import-ant, could fashion be rendered compatible with domesticity? In the female press, in the writings of the *philosophes*, and in the more accessible discussions of aesthetic issues in journals and almanacs such as the *Bibliothèque des sciences et des beaux arts* and the *Almanach historique et raisonné*, discussions of taste, genius, imagination and *esprit* became a major forum for discussions of gender difference. Pervasive beliefs concerning women's ability to seize and quickly absorb the visual world around them were used, not only to deny women access to the fine arts, but, as I will explore in more depth in the next chapter, to naturalize their new roles as consumers.

Among the many contemporaries who wrote on women's taste and imagination, Rousseau famously spelled out the difference between men and women's sensa-tions most clearly when he wrote, "boys seek out movement and noise; drums, sabots, little carriages: girls prefer that which they can see and use as an ornament; mirrors, jewels, rags, and above all dolls."[76] Throughout his novel *Émile*, Rousseau stressed that women excel at fine observations; he advised that if one wanted to assess material objects or anything pertaining to the senses one should consult women; but when one wanted to judge an issue of morality or reason, one should consult men.[77] Boudier de Villemert echoed Rousseau in his *Le nouvel ami des femmes* claiming, "Man is the arm, he bears the weight of the work; but woman is the eye, she surveys everything all the time."[78]

The Enlightenment emphasis on the liveliness, yet passivity, of women's sense of sight and imagination provided a partial explanation for women's susceptibility to the allure of commodities. In addition, the developing science of aesthetics and the popular debate over the nature of taste helped contemporaries understand how commodities acted on individuals, by attracting them, seducing them, and creating desire. As we have noted earlier in this chapter, by the mid-eighteenth century, the neoclassical reaction against the sensuous lines and decorative curves of rococo art led to a new conception of art which distinguished sharply between the fine arts and the agreeable arts. This distinction drew a line between objects that worked on the eyes and objects those that worked on the soul, between decorative objects that captured the passive viewer through sensual delight and true works of art that required contemplation by the intellect. Although sensationalist philosophy, which was predicated on the idea that all knowledge comes from our senses, might have led to the conclusion that men's and women's senses and perceptions were equal, the writings of many Enlightenment writers re-inscribed a new gender hierarchy of the senses. For Rousseau and Boudier de Villemert, women's sensory apparatus was more receptive to stimulation than men's, but women lacked the intellect to move from the world of senses to higher reason. Women's psychology and sensory apparatus made them ideally suited to consume because their passivity rendered female consumers particularly vulnerable to being captured through sensual delight by agreeable and frivolous objects.

Several female journalists offered a substantial revision of this denigration of women's capacity for artistic and moral genius. The editor of *Journal de monsieur*, Mme la Présidente D'Ormoy, suggested that all that was necessary for women's pursuit of the arts and sciences and to make oneself a *"femme forte*, worthy of esteem and respect" was to "take a few hours away from one's *toilette*."[79] Yet in their fear that the pursuit of fashion would interfere with higher intellectual, moral, and artistic pursuits D'Ormoy and her fellow female journalists shared many of Rousseau's ideas about the dangers posed by fashionable Parisian commercial culture. Throughout its issues of 1774 the *Journal des dames* published the epistles of a woman who identified herself as "La Solitaire des Isles d'Hières" and proclaimed "I am the Jean-Jacques of our sex." Contrasting the pleasures and virtues of a tranquil country life with the luxury and corruption of Paris, she could think of no better way to evoke the differences than to compare her sartorial simplicity with the artifice of her Parisian counterparts. Addressing her letter to a Parisian noblewoman, "La Solitaire" wrote, "I imagine seeing you in a pretty ball gown when I read what you tell me of your amusements. Yes, Madame, that is only a disguise that you have taken to shun the eye of reason which pursues you; but sooner or later you will abandon it, and then you will put on the plain dress of wise nature." [80] To advance its reformist mission the *Journal des dames* published many stories and anecdotes about virtuous women who had forsaken their hairdressers and *modistes*, sacrificing their fashions for their family's welfare. In a typical story, a young orphan named Julie transformed sartorial splendor into domestic virtue and won the heart of a rich and loving suitor by trading her showy fashions for a simple dress.[81]

Conclusion

Although hairdressers might proclaim their artistry, and "the divine Scheling" might boast of discovering a new color unknown even to painters, by the end of the century the artisans of Paris were even further removed from the fine arts than when the century had begun. By the eve of the Revolution attempts to elevate the clothing trades to the level of the fine arts and sciences were relegated to the realm of satire and fun, suggesting a growing recognition, even by craftspeople themselves, that the gulf between the world of craft and commerce and the world of art was too great to bridge. Those who made and sold fashions seem to have accepted a trade-off: they would concede that their work was frivolous and that the enslavement of their "genius" to the demands of consumers and the market corrupted their taste and divorced them from the realm of high art. In return society would acknowledge the utility and tremendous economic importance of their trades. By the later eighteenth century few tailors, dressmakers, or *marchandes de modes* would disagree that the agreeable arts of fashion participated in the realm of the *arts utiles* rather than in the realm of the *beaux arts*; and if artisans no longer looked to academies of the arts to certify their genius, they were increasingly willing to look to academies of science to certify the utility of their products and to pronounce the importance of their commerce for the French economy. Whereas once the *arts utiles* and the *arts frivoles* had been considered two distinct categories, by the eve of the Revolution many French people had conceded that the very frivolity of fashions made them extremely useful to the French economy. Denied access to the serious realm of the fine arts, fashion found a warm welcome in the realm of commerce.

Contemporaries' conclusions about women's distinctive taste had a profound impact on the roles that were available to women in French society, restricting women's participation in many areas of production and potentially valorizing a new space for women as consumers. These new conclusions about fashion helped create a new vocabulary of social distinction: taste would become a powerful new code which separated working-class artisans from elite artists and connoisseurs, women from men, and the slavish and frivolous subject from the independent and enlightened citizen. One's relationship to a whimsical, yet tyrannical, *Mode* – to modern commercial culture – marked not only one's rank in the new "society of taste," but one's political, economic, and moral station as well. Not only philosophers and theorists, but ordinary craftspeople, merchants, and female editors helped shape the discourse on artisans' and female consumer's taste, creating a new society of taste capable of feminizing fashion without effeminizing the nation.

Notes

1. *Éloge Funèbre et historique de très-court, très épais, et tout-adroit citadin Monsieur maître Nicodême Patalèon TIRE-POINT, Bourgeois de Paris, maître et marchand Tailleur d'Habits, ancien Juré de sa communauté. . .* (Paris, 1776).
2. *Éloge Funèbre*: 23.
3. *Oraison Funèbre de très-habille, très-elegant, très merveilleus CHRISTOPHE SCHELING, maître tailleur de Paris, Prononcée le 18 Février 1761 dans la sale du célèbre Alexandre, Limonadier au boulevard* (Paris: 1761): 5.

4. *Oraison Funèbre*: 23, 40.
5. Freemasonry became respectable after the mid-eighteenth century and by the 1770s and 1780s there were over 200 lodges in Paris. On Freemasonry, see Margaret Jacob, *Living the Enlightenment: Freemasonry and Politics in Eighteenth-Century Europe* (Oxford: Oxford University Press, 1991).
6. Mercier, *Tableau de Paris*, t. 3: 225.
7. Mercier, t. 7: 132.; Jean-Jacques Rousseau, dictionary entry "Goût," quoted in Philip E.J. Robinson, *Jean-Jacques Rousseau's Doctrine of the Arts* (Bern, 1984): 306.
8. For a discussion of the role of taste in gender and class formation in England see, Robert W. Jones, *Gender and the Formation of Taste in Eighteenth-Century Britain: The Analysis of Beauty* (Cambridge: Cambridge University Press, 1998) and Kevin Sharpe and Steven N. Zwicker, eds. *Refiguring Revolutions: Aesthetics and Politics from the English Revolution to the Romantic Revolution* (Berkeley: University of California Press, 1998).
9. Tjitske Akkerman, *Women's Vices, Public Benefits: Women and Commerce in the French Enlightenment* (The Hague: Het Spinhuis, 1992).
10. See Sarah Maza, "Luxury, Morality, and Social Change: Why There Was No Middle-Class Consciousness in Pre-revolutionary France," *Journal of Modern History* 69 (1997): 199–229.
11. See Jean-Louis Flandrin, "Distinction through Taste," in *A History of Private Life: Passions of the Renaissance* ed. Roger Chartier (Cambridge, MA: Harvard University Press, 1989): 305; Michael Moriarty, *Taste and Ideology in Seventeenth-Century France* (Cambridge: Cambridge University Press, 1988). Although contemporaries argued that taste was "classless," many texts disparaged the taste of certain groups in society such as women and artisans. Moriarty argues that in the seventeenth century the discourse on taste played an important role in the creation of the new model of the courtier, the *honnête homme*, which fused the nobility of the sword, nobility of the robe, and the haute bourgeoisie.
12. David Hume, "Of the Standard of Taste," in *Essays Moral, Political, and Literary* (Oxford: Oxford University Press, 1963): 237.
13. On this point, see Richard Shusterman, "'Of The Scandal of Taste': Social Privilege as Nature in the Aesthetic Theories of Hume and Kant," in *Eighteenth-Century Aesthetics and the Reconstruction of Art*, ed. Paul Mattick, Jr. (Cambridge: Cambridge University Press, 1993): 96–119.
14. Julien Joseph Virey, *De l'influence des femmes sur le goût dans la littérature et les beaux arts pendant le XVIIe et le XVIIIe siècle* (Paris, 1810): 51–52, 65.
15. Quoted in Michael Levey, *Rococo to Revolution: Major Trends in 18th–Century Painting* (London, 1966): 121.

16. Pierre Joseph Boudier de Villemert, *L'ami des femmes* (1758), quoted in Caroline Rimbault "La presse féminine de langue française au XVIIème siècles: place de la femme et système de la mode" (Thèse de 3ème cycle, Ecole des Hautes Etudes en Sciences Sociales, Paris, 1981): 91.

17. *Sur la peinture* (The Hague, 1782), 73.

18. Ibid., 26.

19. Du Bos, *Réflexions critiques* (Paris, 1770), t. 2: 1. In the seventeenth century Roger de Piles also contended that the artist was obliged to attract and please. See Mary D. Sheriff, *Fragonard: Art and Eroticism* (Chicago: University of Chicago Press, 1990): 127.

20. *Réflexions sur quelques causes de l'état présent de la peinture en France* (Paris, 1752): 195, 207.

21. Michael Fried, *Absorption and Theatricality* (Berkeley: University of California Press, 1980): 131, 108.

22. Fried, *Absorption and Theatricality*: 109.

23. *Réflexions sur quelques causes*: 201.

24. *Almanach historique et raisonné* (Paris, 1777): 125.

25. Jacques-Louis David, quoted in Thomas Crow, *Painters and Public Life* (New Haven, CT: Yale University Press, 1985): 230.

26. On Diderot's and the *Encyclopédistes'* ambivalence toward artisans and their work, see Cynthia Koepp, "The Alphabetical Order: Work in Diderot's Encyclopédie," in *Work in France, Representations, Meaning, Organization and Practice* ed. S. Kaplan and C. Koepp (Ithaca: Cornell University Press, 1986): 229–57, and Robert Darnton, *The Business of Enlightenment: A Publishing History of the Encyclopédie, 1755–1800* (Cambridge, MA: Harvard University Press, 1979): 242.

27. In the late eighteenth century Mercier complained of artisans who gained approbations from the Academy of Sciences for their products. Mercier, t. 11: 261.

28. Watin, *L'art du peintre, doreur, vernisseur* (Paris, 1773): xv.

29. Predictably, there was a split between *maîtres* and *maîtresses* who resisted Turgot's reforms and journeymen who welcomed them. See *Réflexions des maîtres Tailleurs de Paris, sur le projet de supprimer les Jurandes* (Paris, 1776), BHVP 10374 in-4 and *Mémoire à consulter sur l'existence actuelle des six corps, et la conservation de leurs privileges* (Paris, 1776), BHVP 103070 in-4. On the seamstresses' support for their guild, see Crowston, *Fabricating Women*.

30. Quoted in Steven Kaplan, "Social Classification and Representation in the Corporate World," in Kaplan and Koepp, *Work in France*: 221.

31. Steven Kaplan, *Provisioning Paris: Merchants and Millers in the Grain and Flour Trade during the Eighteenth Century* (Ithaca: Cornell University Press, 1984), Chapter 1.

32. Kaplan, "Social Classification and Representation in the Corporate World": 221.

33. Gail Bossenga has re-examined the relationship between guild production, illegal work by *chambrelans*, and proto-industrial labor and has found that the boundaries between the three types of production are not as sharply drawn as historians once thought. As Cissie Fairchilds has written in the introduction to Gail Bossenga's article, "not all commercial capitalists became converts to laissez faire, just as not all artisans adhered to the principles of corporatism." See "Protecting Merchants: Guilds and Commercial Capitalism in Eighteenth-Century France," *French Historical Studies* 15, no. 4 (Fall 1988): 691, 693–703.

34. On journeymen's associations, see Cynthia Truant, *The Rites of Labor: The Brotherhoods of Compagnonnage in Old and New Regime France* (Ithaca: Cornell University Press, 1994).

35. For a contemporary account of one of the most famous academies, see Jean Le Rond d'Alembert, *Histoire des membres de l'Académie française morts depuis 1700 jusqu'en 1771* (Paris, 1787). On academic life in the provinces, see Daniel Roche, *Le Siècle des Lumières en province: Académies et académiciens provinciaux, 1680–1789* (Paris and The Hague: Mouton 1978).

36. *Journal dédié a Monsieur* (November 1776). All quotations from Sarrasin are found on p. 365.

37. Bailly, *Avis aux mères qui aiment leurs enfants*: 50. In suggesting the health benefits of confining corsets, Bailly dissented from the most enlightened medical knowledge of his day. Doctors such as Alphone Leroy, a member of the medical faculty at the University of Paris, had been urging women throughout the 1770s to reject the use of corsets and the tight swaddling of children. A. Leroy, *Récherches sur les habillemens des femmes et des enfans, ou examen de la manière dont il faut vêtir l'un et l'autre sexe* (Paris, 1772): 1.

38. Bailly, *Avis aux mères qui aiment leurs enfants*: 21, 22.

39. Mercier, *Tableau de Paris*, t. 11: 261.

40. Legros, *L'art de la coiffure des dames* (Paris, 1765), reviewed in the *Journal des dames* (April 1766); a review of Legros's *Supplément de l'art de la coiffure* (Paris, 1768) appears in the *Journal des dames* (July 1768): 75. See also *L'encyclopédie perruquière* (Paris, Amsterdam, 1757), BHVP, 5534 in-16. Legros died tragically in 1770, suffocated in the crowd attending the festival given in honor of the Dauphin's marriage. Bachaumont, *Mémoires secrets* (June 4, 1770): t. 19: 187.

41. Desplanques, *Barbiers, Perruquiers, Coiffeurs*: 5, 95.

42. Legros, *L'art de la coiffure des dames:* 15.

43. Ibid.

44. *Coiffeurs* practiced as a free profession until 1768–69 when they were ordered join the corporation of the *barbiers-perruquiers.*

45. Legros, *L'art de la coiffure des dames:* 14.

46. Another hairdresser, Guillaume, had set up a subscription service to sell wigs in the 1770s. See Archive de la Seine *Registre des travaux d'entretien par abonnement, 1772–1776*, AS, D5B6, 2146.

47. Legros, *L'art de la coiffure des dames:* 72.

48. Desplanques cites a hairdresser named Laurent working at la Croix-Rouge as the first to use busts in his window displays and Dupin, who worked on the corner of the rue de Grenelle-Saint-Honoré next to the rue du Coq, as the second to adopt this practice. Desplanques, *Barbiers, Perruquiers, Coiffeurs*: 95.

49. Jean-Baptiste Descamps, *Sur l'utilité des établissemens des écoles gratuites de dessin en faveur des métiers* (Paris, 1767): 9.

50. Descamps, *Sur l'utilité*: 16.

51. See also, "Projet pour l'établissement d'écoles gratuites de dessin," *Mercure de France* (March 1746): 67–78. At the Archive de la Seine see collections legislatives, écoles de dessin (1764–84), 2AZ 2(A1); école royale de dessin (1767); école royale de dessin, distributions de prix (1778–82), 2AZ, 41 (D3). The best introductions to the *écoles de dessin* are Harvey Chisick, "Institutional Innovation in Popular Education in Eighteenth Century France: Two Examples," *French Historical Studies* 10 (1977): 43–73 and Reed Benhamou, "Cours Publics: Elective Education in the Eighteenth Century," *Studies on Voltaire and the Eighteenth Century* (1985). For a broad look at the education of the popular classes in eighteenth century, see Harvey Chisick, *The Limits of Reform in the Enlightenment: Attitudes toward the Education of the Lower Classes in Eighteenth-Century France* (Princeton: Princeton University Press, 1981). Beauvais founded a school of design in 1750, Lille in 1755, Lyon in 1756, Amiens in 1758, Paris in 1766, Saint Omer in 1767, and Troyes in 1776. Rennes, Nantes, Orleans, Saint Malo, Lorient, Tour, Saint Quentin, and Arras had founded schools by 1789. All of the proposals to found free schools of design presume that only male students will attend. Chisick, "Institutional Innovation in Popular Education": 43.

52. A. Gourdon, "Projet d'etablissement d'une école académique de dessin dans le port de Toulon," A. Mar., G 86, fol. 79. Quoted in Chisick, "Institutional Innovation in Popular Education": 52.

53. Jean-Jacques Bachelier, *Projet d'un cours d'arts et métiers* (Paris, 1789): 16. Quoted in Chisick, "Institutional Innovation in Popular Education": 44.

54. Barnabé Farmian DeRozoi, *Essai philosophique sur l'établissement des écoles gratuites* (Paris: Quillau, 1769): 34.

55. Descamps, *Sur l'utilité*: 13.

56. Ibid., 23.
57. DeRozoi, *Essai philosophique*, 63.
58. Ibid., 82.
59. Ibid.
60. Ibid., 88–9.
61. The proposal in the *Magasin des modes* included a four-page preface arguing for the importance of academies of fashion. The editor promised to provide a full plan of the organization of the academy in the next edition, but such a plan does not appear in any of the succeeding issues of the journal.
62. The medal of the academy of fashion represented a boat in the middle of the ocean being tossed and turned in four different directions, with Amour at the helm and a group of women blowing bubbles in the stern. The message read "Mors aut salus ex ventis (un vent les établit, un autre les détruit)."
63. J.H. Marchand, *Les panaches ou les coiffures à la mode: Comédie en un acte* (Paris, 1778): 67.
64. *Magasin des modes nouvelles* (January 20, 1787): 55.
65. On the faddishness of the later Enlightenment see, Robert Darnton, *The Literary Underground of the Old Regime* (Cambridge, MA: Harvard University Press, 1982), Chapter 1.
66. *Magasin des modes nouvelles* (January 20, 1787): 52.
67. The publication of one of these proposals in the fashion press, the trade press for the *marchandes de modes*, tailors and dressmakers of Paris, suggests a serious side to the proposals. Certainly the fashion press contained many frivolous and diverting articles, but the proposal to unify the fashion industry within the structure of a single academy closely resembles the attempt by the editors of the fashion press to establish a unified fashion industry in which they controlled the production, marketing and dissemination of fashions.
68. Marchand, *Les panaches*: 69.
69. *Magasin des modes nouvelles* (January 20, 1787): 53.
70. Caffiaux, *Défense du beau sexe* (Amsterdam, 1753): 217–19.
71. Joubert de L'Hiberderie, *Le dessinateur pour les fabriques d'estoffes d'or, d'argent et de soie* (Paris, 1765): xxvi.
72. *Bibliothèque des Femmes* (1759): 21.
73. For more information about Mme de Beaumur, see Nina Rattner Gelbart, *Feminine and Opposition Journalism in Old Regime France: "Le Journal des dames"* (Berkeley: University of California Press, 1987).
74. Marie-Emilie Mayon Montaclos (also called the Baronne de Princen) was an accomplished poet and dramatic author. She was born in Aix in 1736 and died in 1812. Louis-Sébastian Mercier took over the editorship of the *Journal des dames* after Mme de Montaclos. For articles on women and the arts, see *Journal des dames* (June 1764): 118; (July 1774): 13; (October 1774): 240–2.

75. *Journal des dames* (October 1774): 130; J.-Fr. de Bastide, *L'homme du monde éclairé par les arts*, 2 vols. (Paris, 1774).
76. Rousseau, *Émile*: 459.
77. Rousseau, *Émile*: 426, 486, 488.
78. Pierre Joseph Boudier de Villemert, *Le nouvel ami des femmes* (Amsterdam, 1779): 168. Immediately after this passage Boudier de Villemert quotes Rousseau at length on the proper relations between husbands and wives.
79. *Journal de monsieur* (January 1779): 97.
80. *Journal des dames* (December 1774): 192.
81. Ibid. (May 1774): 130 and (July 1774): 79–80.

–5–

Coquettes and *Grisettes*

Modes, Marchandes de: It is a large community, born of the luxury of women, fed by coquetry, and thriving as long as the taste for frivolity is the ruling passion. To the eyes of the observer who seeks to discover the cause of moral corruption, the infinite number of boutiques of the *Marchandes de modes*, the art with which one decorates these boutiques, the different finery that one exposes there to the eyes of passersby, are all sources of danger. What young woman has the strength to shield her eyes, when everyday she sees the productions of genius of the *Marchandes de modes*? Certainly there are few. Almost all women stop gladly in front of these sanctuaries of frivolity and coquetry, and how can they resist the attraction they feel when seeing women of all ages and all conditions entering these enchanting places? Can one delude oneself into thinking that a young girl will have the courage not to give in to such a natural desire to embellish her youthful charm, when she sees old women whose foreheads are lined with wrinkles, wearing elegant hats and adorning their gray hair with gauze and flowers? No, she will follow this dangerous example, and will justify herself by the common behavior of almost all women.

– Nicolas-Toussaint Lemoyne Desessarts, *Dictionnaire universel de police (1785–9)*

When the lawyer and social critic Nicholas Desessarts lashed out at the fashionable shops of Paris, he took part in a long tradition of writings in early-modern Europe on consumption and the problem of luxury.[1] Yet, Desessarts' diatribe against women's irresistible attraction to the boutiques of the *marchandes de modes* of Paris also signals a new way of thinking about women, commerce, and consumption that took shape by the eve of the French Revolution. Desessarts suggests that all women, whatever their age or condition, are unable to resist the *marchandes de modes*' boutiques. Luxury is no longer merely the vice of particular social groups, such as frivolous courtiers or vain bourgeoises. In the later eighteenth century a conceptual framework was constructed which made it possible to think of the excessive desire to consume as a particularly feminine trait, a weakness shared by all women from Marie Antoinette to the fishmongers of *la halle*.

Because Desessarts was concerned with creating an orderly, well-policed city, he worried about the public consequences of women's frenzy for fashion. Yet, many individuals in France drew more nuanced conclusions than did Desessarts and focused on the private as well as the public consequences of women's taste for fashion. When they saw large numbers of women going in and out of dress shops they began to build a new understanding of the connection between domesticity and consumption. Although for much of the eighteenth century women's desire to consume luxury goods was construed as a threat to domestic peace and prosperity, by the later eighteenth century a new position emerged in which women's consumption of clothing was a necessary complement, rather than a threat, to their femininity and domesticity. By the early years of the Revolution the once wild and destructive force of women's desire for fashions had been tamed and domesticated: what had been the problem of luxury (*le luxe*) was now construed as the taste for clothing, and inherent part of femininity and a necessary complement to domesticity.

Desessarts' description of the *marchandes de modes'* boutiques suggests an entry point not only for examining the construction of a new ideology linking women with consumption, but also to a new understanding of the source of the contagion of fashion. While moralists might trace women's love of luxury back to the Garden of Eden, attributing it to the age-old vanity of women, Desessarts points in a more specific and contemporary direction, the fashion boutiques that sprang up along the streets and under the arcades of eighteenth-century Paris. According to Desessarts, the source of danger was the boutiques themselves, which seduced women with new kinds of decorations and window displays, providing havens for women and frivolity. The *marchandes de modes'* boutiques, "born of the luxury of women," enchanted and seduced all who entered.

Women and Luxury

"Dress of velvet, belly of bran" – so went a popular eighteenth-century saying.[2] The suggestion that women were obsessed with the desire to consume fashions and luxuries, even at the cost of food for themselves and their families, was a commonplace echoed throughout the eighteenth century. As Louis-Sébastien Mercier warned in his *Tableau de Paris*:

> The day after a bourgeois wedding, or at the most eight days later, what a change comes over the mind of the loving husband! From what a height plunge the hopes of the honest artisan! He thought he had married an economical, orderly woman who is attentive to her domestic duties. Suddenly he discovers her wasteful nature; she can no longer bear to remain at home; she combines her expenditures with her laziness. Frivolity and craziness replace the useful occupations she had been raised to practice since she was a child. Far from bringing peace and comfort to the household by her prudent work, she surrenders to her frenzy for fashion.[3]

Some observers commented that in view of the mania of French women for fashions, it was no wonder that many men decided that the only sure route to domestic contentment was to remain unmarried. "Why would one want a wife," asked the physician Jean-François Butini in his 1774 treatise on luxury, "when they spend all their dowry on clothing?"[4] The conflict between a woman's desire for luxurious fashions and the fulfillment of her domestic role as wife, mother, and caretaker of the household was perhaps nowhere better expressed than in a manuscript written in 1740, "The Superiority of Men over Women, or the Inequality of the Two Sexes," which contrasted two very different types of consumption, children's consumption of food and women's consumption of fashions. The author of this tract complained that, "When a new fashion arrives, women want to have what other women have, without stopping to think or consider if it is above their station; if there is a new fabric, they must have it no matter what the price, even if their husband cannot afford it, . . . they will have it. Their children might die of hunger, but they will have bellies of luxury and clothing of silk."[5]

Although moralists had written on the perils of luxury for French society throughout the seventeenth century, it was only in the early eighteenth century, in the wake of Mandeville's *Fable of the Bees* and the popularization of Mandeville's justification of luxury by Voltaire, that the debate on luxury heated up.[6] On one side of the debate stood those who wished to place luxury in a traditional moral framework in which superfluous expenditures not sanctioned by one's station were associated with social disorder, the ruin of families, sexual license, and debauchery. On the other side stood those who were beginning to define luxury in a way more familiar to the modern reader: stripping away the traditional, Christian moral framework, luxury was redefined simply as the commercial exchange of any much-desired but not strictly necessary commodity. Luxury, defined in this manner, was neither inherently good nor evil – it was up to the individual to assess the relative advantages and disadvantages of this type of commercial exchange for the health and happiness of individuals and of society at large.

Discussions of women and of gender differences figured prominently in many treatises on luxury; even the driest physiocrat, in a tract extolling the virtues of agricultural productivity, was likely to stray into lurid descriptions of the egregious luxury of women, who seemed to stand at the core of the problem of luxury for French society.[7] As Gabriel Sénac de Meilhan wrote in 1787, sumptuary laws have always been directed against women: "It is women's dress that various regulations have thought it necessary to attack. This is reasonable since the principle of luxury resides in women and men's taste for luxury only follows women's."[8] The association of women with luxury is not, of course, unique to the eighteenth century, but has been a constant refrain throughout the Christian West. From the time of the early Church Fathers, when Augustine and Jerome lashed out at the luxuries of the women of Rome, the association of women with luxury goods such as fine fabrics, jewels and perfumes has been a staple of moralistic writings. But in the eighteenth century one sees a new set of concerns about the perils of women's luxury for French society, new types of arguments for associating women with luxury, and a new culture of the marketplace in which expenditures on luxury items took place.[9]

For most of the seventeenth and eighteenth centuries the main argument used against luxury and excessive expenditures was that luxury confounded the social orders. Most of the harshest critics of luxury were not opposed to ostentatious display in and of itself – the magnificence of king and court was condoned as a visible sign of their love of greatness and their elevated souls – but were against the display of wealth inappropriate to one's station. Women's luxurious fashions were singled out for particular censure as a cause of social confusion. In a 1651 tract titled *The Paradoxes of State Serving to Instruct Bons Esprits*, the author complained,

> If people are poor, should one see neckerchiefs worth twenty or thirty *écus* on the simple wives of meat sellers; should one see footmen dressed in livery carrying the trains of lowly merchants' wives; should one see dresses worth three or four hundred francs on female linen workers and the daughters of colporteurs; should one see gold and silver braid shamefully debased on the work clothes of female candle makers? Is it not true, to finish this troubling deduction, that clothing should be an infallible mark that distinguished conditions and estates? But instead, when walking from the Luxembourg to the Tuileries, one can scarcely distinguish a Duchess from the bookseller, a Marquise from a lady baker, and a Countess from a female meat seller.[10]

Over a century later, fears of social confusion through ostentatious and luxurious dress were still rampant. In 1784 the Parisian bookseller Antoine-Prosper Lottin complained that one could no longer distinguish people by their clothing and that society had become a spectacle, a perpetual masked ball, "where everyone wants to lose the marks of their estate and tries to disguise themselves with the mask of a higher station."[11]

Although worries that luxury would upset the social hierarchy persisted throughout the century, over the course of the second half of the eighteenth century a new set of concerns about luxury appeared. Above all else, writers of treatises on luxury written in the 1770s and 1780s fretted that luxury, and the debauchery associated with it, would lead to depopulation. As the physician Samuel August Tissot explained, when a society is obsessed with luxury, men and women restrict the number of offspring they have so that they will not be forced to divide their wealth between so many children. Moreover, the dissolute lives produced by luxury ruins people's health, rendering them sterile, and luxury creates the demand for more servants and artisans, who lead soft, debauched lives in the city and produce sickly children.[12]

Although when presented in this light luxury was clearly a problem for society at large, many of the tracts discussing depopulation stressed the private and personally devastating impact of luxury on the happiness of individuals and families. As Jean-François Butini explained, "Not only does luxury render married couples sterile, but even more, it attacks this sacred union which, when reason has woven the knot, brings so much sweetness to life."[13] Unlike worries about the effect of luxury on the social hierarchy, the new emphasis in the second half of the eighteenth century on depopulation linked the problems of luxury to the domestic realm of home and family.

While the gravest effect of women's love of luxury was increasingly seen in the private sphere of family and domesticity, to understand where contemporaries placed the blame for women's luxury we must leave the private realm of family and look to women's public role. Critics attributed women's desire for luxurious clothing to their vanity in public, their theatricality and their insatiable desire to stand out in the crowd. As Boudier de Villemert claimed in his 1779 book, *The New Friend of Women*, "What elevates the worth of trinkets in the minds of women is their violent desire to attract the attention of the crowd: once this mania enters a woman's head even once, it excludes all other thoughts except for pomp and display, and they only live to be looked at."[14] Or, as the physician Butini wrote in 1774,

A vain woman loves luxury because it gives her an audience: deprived of useful work, education, and all positions that lead to fame, she embraces their substitute: this sort of woman will arrive today sumptuously dressed at the theater to share the public's attention with the actors and then tomorrow will throw herself in the cloister, as long as her retreat creates a noisy public sensation.[15]

In the past decade women's historians and gender scholars, most notably Joan Landes, have brought to our attention the connection between fears of the spectacular and theatrical function of aristocratic, public women in the *ancien régime* and the Revolutionaries' restriction of women's public participation and their elevation of women's roles in the private sphere of home and family.[16] The eighteenth-century debate on the dangers of women's desire for luxuries, however, concerned a much broader group of women than aristocratic women and included a host of fears in addition to the fears of aristocratic women's public, theatrical displays of power. Along with attacking the luxury of aristocratic women, many tracts on luxury also lashed out at the ostentation of butchers' wives and barge women and focused on the private sphere and economic repercussions as well as on the public sphere and political disruption. Focusing exclusively on the politically problematic role of aristocratic women risks losing sight of the problematic role in enlightened thought of women across a range of classes in the realm of commerce as well as politics.

Increasingly in the second half of the eighteenth century, women's desire for luxuries was attributed not only to their vanity, their desire to shine and their desire for political clout, but to their desire for novelty and their enslavement to that commercial deity, *la mode*. As Gabriel Sénac de Meilhan phrased it in his *Considérations sur la richesse et le luxe* (1787), "The fickleness of a woman's spirit demands that all that is new overpowers her."[17] Luxury, then, was not defined exclusively as ostentatious dress, that is dressing above one's station in richly brocaded silks, expensive laces and gold and silver embellishments, but more broadly as any clothing that was fashionable and frivolous: cloth need not be spun with golden thread and hairstyles need not be laced with pearls to be objects of luxury, they need only be *à la mode*. Luxury was not driven solely by women's lust for power and social stature, but also by their lust for novelties and frivolities available in the shops of Paris.

Although women had for centuries been associated with inconstancy and change, new theories were devised in the eighteenth century to explain their love of frivolity and novelty. Blaming it all on Eve and original sin was set aside (for the most part) as *philosophes* and enlightened thinkers probed women's minds and psychology to try to understand on a scientific basis women's love of all that glittered and all that was new. As we have seen in the last chapter, this attraction to frivolities and novelties was considered a product of a peculiarly feminine imaginative faculty and sense of sight, and the particular interaction between women and agreeable arts such as fabrics, jewels, and fashions. These new beliefs in the liveliness of women's visual sense and imagination and in the power of objects to create desires in their viewers helped recast certain suppositions about women and luxury. Alongside the traditional model that held that the temptation to consume luxuries derived from sinfulness and lax morality arose a new model that attributed women's attraction to luxury goods to their female psychology and which assigned new importance to the role of the commodities themselves in the process of seduction and the creation of desire. The drama of women confronting and struggling with their desires for luxury goods was no longer the lonely battle of a woman in conflict with her soul but the drama of women surrounded by window displays, fashion magazines, and business cards in the bustling commercial city of Paris. Temptation now came from without as well as from within, and it was a temptation to which women, with their heightened visual sensibility and innate feminine frivolity, were considered particularly susceptible.

Shops and Shopping

Recreating the world of buying and selling clothes in eighteenth-century Paris requires some major bulldozing to clear away our contemporary notions about consumption. To imagine that earlier world, the wrecking ball would have to raze alike the houses of *haute couture* on the avenue Montaigne, the venerable *grands magasins* of the Bon Marché, Printemps, and Galeries Lafayette, and the huge discount chains of Prisunic and Tati.[18] The *marché aux puces* on the outskirts of Paris, now principally serving as the tourist-stop *de rigueur* for the youth of Europe, would have to be moved back into the city and reinstated as a lively emporium for buying clothing. Even the sidewalks and gutters would have to be uprooted to reveal the thick Parisian mud which coated the shoes of the lower classes as they walked the streets and made travel by carriage a necessity for the well-to-do who wished to visit the latest boutique *à la mode*.

Even more difficult to recreate than the physical and architectural landscape of shopping is the act of shopping itself: what was it like to consume in a world in which shops as we know them today – buildings stocked with ready-made clothing sold at fixed prices – were only beginning to appear and when most consumption by the wealthy took place within the private confines of their homes and boudoirs? And what was the experience of shopping like in an age in which the shops that did exist were centers of gallantry and sociability, more like modern-day cafés than boutiques? The fleeting transaction between an eighteenth-century customer and merchant might seem difficult to reconstruct, leaving, as it did, few historical records. In fact, historians have availed themselves of a number of sources to reconstruct the world of commerce in eighteenth-century Paris. In addition to merchants' ledger books, receipts and business cards, a series of bankruptcy cases provides a rich source of information about commerce and consumption. More-over, because shops and shopping were such problematic phenomena in early-modern Paris, the writings of social critics provide clues as to how contemporaries experienced shopping. In addition to the works of moralists and libertines, glimpses of Parisian commercial culture also abound in contemporary works of fiction, memoirs, and travelers' accounts. Doubtless the most insightful and most cele-brated account of eighteenth-century shops and shopping is provided by Louis-Sébastien Mercier (1740–1814), whose *Tableau de Paris* reads like an opinionated travelogue, guiding us through the shops and galleries of Paris from the second-hand clothes dealers of the Saint-Esprit Fair to the luxury boutiques of the rue Saint-Honoré.[19]

The consumption of fashions and clothing in the seventeenth century did not take place, for the most part, in shops. The wealthy ordered clothing to measure through tailors and seamstresses who fitted the garments in their homes and then delivered them to their chambers. And the fashion accessories needed to complete their wardrobes were provided by *marchandes de modes* and *revendeuses à la toilette*, who made daily rounds of the city's wealthiest quarters with baskets brimming with ribbons, scarves, bows, jewelry, and gloves, lending money to cover gambling debts and an ear to hear confidences in addition to fashion advice.[20]

When the poorer classes bought clothing it was usually second-hand, purchased either from the *fripiers* who worked in the Halles quarter, concentrated on the rues de la Grande and de la Petite-Friperie and under the Piliers des Halles, or from the ambulant *revendeurs* and *revendeuses*, who hawked their wares along the quai de la Ferraille, the quai de l'Ecole, the place des Trois-Maries, and the Pont-Neuf.

Before the mid eighteenth century most shops would have been almost un-recognizable as such to a consumer accustomed to modern-day boutiques.[21] Like the buildings in which goods were produced, the shops in which they were sold were open to the street and usually lacked windows or window displays to separate the selling of goods from the life of the quarter. With the boutique often abutting the merchant's and his or her workers' living quarters, domestic and commercial concerns often mingled, blurring the lines between neighborhood, shop and domestic space.[22] Many linen drapers' and mercers' shops were little more than small stands (*échoppes*) lining the street.[23] A host of unprivileged merchants made use of these little stands as well; for, unlike fixed boutiques, these could be quickly set up for illicit trade on Sundays and holidays and then taken down at night to elude the police. In addition to the merchants who conducted their trade from street-side stalls, Paris was filled with itinerant *marchands de frivolités*, colporteurs who stood on the bridges and quais and who entered cafés and *auberges* to peddle their wares, much of them reputedly stolen.[24]

Throughout the seventeenth and eighteenth centuries, although the production of cloth, clothing and fashions was spread throughout Paris, with many women working out of their homes, specific neighborhoods were known as centers for the production of particular goods. In the seventeenth century, for example, the linen drapers congregated around the rue Aubry-le-Boucher and the second-hand clothes sellers around Saint-Eustache.[25] Meanwhile, although each neighborhood had its own seamstresses, tailors and mercers to serve the needs of the local clientele, many *marchandes de modes* and dealers in luxury fashions congregated in the most elegant quarters of the city, in close proximity to their clientele of wealthy bourgeois and aristocrats.

Until the mid-eighteenth century, the Palais de Justice was the most fashionable place to shop.[26] The Palais, which housed the Parlement, the Chambre de Comptes, the Cour des Aides et des Monnoies, contained a great central hall bordered on two sides by arcades, which were lined with shops offering an abundance of luxury goods.[27] The Dutch travel writer J.C. Nemeitz described the arcades of the Palais in his *Séjour de Paris* (1727): "Paris is full of boutiques in many locations where one can find anything one desires to buy; but the Palais is the center and essence of all the beautiful clothing shops. One is amazed at the extraordinary abundance of precious commodities of all sorts enclosed here. The hardest part is deciding in which boutique to makes one's purchases."[28]

In the eighteenth century the Palais was joined by a number of other neighborhoods du luxe – Saint-Germain, the Louvre, the rue Saint-Honoré and the Palais-Royal – as the center of gravity of the Parisian luxury trades shifted westward and crossed to the Right Bank.[29]

In addition to these specific neighborhoods, throughout the seventeenth and eighteenth centuries, annual fairs offered the chance to buy clothing and accessories.[30] Of the two major Parisian fairs in the seventeenth and first half of the eighteenth century, Saint-Laurent and Saint-Germain, the Saint-Germain fair was the most commonly associated with luxury goods and frivolities.[31] Running each year from February 3 until fifteen days after Easter, it offered an opportunity for all segments of Parisian society – ranging from courtiers to valets and lackeys – to mingle while browsing the stalls, gambling and attending the *spectacles*. It was known as the place where "one finds the most beautiful goods, the richest clothing and fabric in Paris."[32] At night, candles lighted the shops for those wishing to linger after the shows had ended. But as a guidebook recommended, "One should make one's purchases in the day, because at night it is difficult to bargain, when one is constrained by the crowds."[33] The guide went on to caution that, although the stalls at the fair where filled with charming goods, one should only look, instead of buy because, "one can always buy the item in the Palais for the same price or even less, because merchants here have to pay dearly for their tents and boutiques and consequently elevate the price of their merchandise."[34]

Whether in the Palais, at the fairs, along the rue Saint-Honoré, or by the later eighteenth century, under the arcades of the Palais-Royal, shopping, for those who could afford it, was a frivolous diversion.[35] In an era in which the wealthy still had most of their clothes made to order and delivered to their homes, venturing out into public to shop had a different meaning from other types of consumption. Shopping was entertainment and, as Nemeitz's warning that one should not actually purchase anything at the fair suggests, "window shopping" (even without the windows) was commonplace. Contemporaries admitted that part of the attraction of shopping was the opportunity to look at exquisite objects, artfully displayed in inviting new shops where "eyes are fascinated by the exterior decorations which deceive and seduce the curious."[36] Successful merchants like Rose Bertin capitalized on the popularity of "window shopping": on one occasion Bertin displayed for the public's delectation 280 dresses commissioned by the Spanish court.[37]

In addition to being entertaining, shopping was also linked spatially and temporally to entertainments. Whether at fairs or in the luxury "shopping districts," the line between shopping and entertainments (some of them licit, some not) was equally blurred. The pleasures of the *bal de l'Opéra* were immeasurably increased when the duc de Chartres ordered that the boutiques of the Palais-Royal be kept open and illuminated all night.[38] And Restif de la Bretonne likened the rue Saint-Honoré to a bazaar in which commerce rubbed shoulders with "tous les abus de la sociabilité":

Figure 13 *Vue d'optique nouvelle, representant la Foire Saint-Ovide place Vendome à Paris,* anonymous, eighteenth century, courtesy of RMN.

> What a wonderful street! What a mixture of luxury, commerce, spectacle, mud, theater, girls, imprudence, urbanity, debauchery, politeness, and fraud – all the abuses of sociability. I wish that one could concentrate here all the vices in a type of bazaar, so that they would not scandalize the rest of the city: there will always be vices in a capital city, but one should treat them like fire and abandon the house and cut off all communication.[39]

The mixture of fashion boutiques, cafés, clubs, and promenading beauties made the Palais-Royal, according to Mercier, "une fête piquante."[40] Whether at the foire Saint-Germain, the Palais-Royal, or the Pont-Neuf, spaces for the consumption of fashions and luxury goods flowed directly into spaces for drinking coffee, gambling, examining curiosities, or watching puppet shows.

Like attending art salons, frequenting cafés, and promenading, shopping was part of the widespread expansion of public life in eighteenth-century Paris. Part of the pleasure was the opportunity to participate in *le monde* and feel *à la mode*. One did not go shopping merely to purchase clothing, but to buy, or at least be, where all the rest of fashionable society was currently buying. The baronne d'Oberkirch, for example, noted with little surprise that the most celebrated jewelry shop of the

Figure 14 "Les Belles Marchandes", *Almanach historique, proverbial et chantant*, 1784, courtesy of the Bibliothèque des arts décoratifs.

day, Au Petit-Dunkerque, near the Pont-Neuf, was so thronged with shoppers that the store had to hire a guard to keep the peace.[41] In addition to the pleasures of seeing and being seen, part of the fun of shopping was the chance to banter with pretty girls and to drive a hard bargain. In this game, as in the games played in the gambling tents, some came out winners and others losers.

Grisettes and *Marchandes*

Sitting at the counter in a line, you see them through the window as you pass. They arrange the pompoms, trinkets, and decorations that fashion creates and varies. You eye them freely, and they meet your eye. Boutiques like these are found on every street. Across from a shop that sells only breastplates and swords, you see a shop with only clumps of gauze, feathers, ribbons, flowers and women's bonnets . . . . One sees in these shops charming young faces next to ugly ones. Thoughts of the harem involuntarily seize your imagination: the pretty ones would be the sultan's favorites and the others would be their guardians.

Louis-Sébastien Mercier, *Tableau de Paris*.[42]

Throughout the eighteenth century both moralists and libertines fretted over the young women who worked in the growing number of fashion boutiques in Paris. Contemporaries thought of them as a distinct social category and called them, collectively, *grisettes*, a term originally derived from the inexpensive cloth worn by shop girls in the seventeenth century.[43] As Mercier explained, "One calls *grisette* young girls who, having neither good birth nor wealth, are obliged to work for their living, and who have no other way of supporting themselves than working with their hands. Bonnet makers, seamstresses, linen workers, etc. are all part of this numerous class.[44] For moralists the increasing numbers of shopgirls was problematic because they were both vulnerable and seductive, in danger of their own moral ruin and of imperiling the morality of others. The author of the *Encylopédie méthodique* worried about the "immense crowd of young girls, seduced by the lure of easy and lucrative work, who dedicate themselves to the work of producing sparkling rags; they are worthy, in more than one way, of the name that one gives them: 'priestesses of Venus'."[45] Although libertine writers were less concerned about the moral lapses of the *grisettes*, they were certainly equally aware of the potential for seduction when hundreds of young women fell daily under the gaze of customers and passersby in the boutiques of Paris.[46] For both moralists and libertines, the fashion boutiques of Paris were equated with harems and brothels (*maisons de jouissance*), feminine worlds charged with sexual excitement and sexual danger.

Other contemporaries, including many *grisettes* and *marchandes de modes* themselves, might have rejected the charge that they were a source of sexual danger; but even those who denied that shopping had become highly sexualized would have agreed that the selling of fashions had become starkly gendered. Although male mercers continued to sell clothing, female business women, the *marchandes de modes*, had become the retail fashion merchants *par excellence*, and even the shops owned and managed by male mercers employed young women to tend the counter. As Mercier exclaimed, writing about retail shops in general, "Woman is the soul of the shop."[47]

By employing women, the fashion merchants' and linen drapers' boutiques did not differ from a wide variety of Parisian shops in which women presided. As Mercier observed, women were omnipresent in Parisian shops:

> A fourbisseur's shop has a woman who will show you and sell you a sword, a pistol, or armor. Women run Clockmakers "and goldsmiths" boutiques. In fact, whether you buy a pound of candy or a pound of cannon powder, a woman will be weighing it for you. Women buy, transport, exchange, sell and re-sell everything; all food passes through their hands: they sell poultry, fish, butter, and cheese. They even open oysters rapidly and dexterously. Women occupy little offices where they sell salt, tobacco, letters, stamps, and lottery tickets.[48]

One must distinguish between two types of women who worked in the boutiques of Paris. On the one hand there were merchants' and artisans' wives or

Figure 15 *Mode du jour: le serial en boutique*, Claude-Louis Desrais, courtesy of RMN.

widows and women such as *maîtresses lingères* or *marchandes de modes* who owned the shop. On the other hand there were the young girls, serving as apprentices or employed as wage laborers, who filled the shops of Paris. As we have seen, the women who were able to attain the *maîtrise* occupied a privileged position in commerce and, despite the number of bankruptcies in eighteenth-century Paris, enjoyed relative economic security. Bernadette Oriol's study of Parisian *lingères* in the mid-eighteenth century indicates that most had been raised in Paris and that their parents were "middle class, or Bourgeois de Paris and merchants of all sorts."[49] They in turn married men of their same economic station and, Oriol calculates, had at the time of their marriage a median wealth of 7,800 *livres*. Mercier ranks these wives of artisans and small-scale retail merchants among the happiest women in Paris, earning enough money through their labor in the family's boutique to indulge their pleasures and attain a more equitable division of power with their husbands:

> These busy women have more power in their households and are happier than the wives
> of bailiffs, lawyers, clerks, office assistants, etc., who do not deal with money, and who
> consequently cannot put a little aside to satisfy their fantasies. The wife of a cloth

merchant, a retail grocer, or a mercer has more money at her disposal to spend on her little pleasures than the wife of a notary who scarcely has twelve *sous* to call her own.[50]

There was a gulf, however, between the lives of the bourgeois, if only petit bourgeois, owners of shops and the young *ouvrières en linge* employed by them as wage laborers. If single these *ouvrières* often lived two women to a room, their quarters often doubling as their workspace. When they married, it was almost invariably to men of a similar station, domestics, wage earners, *compagnons* or *garçons*.[51] Many of these women, generally from less wealthy backgrounds than the *lingères*, lacked the means to become apprentices. Others may have in fact attained the *maîtrise*, but lacked the capital to rent a boutique and buy the supplies necessary to start a business. Without the aid offered by the linen drapers' corporation or confraternity to fall back upon in hard times, these *ouvrières'* economic position was much more precarious than that of the women for whom they worked.[52]

Although there was a considerable gap in wealth and status between *march-andes* and *grisettes*, they were united in contemporary perceptions as uniformly consumed by a love of fashions. Whether motivated by business acumen – what better way to advertise one's taste and skill in making clothing – or coquetry, postmortem inventories suggest that both mistress seamstresses and linen drapers and their *ouvrières* did indeed spend a considerable amount of money on their wardrobes. The dress was the most costly component in a woman's wardrobe and the value of the linen drapers' and workers' dresses ranged from 20 *livres* for "une robe de satin à la reine" to 40 *livres* for "une robe de satin fond violet à petit bouquets, doublée de taffetas bleu," to 130 *livres* which made up the dowry of a young bride. Fashionable dresses were luxury goods roughly similar in cost to a finely-crafted wooden cabinet and in many cases a single dress cost more than a young worker earned in a year. With both female workers and the mistresses who employed them owning, on average, more than four dresses, a considerable percentage of their earnings were devoted to their attire. True to their reputation, *ouvrières'* and *marchandes'* dresses sported the brightest and loveliest colors and designs, silks in "vert, citron, blanc, violet and gorge de pigeon" and gaily striped or floral cottons. The inventories also included a large number of undergarments: many merchants and shop girls possessed three or four dozen blouses and one owned as many as fifty-seven.[53] Both groups of women possessed a large number of accessories such as bonnets, neckerchiefs and handkerchiefs, underscoring the importance of accessories, particularly for women of modest means, in creating a fashionable look.

In addition to being associated with fashionable dress, the *grisette* was linked with a freedom of spirit that, according to harsher commentators, too often lapsed into immorality.[54] Among the more flattering observers of the *grisettes*' free spirits was Mercier, who exclaimed,

> The *grisette* is happier in her poverty than the daughter of a bourgeois. She becomes independent at an age when her charms are still radiant. Her poverty gives her a certain liberty, and her happiness sometimes results from not having been given a dowry. She only sees in marriage to an artisan of her own class subjection, pain and misery; so she early on develops a spirit of independence. For her, fashionable clothing is among the necessities of life. Vanity, no worse a counselor than misery, advises her to add the resources of her youth and figure to those she earns by her needle.[55]

The *grisettes* of Paris endured frequent accusations of loose morality and prostitution. A satirical legal *mémoire, Etrennes aux grisettes pour l'année 1790*, accused the *grisettes* of encroaching on "the commerce exclusively permitted to *filles de joie*," prostitutes.[56] Another pamphlet titled *Etrennes aux grisettes* (a small sub-genre of libertine pamphlets on the *grisettes* used this title) provided a list of names and addresses for over 100 *grisettes*. Occasional annotations, discussing the virtue of a few of the women listed cast aspersion on the virtue of the other entries:

> Bertrand, Angélique, *marchande de modes* rue Neuve des Petits-Champs. This young lady possesses a virtue that is proof against all seduction. With a childlike figure and fifteen or sixteen years old at least, she possesses a gentleness, boldness, and polish that infinitely augments her charms. All lovers are invited to try the conquest, which has already unsuccessfully been tried by a soldier.[57]

Contemporaries were as aware as modern-day social historians that the moral "lapses" of the *grisettes* were often driven by dire economic need, but there was a persistent suggestion that these women actively sought sexual liaisons because of their "goût libertin" or "their need for dresses, hats, and shoes to distinguish themselves from lowly *couturieres*."[58] As the author of the *Encyclopédie méthodique* warned,

> The prodigious consumption which creates the luxury of all the things we speak about particularly multiplies the number of people involved in the luxury trades; in most cases, it would be difficult for workers not to take up the inclinations created by this kind of work. To succeed brilliantly it is necessary to have a taste for the trinkets and frivolities which are the base [of luxury]; soon the desire to enjoy luxuries follows the desire to make them, and all means to procure these goods are avidly seized upon by a giddy youth, drawn into disorder before they have even perceived they are heading there.[59]

The female press, a primary advocate for the new eighteenth-century sensibility of womanhood, was the only voice that sympathetically depicted the *grisettes* as helpless victims of male vice.[60] Most observers assumed that the *grisettes* of Paris were far from passive, but were instead as busy looking out the window, "consuming" the men passing by, as these men were busy looking in at the *grisettes*. As Mercier explained, although the *grisettes* might be chained to the counter with needles in their hands, they

> Incessantly throw their gaze out on the street. No passerby escapes them. A place at the counter, next to the street, is always considered the most favorable, because of the crowds of men who pass by always offering an admiring glance. The girl is thrilled by all the looks men throw her way, and imagines them as lovers. The multitude of passersby varies and augments her pleasure and curiosity. Thus, a sedentary craft becomes bearable, when it is combined with the pleasure of seeing and being seen.[61]

Bargaining and Selling

Running counter to the trend of commercial capitalism, which since the sixteenth century had excluded women (particularly middle-class women) from certain kinds of productive labor, the explosion of retail shops in eighteenth-century Paris increased opportunities for women to work as shop girls and businesswomen. For observers such as Mercier, these shops looked like harems, filled with women busily sewing, decorating hats, and knotting ribbons. But for many women the shops in which they worked must have seemed more like *salons* than *serails*: these feminized, quasi-public spaces provided a rare opportunity for the sexes to mix while women remained firmly in control.[62]

Accusations of prostitution and libertinism aside, for contemporary observers the relationship between *grisette* or *marchande* and male customers was sexually charged. Mercier explicitly likened buying fashions with buying women's sexual favors, remarking that "Shopping is only a pretext; one looks at the shop girl, and not the merchandise."[63] But references to the coquettish playfulness and sexual innuendo that occurred when men bought and women sold are found throughout seventeenth- and eighteenth-century literature and commentary.[64] The Théâtre de Gérandi, for example, staged a comedy in 1652 titled *Arlequin, lingère du Palais* that recorded the banter between a female linen draper and her male client in a boutique in the Palais. For the live audience the depiction of men buying and women selling would have been even more humorous and more sexually charged because Arlequin is a male character, played by a male actor, but dressed as a female merchant:

> *Arlequin*, dressed as a lingère: Chemises, ties, undergarments, towels, messieurs.
> *Pasquariel*:   Here is a linen draper's boutique; I had some items of linen made here and I want to see if she has what I need.

A: Come to our store, Sir, and see the beautiful cloth from Holland . . .

P: (*picking up a chemise*) I would be delighted to buy something at your store. (*Aside*) This girl is pretty, well made. Those beautiful blue eyes!

A: (*who hadn't heard the last words*) Blue, Sir? I guarantee you there are none in my cloth.

P: (*looking at a shirt*) This shirt will do; but it is a little small.

A: Small, sir? You can't think that. It is three quarters and a half long!

P: (*aside*) The beautiful nose!

A: Oh, measure it? Don't trouble yourself. Mine aune is twelve more than other merchants.

P: How much does it cost?

A: It costs ten écus and isn't over priced.

P: Ten écus!

A: Yes, sir, in good conscience, I'm only making one pound . . .

P: I will give you thirty sous.

A: 30 sous! I see that you aren't accustomed to wearing shirts.

P: Here! Take these écus, without bargaining; don't make me go elsewhere.

A: O.K., O.K. take the shirt, but on one condition, do me the honor of coming to see me. Come to the sign of the 'Pucelle'. That's me, sir, who provides the layettes for all the babies of the eunuchs of the grand harem!

P: What is your name?

A: The beautiful Angélique, at your service.[65]

Angélique may claim to be "at Pasquariel's service," but it is not hard to see that she is calling the shots. According to contemporaries, in the sexual banter and commercial bargaining that occurred between female merchants and male customers, the female merchants almost always got their way. As Nemeitz commented in his *Séjour de Paris*, the *marchandes* of Paris were wily and knew how to use their charms to full advantage: "Principally, women know how to praise their merchandise and flatter their buyers so well that you would have to have the firmness of Ulysses not to give in to their attractions."[66] Attracted to the beauty of the *marchande* and encouraged by her flatteries and charms, one nevertheless left the boutique loaded with overpriced trinkets. As Nemeitz warned tourists shopping in Paris, "One's hope is dashed, and at the end of the encounter, one has bought only the shop instead of the woman inside it."[67]

The novelist Marivaux illustrates in an account of a flustered provincial gentleman and a Parisian *marchande* that even without resorting to overt coquetry female merchants' bargaining style usually overcame the resistance of customers:

One day, a provincial gentleman, newly arrived in Paris, entered a boutique of one of these female merchants to make an expensive purchase. First he gets a gracious hello and an eager display of merchandise. But nothing pleases him; he wants to refuse it, but does not dare say it: his recognition of all the merchant's kindness stops him. The more he hesitates the more the merchant burdens him with more kindness. Seeing her make so much effort, and not having the strength to be ungrateful, he gets up and takes out his purse; take it, Madame, he tells her, I don't like your merchandise and I have no desire to buy it, but you have so overwhelmed me with your kindness that you are driving me crazy; I don't have the nerve to leave without buying; so here is my purse.[68]

Buying and selling constituted a complicated and often stylized game of skill and cunning in which contemporaries believed the merchant almost invariably came out ahead monetarily.[69] Male merchants were shrewd, but female merchants were perceived to be even more successful at enticing customers to buy because they could supplement the usual cajoleries of the merchant with a hint of more intimate commerce and of future returns on the investment. When contemporaries wrote about shopping they almost always portrayed the shopkeeper as a woman. The buyer, however, was virtually always assumed to be a man.

Both pictorial and written accounts from the seventeenth and eighteenth centuries portray men shopping in the most fashionable boutiques of Paris. Although inventories after decease reveal that men's ownership of clothing trailed behind their sisters' and wives' both in relative numbers and varieties of garments and accessories, aristocratic and wealthy bourgeois men's consumption of clothing, particularly linen shirts, cuffs, handkerchiefs, buttons and buckles, increased rapidly in the eighteenth century. Although these items could be commissioned, they were precisely the kinds of products that were available, ready-made in mercers' and *marchandes de modes*' boutiques. Moreover, even if men did commission jackets or elaborate vests, they frequently ventured into mercers' and *marchandes de modes*' shops to select the fabric. Another occasion for men to shop was to buy gifts, such as lace gloves or jewelry for their mistresses, or, in the case of the many provincial and foreign visitors to Paris, souvenirs.[70] On other occasions men were portrayed shopping with their mistresses or female friends, with shopping, like the promenade, providing an occasion for innocent mingling of the sexes.[71]

Paradoxically, although those who wrote on the subject of luxury denounced women's obsession with consuming fashions, when they imagined the act of commerce, they often imagined a male consumer and a female merchant. The model for shopping was courtship (although in the harsh light of its critics it might look more akin to prostitution), a decidedly heterosexual encounter between carefree, but self-interested, *grisettes* and desirous male customers. Unlike many instances of monetary exchange, in this model both parties could find satisfaction. The man might end up buying over-priced *bagatelles*, but since he was not really shopping for material goods or looking for a bargain he did not feel cheated. The shop girl, of course, according to contemporary stereotypes of the amorous *grisette*, walked away from the encounter doubly satisfied.

Although foppish *petits-maîtres* who were obsessively interested in fashion were heaped with scorn in the eighteenth century, few contemporaries suggested that men were seduced by the shops of Paris to the same extent that female customers were. And, although writers on luxury were all too aware that Paris abounded with vain and frivolous men, they rarely portrayed men as the kind of irrational consumers, seduced by trinkets and gloss, that women were. Although women's shopping habits were considered a social problem, men's were not. The model of shopping as courtship worked to normalize, rationalize, and naturalize male shopping: men did not shop to buy clothing, and they did not shop because goods and shop displays irrationally seduced them: men shopped for women.

Since so much of the game of buying and selling revolved around a sexual dynamic, contemporaries had a difficult time imagining what it was like for women to sell to other women. As they struggled to conceptualize the dynamics of this encounter they settled on two different scenarios, corresponding to upper- and lower-class styles of consumption. In the former, the central tension between shop girl and female customer is not over the price or quality of the goods, but over their sexual rivalry as women. As Mercier fantasized, *grisettes* who spend their days adorning the heads of their beautiful rivals "must quiet the secret jealousy of their sex. Because of their estate, they must make beautiful all those who pay them and who treat them with such haughtiness."[72] One way to explain, at least metaphorically, why the *marchandes de modes* charged so much for their trinkets and fashions was that, driven by female jealousy, they wanted to make their rivals pay dearly for their pretty clothes. As Mercier explained, "Female fashion merchants harshly punish women for their eternal taste for stylish rags; they always make them pay four times their real value."[73]

Mercier also presents a colorful image of a second way in which contemporaries might understand the relationship of women buying and women selling fashions, an image of petit bourgeois and "excessively economical" women buying second-hand clothing from the wives and sisters of *fripiers* who hawked their wares at the weekly Saint-Esprit fair on the place de Grève. For Mercier there was something unseemly, even ugly, about the second-hand clothing trade to begin with ("The buyer does not know where the corset came from: the poor and innocent girl, under the eye even of her mother, puts on a corset in which just the night before a lewd prostitute had danced."), which was exacerbated by the sight of dozens of women rifling through stacks of clothes and then undressing to try them on in a very public place. Mercier found encounters between female customers and female merchants coarse and unpleasant: "From far away one could hear the sharp, false and conflicting voices arguing with each other." And while in the relationship between merchants and male clients, according to common perception, wily merchants outsmarted guileless customers, at the Saint-Esprit fair female merchants met their match with female customers. As Mercier explained, "Since women were both the buyers and the sellers, their wiliness was almost equal on both sides."[74]

From *Boutiques* to *Magasins*

Although many courtiers and aristocrats shopped in Paris, shopping was not a refined experience in the seventeenth and early eighteenth centuries. Even the most fashionable and celebrated shops of seventeenth-century Paris, the boutiques of the Palais de Justice, were narrow, cramped and poorly lighted. With only a tiny wall behind the counter on which to hang their wares, *lingères* and silk merchants had to use considerable ingenuity to attract customers. A frequently used merchandising strategy seems to have been a loud voice, and as a Dutch visitor to Paris commented in 1727, "The shouts of women, girls and men in the boutiques as they tried to attract passersby, continued without ceasing."[75] In even the most exclusive shops of the Palais de Justice, not to speak of the boutiques of the Parisian fairs, the Pont-Neuf, or under the Pilier des Halles, one's ears were battered, one's person jostled and one's belongings endangered.

But perhaps more troublesome than the blows to one's ears were the shocks to one's sense of propriety when visiting these festive public spaces to shop. For whether at fairs, along the rue Saint-Honoré or in the Palais-Royal, one shopped amid a "fête piquant" in which the sexes and social classes mixed freely. Mercier explained that in the evening, when the fashionably dressed women of Paris emerged in the Palais-Royal to promenade, "A mother out walking with her two young daughters would never dare cross the noisy walkway; the virtuous wife, the honest female citizen, would never dare appear next to the bold courtesans, with their dress, their bearing, their airs and even their words. All of that would force them to flee."[76]

It is often difficult to discern to what extent Mercier's observations were colored by his wishful thinking. He might like to believe that the virtuous bourgeois wife would scorn the pleasures of promenading and peering at displays of silks and ribbons in the Palais-Royal, but businesswomen, artisans' wives, and shop girls were, of course, active participants in the culture of commerce and neighborhood sociability.[77] To a large extent, however, except for a few aristocratic women, historians still do not know the extent to which women participated in the "public" world of eighteenth-century Paris. Anecdotal evidence can be found supporting both the conclusion that all virtuous women were sequestered in their homes (or convents) and that Parisian women of all classes passed much of their day out in public. As Nemeitz observed, "There is no society in Paris where there are not women and girls. Those women who are even just a little above the common classes spend their mornings at their *toilette*, after dinner and the evening paying social visits, attending spectacles, promenading and playing cards."[78]

Figure 16 *La promenade publique*, Philibert-Louis Debucourt, courtesy of RMN.

When Desessarts warned that "women of all ages and all conditions" could be seen entering *marchandes de modes'* shops, one can conjecture that, like many moralists who invoked the phrase "women of all conditions," he was not particularly worried about aristocratic women; for their patronage of *marchandes de modes* was not so much a luxury as a necessity for upholding their position and the etiquette of their estate. Few contemporaries, for example, would have found fault with baronne d'Oberkirch for ordering a ceremonial *habit de cour* chez Baulard. (Although by the eve of the Revolution they would certainly criticize Marie Antoinette's lavish expenditures on clothing.) The acceptability of aristocratic shopping and consumption is evidenced by contemporary engravings, which from the early seventeenth century onward portray aristocratic women out shopping, depicting the activity as a normal part of aristocratic life. If the "ideal" shopper was in some respects male, a complementary model also existed which viewed the quintessential shopper as aristocratic.

Shopping, according to critics like Desessarts, posed little threat for men or aristocratic women but posed a great threat for bourgeois and working women. While shopping in public, like promenading, may have been as acceptable a diversion for courtiers and aristocrats as attending a fair or the theater, it was not an activity in which virtuous, bourgeois mothers should (at least in theory) choose to participate, mingling as it did the sexes and the classes. By the later eighteenth century, however, the luxury boutiques of Paris had been transformed into, if not the safe havens provided by the department stores of the nineteenth century, then at least into more acceptable public spaces which women of means could enter without fear of reproach.

Although most Parisians of the popular classes continued to buy their clothing at small stalls, in second-hand shops and from itinerant *revendeuses*, a number of luxury fashion shops had opened with larger, well-lighted, and decorated interiors.[79] These shops, bearing exotic or aristocratic names such as "Au Grand Mogol," "Au Pavillion d'or," and "Au Trois Mandarins,"[80] sprang up in the wealthiest sections of Paris, the rue Saint-Honoré, the rue de la Monnaie near the Louvre, and the Saint-Germain *quartier*. With the reconstruction of the arcades of the Palais-Royal eagerly awaited by Parisians, the two wooden galleries of shops known as "camp des Tartares" were transformed, making way for larger, more permanent shops.[81] These well-lighted shops were outfitted with large counters upon which to display the goods, wardrobes and chests in which to store them, mirrors, and rudimentary window displays. They were large, permanent buildings, *magasins* rather than *boutiques*. The work of painters, glaziers, and woodworkers must have made an almost constant din along streets such as rue Saint-Honoré and the streets in the Saint-Germain quarter, rues de Bac, de Four, Saint-Dominique and Saints-Pères, as merchants outfitted their shops, for bankruptcy records from the eighteenth century almost invariably mention large sums of money owed to cabinet makers, glass makers, painters, and masons who furbished the shops of *merciers* and *marchandes de modes*.[82]

As luxury shops became more permanent and elaborate structures they not only looked different from the small-scale boutiques of the seventeenth century, but the process of shopping itself changed. The merchant now more commonly set prices in advance, and haggling was relegated to less expensive shops and markets. Ready-made clothing, which had existed since at least the seventeenth century, became more common, particularly suited, as it was, to kinds of goods made by *lingères* and *marchandes de modes*.[83] Buying on credit, a long-standing practice, became even more commonplace as merchants extended credit in their attempt to lure new, often bourgeois, clients.[84] In addition, fashion merchants increasingly found ways around restrictions against advertising and other forms of overt competition within their trades by using business cards, receipts, and the fashion press.[85] Business cards contained much more than the address of the merchant's boutique; for instance, a card proclaimed the virtues of Mme Leclere's shop:

> The White Rose, in the center of the Quai de Grêvres in Paris. Madame LECLERE has a fashion shop with the latest styles and newest tastes, such as pretty bonnets and other items; fabric by the yard, black and white lace, beautiful hairstyles, cuffs, all colors of gauze and the very best fabric; new scarves, taffetas of all qualities, ribbons for every season, some embroidered with gold, silver and silk for ladies' shoes; coiffures and decorations of embroidered Marly; handsome linens from Saint-Quentin, plain and

brocaded; pretty flowers for dress in winter; pretty ivory fans . . . in winter all sorts of muffs in satin, feathers and fur; capes and fur cloaks. She decorates dresses and sends them to the provinces. All at a reasonable price.[86]

Late-eighteenth-century merchandising tactics and interior displays were rudimentary compared with their nineteenth-century counterparts. As late as 1807 Louis-Marie Prud'homme found the *marchandes de modes'* window displays novel enough to note, "Women's bonnets and hats are displayed in *marchandes de modes'* boutiques like hams and sausages in butchers' shops."[87] Even the most cursory glance at pictures of the Palais-Royal suggests that shopping still took place in the context of a festive and gallant mingling of the sexes. (Women were advised to do their shopping in the morning to avoid these "perils.") Even though the shops were now bigger and shopping had become, to a certain extent, "rational-ized" with set prices, observers such as Mercier nevertheless complained that shopping was still not a serious and rational business in Paris. The process of buying and selling remained an elaborate game of sizing up the customer and of flatteries and pretensions. Mercier complained that in contrast to London, where buying and selling was conducted in a straightforward manner,

> Enter a shop in Paris and you must sit down, pay your respects, and make a thousand comments while buying your goods, even going so far as to talk about your family life and public affairs; you must discuss and debate what you are buying: one is too much, one is too little; often times you leave the store after a long discussion without having bought anything, dizzy from the merchant's babble. The merchant sulks because he hasn't sold anything until he latches on to a new customer who enters his store. In London, you enter a shop without saying hello or even tipping your hat; you ask simply for what you want; you get no response or greeting; one simply gets what you asked for and presents it to you. The price is not negotiable; it is your choice to take it or leave it. You pay: that says it all.[88]

As shops became more inviting and hospitable spaces for women during the course of the eighteenth century, shopping nevertheless remained just as entertaining and diverting. The memoirs of the baroness D'Oberkirch, for example, describe numerous visits to shops, as her days mixed strolling through the Tuileries with visits to the newest boutique *à la mode* in the Palais-Royal, or a visit to the Comédie-Italien followed by a brief visit to a shop. However, although shopping was still an entertaining diversion, the relationship between client and merchant had changed since the days of the small *lingère's* stall in the Palais de Justice. In part, this was a product of the growth of Paris and the increasingly impersonal relations between merchants and their clients and in part, it resulted from the growing importance of the *marchandes de modes'* trade and the growth of a kind of "cult of celebrity" around the most famous merchants in Paris.[89]

Figure 17 *Marie-Antoinette, reine de France, en robe de cour*, Claude-Louis Desrais, courtesy of RMN.

The most celebrated *marchande de modes* in late-eighteenth-century Paris, Rose Bertin, was proprietor of a shop under the sign, "Au grand mogul," on the rue Saint-Honoré. The sumptuousness of her creations was signaled to her clients as they entered her shop with its grand windows framed with simulated lavender and yellow marble.[90] Her business was so extensive that she employed thirty workers and when she filed for bankruptcy in 1787 she claimed that her clients owed her 2,000,000 *livres*.[91] Bertin was as notorious for her haughtiness and pretensions as for her elaborate hats; the *Correspondance secrète* reported in April 1778 that when a *femme de qualité* entered Bertin's shop to request several bonnets to be sent to the provinces, "The merchant, resting on a chaise longue and wearing an elegant dress, scarcely deigns to greet her wealthy customer with a very slight tilt of her head."[92] As the Baronne d'Oberkirch described Bertin, "The speech of this woman is very amusing, mixing haughtiness, baseness, and insolence."[93]

Bertin's constant reminders to her clients that she provisioned the queen may have seemed arrogant to some, but her haughtiness also made good business sense. She possessed the business expertise to realize that there was no better way to attract clients – court aristocrats, provincial aristocrats, and the bourgeoises of Paris – than to associate her business with royalty, and in particular, with Marie Antoinette. Bertin's shop was filled with portraits of the queens of France, Sweden, Spain, Portugal and Naples and the Empress of Russia. But the loss of her shop and her hasty forced flight to England with the coming of the Revolution reveal the dangers as well as the benefits of linking one's business with aristocratic luxury. Although associating one's business with aristocratic patrons continued to seduce bourgeois clients well into the nineteenth (and even the twenty-first) century, many *marchandes de modes* were astute enough to realize that associating themselves with a classless but highly gendered taste, rather than aristocratic luxury, would prove even more attractive to a broader spectrum of women.

The status of the *marchandes de modes* and the nature of shopping had been transformed since the seventeenth century when merchants hawked their wares along the Pont-Neuf or from behind narrow counters in the Palais de Justice. As the model of aristocratic male consumers slowly gave way to a new model of bourgeois, female shoppers, shopping seemed to have become more "rational," with permanent stores, fixed prices, and advertising. If shopping was no longer viewed as a kind of courtship, relations between female merchants and female customers were nevertheless mystified in new and seductive ways. The *marchandes de modes* were extolled as creative geniuses and the boutiques themselves, once merely a backdrop for the merchants, took on a life of their own, setting the standards for what was fashionable, dazzling customers, and convincing them that they had little choice but to bow down and pay homage to the creations of the *marchande de modes*, now ready-made and available for a fixed price.

Notes

1. Desessants, *Dictionnaire Universel de Police* (Paris, 1785–89), 624–5. On eighteenth-century ideas about luxury, see Christopher Berry, *The Idea of Luxury: A Conceptual and Historical Investigation* (Cambridge: Cambridge University Press, 1994); Anthony Pagden, ed. *The Languages of Political Theory in Early-Modern Europe* (Cambridge: Cambridge University Press, 1987); Albert Hirschman, *The Passions and the Interests* (Princeton: Princeton University Press, 1977); John Sekora, *Luxury: The Concept in Western Thought from Eden to Smollet* (Baltimore: Johns Hopkins University Press, 1977); Ellen Ross, "The Debate on Luxury in Eighteenth-Century France" (Ph.D. thesis, University of Chicago, 1975).
2. Philibert-Joseph LeRoux, *Dictionnaire comique* (Lyon, 1752): 201.
3. Mercier, *Tableau de Paris* t. 4: 74. Mercier returned to this theme throughout his *Tableau de Paris*. In Volume 6 he explained that many Parisian men preferred to have a housekeeper and mistress, rather than a wife, because of women's unbridled taste for fashionable clothing and tendency toward dissipation.
4. Jean-François Butini, *Traité du luxe* (Geneva, 1774): 89.
5. Bocquel, "Supériorité de l'homme sur la femme ou l'inégalité des deux sexes," (1740), 101. BA, manuscript 3656.
6. Although eighteenth-century economists and social theorists were trying to understand abstractly the nature of consumption, contemporaries for the most part did not think in terms of abstract categories such as "consumers" and "consumption." In general, French men and women differentiated between three kinds of consumption: the consumption of necessities such as food, shelter, and protective clothing; that of items that made life more agreeable, but which were not strictly necessary; and that of items that were frivolous luxuries. For a discussion of these three categories of consumption, see Antoine-Prosper Lottin, *Discours sur ce sujet: Le luxe corrompt les moeurs* (Paris and Amsterdam: Desanges, 1784): 38–9.
7. For an examination of the connection made between women, luxury and culture in the eighteenth century, see Sylvana Tomaselli, "The Enlightenment Debate on Women," *History Workshop Journal*, no. 20 (1985): 101–24.
8. Gabriel Sénac de Meilhan, *Considérations sur la richesse et le luxe* (Amsterdam and Paris, 1787): 145–6. Hoping to follow the success of Necker's *Compte rendu*, Senac de Meilhan wrote his *Considérations* to further his design to become minister of finances. See André Vielwahr, *La vie et l'oeuvre de Sénac de Meilhan* (Paris: A.G. Nizet, 1970): 69.
9. There exists a complementary tradition of associating women with avarice. For discussions of women and avarice, see Pierre de Marivaux, *Le spectateur*

Français, douzième feuille, (December 6, 1722), and Mme de Pringy, *Les différents caractères des femmes* (Paris, 1699): 109, 132–4.

10. *Les paradoxes d'état servant d'entretien aux bons esprits* (1651): 37.

11. Lottin, *Discours sur ce sujet*: 10–11. Lottin, a follower of Rousseau and one of the harshest critics of the Parisian women's *luxe* and frivolity, wrote under the pseudonym M. de Saint Haippy.

12. Samuel August André David Tissot, *Avis au peuple sur sa santé*, 4th ed. (Lyon, 1769): 42–46.

13. Butini, *Traité du luxe*: 86–7.

14. Boudier de Villemert, *Le nouvelle ami des femmes*: 98.

15. Butini, *Traité du luxe*: 27.

16. Landes, *Women and the Public Sphere*. For a critique of Landes's arguments, see Olwen Hufton, review of *Women and the Public Sphere*, *American Historical Review* 96 (April 1991): 528.

17. Sénac de Meilhan, *Considérations*: 143.

18. On the birth of the department store in nineteenth-century Paris, see Michael Miller, *The Bon Marché: Bourgeois Culture and the Department Store* (Princeton: Princeton University Press, 1981). Other important studies of nineteenth-century commerce and consumption include Leora Auslander, *Taste and Power: Furnishing Modern France* (Berkeley: University of California Press, 1996); Philip Nord, *Paris Shopkeepers and the Politics of Resentment* (Princeton: Princeton University Press, 1986); Theresa McBride, "A Woman's World: Department Stores and the Evolution of Women's Employment," *French Historical Studies* 10 (Fall 1978): 664–83; Victoria Thompson, *The Virtuous Marketplace: Women and Men, Money and Politics in Paris, 1830–1870* (Baltimore: Johns Hopkins University Press, 2000); Lisa Tiersten, *Marianne in the Market: Envisioning Consumer Society in Fin-de-Siècle France* (Berkeley: University of California Press, 2001); Rosalind Williams, *Dream Worlds: Mass Consumption in Late Nineteenth-Century France* (Berkeley: University of California Press, 1982). On shopping in nineteenth-century Britain, see Erika Rappaport, *Shopping for Pleasure: Women in the Making of London's West End* (Princeton: Princeton University Press, 2000).

19. For an introduction to Mercier's discussion of women in the *Tableau de Paris*, see John Lough, "Women in Mercier's *Tableau de Paris*," in *Woman and Society in Eighteenth-Century France*, ed. Jacobs, Barber, Block, et al., (London, 1979): 110–22. For an important collection of recent scholarly essays on Mercier, see Jean-Claude Bonnet, ed. *Louis-Sébastien Mercier (1740–1814): Un hérétique en litterature* (Paris: Mercure de France, 1995).

20. On the *revendeuses à la toilette*, see Mercier, *Tableau de Paris*, t. 2: 188–9.

21. For definitions of "boutique" and "magasin," see *Encyclopédie, ou diction- naire raisonné*.

22. On the character of artisanal boutiques and living quarters, see Daniel Roche, ed., *Journal de ma vie, Jacques Louis Ménétra, compagnon vitrier au XVIIIe siècle* (Paris: Editions Montalba, 1982): 374.

23. For information on the legal status of "échoppes", see Marcel Marion, *Dic- tionnaire des institutions de la France au XVII et XVIII siècles* (Paris: A. et J. Picard et Cie, 1968): 195.

24. For a detailed examination of the stealing and reselling of garments, see Roche, *The Culture of Clothing*, Chapter 12. On regulation of colporteurs, hawkers and street displays, see *Ordonnance de Police qui fait défense de tous particuliers. . .d'étaler et de vendre aucunes marchandises dans les rues* (Paris, 1776), AN, AD XI, 11, fol. 66.

25. On the rue de la Lingerie, see Du Pradel *Le livre commode*, t. 2: 16.

26. On the boutiques of the Palais in the early seventeenth century, see *Registres des délibérations du Bureau de la ville de Paris* (Paris: Imprimerie Nationale, 1952), t. 17, nos. 232, 148. In this document, twenty-eight merchants describe the location of their boutiques in the Palais and the amount of their losses in the fire at the Palais on the night of March 6, 1618.

27. Built by Louis IX, these arcades were variously referred to as, "La Galerie mercière," "Salle aux merciers," "Galerie du Palais," and "Mercerie du Palais."

28. Joachim Christoph Nemeitz, *Séjour de Paris* (Leiden: J. Van Abcoude, 1727): 338.

29. For a bibliography of seventeenth- and eighteenth-century accounts of the Palais-Royal, see Victor Champier and G.-Roger Sandoz, *Le Palais-Royal d'après des documents inédits* (Paris, 1900). Particularly interesting accounts are found in Piganiol de La Force, *Description de Paris* (Paris, 1742); John Andrews, *Letters to a Young Gentleman on his Setting out for France* (London, 1784); and Mayeur de Saint-Paul, *Tableau du nouveau Palais-Royal* (Paris, 1788). The *Almanach du Palais-Royal pour 1785* (Paris, 1785) provides information on merchants and shops. Although the *Galerie Mercière* of the Palais de Justice burned down in 1776 and the Palais lost some its vogue as the commercial geography of Paris shifted towards the rue Saint-Honoré and the Palais-Royal on the Right Bank, the Palais de Justice continued to house the shops of luxury merchants. Mercier described the commercial bustle of the Palais in his *Tableau de Paris*, t. 2: 23.

30. On Parisian fairs, see Robert Isherwood, *Farce and Fantasy: Popular Enter- tainment in Eighteenth-Century Paris* (Oxford: Oxford University Press, 1986).

31. On the Foire Saint-Laurent, see Nemeitz, *Séjour de Paris*: 99.

32. Nemeitz, *Séjour de Paris*: 100.

33. Ibid., 101.

34. Ibid., 107–8. On the high price of goods in luxury boutiques, see Nemeitz *Séjour de Paris*: 340 and Mercier, *Tableau de Paris*, t. 10: 233.

35. On the shop as a place of entertainment, see Chanoine François Pedoue, *Le bourgeois poli* (1631). Cited in F. Braudel, *The Wheels of Commerce*, trans. Siân Reynolds (New York: Harper and Row, 1982): 71.

36. Mercier, *Tableau de Paris*, t. 10: 233.

37. Bernier, *The Eighteenth-Century Woman*: 126.

38. Oberkirch, *Mémoires de la baronne d'Oberkirch*: 118.

39. Nicolas Restif de la Bretonne, *Les nuits de Paris* (London, 1788–94), 2: 470

40. Mercier, *Tableau de Paris*, t. 10: 244.

41. Oberkirch, *Mémoires de la baronne d'Oberkirch*: 225.

42. For another example of the image of the *marchandes de modes'* boutique as a harem, see Mercier, t. 11:110.

43. In the seventeenth century the young women who worked in the *lingères'* boutiques of the Palais were also known as *noguettes*. See *Dictionnaire de Trévoux*. By the eighteenth century the term was used more broadly to include any carefree young urban woman.

44. Mercier, *Tableau de Paris*, t. 8: 133. Furetière, *Dictionnaire universel*, s.v. "*grisette*." For a history of the grisette, see Joëlle Guillais-Maury, "Une Histoire de grisette" (Maîtrise, Paris VII, 1980) and "La grisette," in *Madame ou mademoiselle? Itinéraires de la solitude feminine, dix-huitième à vingtième siècle* ed. Arlette Farge and Christine Klapish-Zuber (Paris: Montalba, 1984): 233–50.

45. *Encyclopédie méthodique*, t. 1: 135.

46. See Pierre Jean Baptiste Nougaret, *Les jolis pêches d'une marchande de modes*, 4th ed. (Paris, 1801) and Nicolas Restif de la Bretonne, "Les jolies femmes de commerce," in *Les contemporains* (Paris, 1782), 3: 65.

47. Mercier, *Tableau de Paris*, t. 9: 173.

48. Ibid., t. 9: 173–4.

49. Oriol, "Maîtresses marchandes lingères": 22.

50. Mercier, *Tableau de Paris*, t. 9: 174–5.

51. Oriol, "Maîtresses marchandes lingères": 49.

52. For an attempt to alleviate the suffering of working women who fell sick or on hard times, see *Prospectus d'une maison d'association en faveur des filles de boutique, ouvrières et domestiques* (1762) BM, 43004.

53. Oriol, "Maîtresses marchandes lingères": 82.

54. Representations of *grisettes* can be compared and contrasted with representations of *poissardes*. The term *poissarde* originally designated female fishmongers, but then was later broadened to include any woman who sold at *des halles*. Ultimately, the term was used to describe any urban woman of the

popular classes. While some observers such as Greuze and Diderot commented on the beauty and gaiety of the *poissardes*, others characterized them as crude and "masculine." See Yvonne Knibiehler and Catherine Fouquet, *La beauté, pour quoi faire?* (Paris, 1982): 28. On the market women of Paris, see Rene Marion, "The Dames de la Halle: Community and Authority in Early Modern Paris" (Ph.D. dissertation, Johns Hopkins University, 1995).

55. Mercier, *Tableau de Paris*, t. 8: 134.

56. *Etrennes aux grisettes pour l'année 1790: Requête presentée à M. Sylvain Bailly, Maire de Paris, par Florentine de Launay contre les marchandes de modes, couturières, et lingères et autres grisettes commerçante sur le pavé de Paris*, BHVP, 603159 in-8, and BN, 8 Li5.9I.

57. *Etrennes aux grisettes, noms et demeure des grisettes* (1790), BN, L5i 91A. For another satire on the morality of the *grisettes*, see *Brevet d'Agnès Pompon, apprentisse fille de modes*, BN, 8 Z. Le Senne, 4365(1).

58. Mercier, *Tableau de Paris*, t. 11: 111–12.

59. *Encyclopédie méthodique*, t. 1: 135.

60. See the report of a rape and seduction of a fifteen-year-old *ouvrière en linge*, Marie-Anne Marchebout, *Journal dédié à Monsieur*, no. 9 (May 1777): 111.

61. Mercier, *Tableau de Paris*, t. 6: 309.

62. As Olwen Hufton reminds us in a recent review of Joan Landes's *Women in the Public Sphere*, the *salon* was a private, not a public, space. *American Historical Review* 96, no. 2 (April 1991): 528. On women's enlightened government of the upper-class salon, see Dena Goodman, *The Republic of Letters: A Cultural History of the French Enlightenment* (Ithaca: Cornell University Press, 1994).

63. Mercier, *Tableau de Paris*, t. 6: 311.

64. For an account of a dialogue which took place in 1702 in a boutique near the *charnier des Innocents* between a beautiful *mercière* and the Prince d'Orléans as he tried to seduce her, see Cardinal Guillaume Dubois *Mémoires du Cardinal Dubois sur la ville, la cour et les salons de Paris sous la Régence*, BN, Fol. Z Le Senne 789 (1). For visual images of *couturières* and *chapelières* flirting with male customers see *Les belles marchandes, almanach historique* (Paris, 1784) which contain a picture of one female merchant for each month of the year with captions.

65. *Arlequin, lingère du Palais* (1652), cited in Bouvier, *La lingerie et les lingères*: 176–8.

66. Nemeitz, *Séjour de Paris*: 339.

67. Ibid.

68. Pierre Marivaux, "Lettres sur les habitants de Paris," in *Journaux et oeuvres diverses de Marivaux*, ed. Frédéric Deloffre and Michel Gilot (Paris: Bordas, 1988): 16.

69. See the merchant Jacques Savary's advice to apprentices on how to comport themselves honestly and politely with customers, *Le parfait négociant*: 61.
70. For advice on how to seduce a *mercière*, see the advice of the Cardinal Dubois in "*Mémoires du Cardinal Dubois*, Chapter 29.
71. In *Le nouveau magasin françois pour le mois d'avril, 1750*, 152, an article titled, "Lettre à madame ***," tells the story of an aristocratic man's experience shopping and his encounters with a *grisette*.
72. Mercier, *Tableau de Paris*, t. 6: 310.
73. Mercier, *Tableau de Paris*, t. 12: 269. Contemporaries also believed that the *marchandes de modes*' female clients regarded their merchant's other female clients as rivals. See the play *La matinée d'une jolie femme*, quoted in *Journal de la mode et du goût* (January 20, 1793): 2.
74. Mercier, *Tableau de Paris*, t. 2: 267–8.
75. Nemeitz, *Séjour de Paris*: 338. A number of authors, including Montesquieu, made reference to the commercial din of the Palais. Charles de Montesquieu, *Persian Letters* (1721), letter 87.
76. Mercier, *Tableau de Paris*, t. 10: 234. For a particularly scathing and highly subjective account of sexual license at the Palais-Royal, see Restif de la Bretonne, *Le Palais-Royal* (Paris, 1790). On the convergence of elite and popular culture on the boulevards and in the fairs of Paris, see Isherwood, *Farce and Fantasy*.
77. For a useful exploration of the problematic relationship of an emerging "public sphere" and "private life" in early-modern France, see Dena Goodman, "Public Sphere and Private Life: Toward a Synthesis of Current Historiographical Approaches to the Old Regime." *History and Theory* 31, no. 1 (1992).
78. Nemeitz, *Séjour de Paris*: 65.
79. The French lagged behind the British in shop displays. For a description by a French visitor on the lavish use of glass in British shops, see *Voyage en Angleterre* (1728), quoted in Braudel, *The Wheels of Commerce*: 69. On the counters and display cases needed in an eighteenth-century French mercers' boutique, see Savary, *Le parfait négociant*: 250.
80. Au Grand Mogol was run by Mlle Bertin on the rue Saint-Honoré, Au Pavillon d'or by the *couturière* Mme Teillard, and Des Trois Mandarins by Sieur Jubin near the théatre des Variétés.
81. The Camp of the Tartars was a temporary wooden shopping arcade built on the site of the Palais-Royal in the 1780s. It gained a reputation, according to Robert Isherwood as, "the hangout of debauched youths, thieves, *petits-maîtres*, swindlers, prostitutes, and financiers. A decent woman or a 'reasonable man' could not be found amid the shoving and pushing, according to Mayeur de Saint-Paul . . . . The Camp of the Tartars inaugurated the new

Palais-Royal and the launching of a festival of popular culture cheek by jowl with the palace of princes of the blood." Isherwood, *Farce and Fantasy*: 222.

82. See, for example, the bankruptcy proceedings of Marie Denise Prévost in February 1785. Of the approximately 13,000 *livres* spent on her business over a three-year period (including taxes, wages for two *fille de boutique* and a cook, rent and expenses incurred while sick) 2,500 was paid to workers to refurbish her boutique. AS, D4B6, carton 18, doss. 865. See also the dossier of dame Godart, a *marchande de modes* on the rue Croix des petits champs, who spent 3,000 *livres* on mirrors, counters and *armoires*. AS, D4B6, carton 81, doss. 5393.

83. On the flourishing trade in ready-mades in the eighteenth century see Nemeitz, *Séjour de Paris*: 335–6. The *tailleur* Dartigalongue announced the sale of ready-mades in *Affiches, annonces et avis divers* no. 4 (April 1770): 55. Mercier claimed in the 1780s that one could dress oneself much more cheaply with set price, ready-mades but that young people often rejected this option because it required a cash payment. *Tableau de Paris*, t. 10: 271. See also t. 10: 241–2.

84. Some historians have suggested that buying on credit exploded in 1788 and 1789. As the aristocratic market for fashions dried up in the last years of the *ancien régime*, due in small part to a new, simpler sartorial style and in large part to mounting debts, Parisian merchants extended more credit to their customers. The growth of credit may have been driven by the increasing demand of female consumers as well as supply. Contemporary observations suggest that women were more prone to buy on credit than were men. See Dancourt's *Les bourgeoises à la mode*, in which Araminte threatens her lover that if he does not pay her debts she will commit herself to the convent. See also Mercier, t. *Tableau de Paris*, 12: 270. According to the *Coutume de Paris*, although in theory a wife was not supposed to alienate any portion of the estate or make any contracts, her debts had to be paid by her husband. See *Traité de la puissance du mari sur la personne et les biens* in R.-J. Pothier, *Oeuvres de R.-J. Pothier* (Brussels, 1831): 8. See also Savary, *Le parfait négociant*, 319, on husbands' responsibility for their wives' debts.

85. Although clothing workers and merchants had been forbidden to advertise throughout the eighteenth century, in the 1760s and 1770s the number of *sentences de police* forbidding clothing workers and merchants to advertise the prices of their wares suggests that, in fact, the practice was becoming more widespread. See BN, fr. 22116, fols. 112, 169 and 171 and AN, AD XI, 26.

86. This card also noted that the *marchande* had a boutique at the Saint-Germain and Saint-Ovide fairs. "Publicité commerciale à Paris," AS, D43Z, vol. 1, fol. 10.

87. Louis-Marie Prud'homme, *Miroir historique, politique, et critique de l'ancien et du nouveau Paris*, 6 vols., 3rd ed. (Paris, 1807), t. 5: 238.

88. Louis-Sébastien Mercier, *Parallèle de Paris et de Londres*, ed. C. Bruneteau (Paris, 1982): 144. See also Mercier, "Surfaire," *Tableau de Paris*, t. 5: 231.

89. Establishing a regular clientele was considered an indispensable part of succeeding in one's business. A regular customer was called a *chaland*. See Savary des Bruslons, *Dictionnaire universel du commerce*.

90. For a description of Bertin's shop see Bernier, *The Eighteenth-Century Woman*: 126.

91. *Correspondance secrète*, t. 6: 146. Quoted in Franklin, *La vie privée d'autrefois*, vol. XV: 258.

92. Ibid.

93. Oberkirch, *Mémoires de la baronne d'Oberkirch*: 52.

– 6 –

Selling *La Mode*

"Verses on Novelty"

In a land where madness reigns
One day Novelty appeared:
Immediately everyone rushed to her.
Everyone said that she was pretty
"Oh! Madame *la Nouveauté*,
Stay in our country;
More than Intelligence, more than Beauty
You will always be cherished here."
"O.K", the goddess responded to all the fools,
"Gentlemen, I will live here."
And she promised to meet them
The next day at the same time.
The next day came, she showed up
As brilliant as the day before.
The first one to see her
Cried, "God, she is old."

Cabinet des modes, March 15, 1786.

Since the Renaissance fashion and adornment had almost continually provoked censure – as both cause and symptom of vanity, immorality, and excessive luxury – but in the eighteenth century French men and women became even more acutely aware of the problems that the changeable, arbitrary reign of fashion might pose for society. As we have seen in earlier chapters, there were many reasons for this heightened concern about fashion, including the rapid growth of the commercial economy of cities such as Paris, the breakdown of a fashion culture centered at court and dictated by royal authority and etiquette, and the participation of a new class of female artisans and shop girls in the culture of fashion. Although few contemporaries would have explicitly associated debates over fashion with lofty debates about citizenship and sovereignty, fashion was an important part of elite sociability and may have played a larger role than historians have realized in creating a sense of citizenship and public participation in a new society of taste.

Worries about the protean nature of fashion focused on the arbitrary and despotic nature of *la mode*, and witnessed the projection of eighteenth-century political critiques of the nature of monarchy and despotism onto the culture of fashion.

Gender was deeply entwined with eighteenth-century political critique; not surprisingly, the most explicit concerns about fashion's despotism related to the trouble it caused between the sexes. Among the most serious concerns were fears that women would deplete the family's fortune in order to keep up with *la mode*, that they would deceive men with their clothing and artifice (disguising deformities and blemishes to trick men into marriage or concealing pregnancies with hoop-skirts), and that young, working girls in Paris would sacrifice their virtue to their desire for pretty dresses and trinkets. Not until the Revolution were the problematic relationships between despotism and *la mode*, and between women and fashion, resolved through the ascendancy of a discourse on women and fashion that rested on three interconnected assumptions: first, that fashions could be "natural" rather than artificial and dissimulating; second, that fashionable dress could express one's inner taste rather than external ostentation; third, that the arbitrary, despotic nature of fashion was not really threatening to men and society because *la mode*'s power was restricted to the circumscribed domain of the frivolous and the feminine.

An examination of the way in which *la mode* was discussed in the late-eighteenth-century fashion press offers a glimpse of how women came to be positioned at the heart of the problem of the "règne de la mode," the arbitrary rule of fashion over the citizens of commercial cities such as Paris, and how a new definition of femininity was offered as the solution. The fashion press played a crucial role in disseminating a new vision of the relationship between women, fashion, and commercial culture. While enthusiastically promoting *la mode*, the fashion press worked, if not completely to harness fashion, at least to relegate it to a smaller, less dangerous purview. Fashion was defined as frivolous and ephemeral, and consigned to the realm of taste rather than the serious realm of art and politics, to the *toilette* rather than the Conseil d'État, and to public promenades in the Tuileries and the shops of the Palais-Royal rather than to learned academies. Fashion was tamed and made sense of by linking it to femininity and defining it as one of the principal, innate, but relatively unimportant, concerns of all women. Although the fashion press supported *la mode*'s dominion over women, the editors depicted fashion as a gentle, maternal, and enlightened despot; the fashion press "sold" *la mode* to women, and to the French generally, by encouraging women to imagine that while they were subject to fashion's whims, they might claim some citizenship in her sovereignty.

The French Fashion Press

Unlike in the seventeenth century, when the only treatment of fashion in the periodical press was found in biannual issues of the *Mercure*, by the late eighteenth century several journals reported on the latest fashions.[1] The first daily newspapers in France, the *Journal de Paris* and *La feuille sans titre*, both included information on fashion, along with news of literature, music, theater, *faits divers*, and developments in the arts and sciences.[2] The weekly *Feuille nécessaire* (1759) and its successor, the *Avant-Coureur* (1760–73), also reported on new clothing styles. The *Le courrier de la nouveauté*, whose prospectus was published in 1758, and Joseph Boudier de Villemert's *Le courrier de la mode* (1768–70) were founded with the plan to devote themselves exclusively to presenting the latest fashions.[3] In the provinces, both the *Journal de Normandie* and the *Affiches des evêches de Lorraine* provided news of the latest fashions from Paris. Numerous collections of fashion engravings also regularly appeared, such as *La publication mensuelle des modes, ou bibliothèque pour la toilette des dames* and the *Galerie des modes*, which published over 400 engravings of contemporary fashions between 1778 and 1787.[4] Furthermore, French consumers could participate in the general late-eighteenth-century Anglomania by following British fashions in the well-established British periodical press.[5]

The most extensive coverage of fashion appeared in Jean Antoine Brun's *Cabinet des modes*, which every fifteen days, from 1785 to 1786, provided its subscribers with three-color engravings and eight pages of text on the latest fashions.[6] From November 1786 to December 1789, Louis Edme Billardon de Sauvigny edited the journal under the title, *Magasin des modes nouvelles*.[7] Beginning in February 1790 Brun returned to the journal, now titled the *Journal de la mode et du goût*.[8] Meeting with financial difficulties at the height of the Terror, Brun suspended publication of the journal in April 1793. Between 1793 and March 1797, when the *Journal des dames* began publication, no French journal provided coverage of fashion.[9]

During its eight years of publication, the *Cabinet des modes*, the first journal to resemble the nineteenth- and twentieth-century fashion press, provided a detailed view of how the "fashion system" worked – how fashions were created, how vogues for new styles were sparked, and how they spread from class to class – and explicit commentary on the nature of *la mode*.[10] Furthermore, the journal was remarkably self-reflexive, regularly discussing its own role in the culture of fashion. Like the *Mercure*, the *Cabinet des modes* was clearly aimed at provincials and foreigners wishing to keep abreast of the latest Parisian fashions. However, the fashion culture in which the *Cabinet des modes* participated was much broader than the relatively circumscribed fashion culture of the *gens de qualité* presented

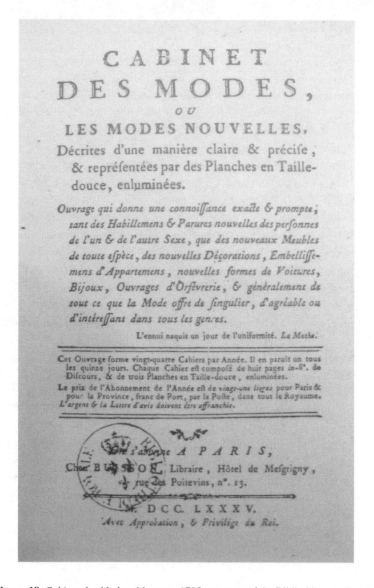

Figure 18 *Cabinet des Modes*, title page, 1785, courtesy of the Bibliothèque nationale.

in the *Mercure*.[11] Although both the textual descriptions and fashion plates situated the clothing in opulent, aristocratic settings, the fashions were rarely distinguished based on class and position and the court no longer provided the sole reference point. The commercial culture of Paris and all its parts – *marchandes de modes*, boutiques, actresses, operas and popular entertainments – had become the center of fashion and the nucleus of *le goût national*, France's most treasured national resource, according to the fashion press. The *Cabinet des modes* served not only the *dame de qualité* who casually perused it while conducting her morning *toilette* but also all those whose livelihood depended on French fashions; it was the first fashion trade journal.

Of the four primary ways in which the *Mercure* had understood fashion to be shaped (class and rank, seasons, royal authority and etiquette, and sex) only the seasons and sex continued to figure prominently in the *Cabinet des modes* as ways of structuring the fashion system.[12] Although Marie Antoinette continued to play an important role inspiring fashions throughout the 1770s and 1780s, (setting, for example, the trend for the simple muslin chemise in the early 1780s), the queen virtually disappears from the story of fashion narrated in the *Cabinet des modes*. One could argue that a half decade before the Revolution, the fashion press had already effectively desacralized king and queen, at least from the point of view of fashion. The sole reference to the queen's influence on fashion was the sad report in August 1792 on her hairstyle: "The queen's hair isn't very long, only about a foot. Women of distinction, and especially those at court, have cut their hair to this length of one foot."[13] Royal sumptuary edicts appear in the fashion press only when the texts of ancient sumptuary edicts are reprinted, presented as arcane, even amusing, documents published to inform the reader of the history of fashion, in contrast to their original intent, in the days of the *Mercure*, to enforce royal authority over dress.[14] The *Mercure* had portrayed the hierarchy of the court through the hierarchy of sumptuous dress at court balls but the *Magasin des modes nouvelles* described the fashions worn at balls in 1787 thus: "Each woman can, forgetting her rank in society, her estate, her birth, and even her fortune, appear at a ball with the richest, most elegant and most beautiful costume without fearing to provoke serious criticism."[15] And, when describing new fashions the journal frequently reported that they were "for all classes."[16]

In the journal's discussion of ball gowns, as throughout, all of the categories which had once shaped fashion, such as class, privilege, or rank, were collapsed onto the category of sex, which became the primary device used by the journal's editors for organizing the fashion culture of late-eighteenth-century Paris. Sex even supplanted qualities such as age in determining dress. In July 1786, the *Cabinet des modes* reported that a woman from the provinces had written to the journal asking "if the new fashion is for all, and if it is the same for women between thirty and forty years old as it is for women between eighteen and twenty." The journal responded, "there is only one fashion and it is the same for all ages; for the most part our women, even those much older than forty, will not have any difficulty wearing it and they will not be blamed for wearing it."[17]

As the categories of class, rank, and court etiquette were collapsed onto sex and gender as the primary determinants of fashion, a new set of variables took their place in shaping what men and women wore: the intimate rhythms and details of daily life – one's personal world of time and place – began to determine one's toilette as *la mode* left behind the public world of court ritual and the pomp of class and privilege and entered the more private world of women, family and the home. No longer changing only with the seasons, the fashion press suggested that the fashionable woman dressed according to the hourly striking of the clock. The *Magasin des modes nouvelles* excused its practice of specifying different *toilettes* for different hours of the day by explaining: "It would be too little for fashion . . . to change only after a certain amount of time, after certain époques . . . ; fashion wants to change many times each day even. That is why she has created the *habit du matin*, *l'habit de dîner*, *l'habit de soir*."[18] In addition to keeping pace with the dizzying movement of *la mode* through the hours of the day, the woman of fashion needed to follow fashion into a variety of realms where it had not heretofore ventured: for example, the *Cabinet des modes* instructed her on dressing for church, dressing her child for a walk in the park, and the proper attire for horseback riding.[19] In commenting on the fashion journals, Louis Sébastien Mercier was struck by the fact that the journal reported on fashions "not only at court, the city or the provinces, but even for the *salon*, the study, the bedroom, the *chaises longues*."[20]

Throughout its eight years of publication, the *Cabinet des modes*'s avowed purpose was to provide "a prompt and exact knowledge of all the new clothing of both sexes."[21] Each issue offered some information on men's attire, and the journal described fashion as a natural interest of men as well as women, writing, "In all times, and in all places, the two sexes, with the desire to mutually please each other, have tried to adorn themselves."[22] Nevertheless, by far the largest amount of space was devoted to women's dress, and the journal portrayed the fashion culture of late-eighteenth-century Paris as a distinctly feminine affair. Letters to the editor were always from female readers and the anecdotes mixed with the journal's fashion plates and descriptive text primarily concerned "le beau sexe." During the eight years of the journal's publication women were for the subjects of 53 per cent of the engravings whereas men accounted for only 11 per cent. During the Revolution, in the final three years of the journal's publication, the ratio of female to male fashions in the engravings became even more lopsided with over 76 per cent of the objects represented belonging exclusively to women's dress.[23] At one point the journal simply admitted, "We have used up all that it is necessary to say about men's fashions, which change so much less." On another occasion the editor explained that, "For some time now men's clothing has not been worth the trouble of bothering with."[24] Reflecting in May 1787 on the imbalance in its treatment of male and female fashions, the editor of the *Magasin des modes nouvelles* conceded that "This work will from now on be particularly destined for women; we must think to satisfy them first of all."[25]

When the journal did portray men's fashions it often noted that the fashion was for "young men," suggesting that except for the young, an interest in fashion was unseemly or inappropriate in men. Whereas women followed fashions because they were innately attracted to "les nouveautés," men, as presented in the fashion press, followed fashion merely as a courting strategy. The *Magasin des modes nouvelles* explained that men's fashions changed less frequently than did women's, "Either because they are less preoccupied with pleasing than women, or because their minds are less inventive in this medium." The journal went on to insist that men should not be reproached for being uninterested in fashion since,

> They are not called by nature or social estate to work at the art of pleasing. To do so would render their sex, too unaccustomed to pleasing, ridiculous. Let them leave these cares to the other sex, which is more delicate and agreeable and which seems born to no other employment than pleasing. That is their charge, and any other that they might have would seem contrary to the views of nature.[26]

The late-eighteenth-century fashion press's presentation of dress and fashion as a distinctly feminine affair rested on a new definition of fashion that the fashion press itself played a vital role in creating and disseminating. According to this new definition, which would have seemed strange to seventeenth-century writers such as Donneau de Visé, the impetus for fashion was not the desire to display luxurious clothing symbolic of one's power and position. As defined by the *Cabinet des modes*, fashion and adornment were products of women's desire to be "*jolie*" and "*belle*" in order to please men, and the constant transformation of colors and styles of clothing was a product of women's persistent desire to present their charms to men in a new and more advantageous light. As the journal wrote, "No matter how honorable a woman is, she always wants to please. And to succeed at that it is necessary that she continually present her charms in a new light. By this means she provides her husband, or lover, the pleasures of variety."[27] This new definition served to naturalize the variety and inconstancy of fashion by linking it to innate characteristics of the relationship between the sexes, men's need for variety and women's desire to please men. Whereas the *Mercure* had presented fashion as a product of culture – of state pomp and etiquette – the eighteenth-century fashion press stressed that the desire to be fashionably dressed was grounded in nature. This point was underscored in the journal with frequent examples of savages and native American women who painted their bodies and adorned themselves to attract the attention of men, and with historical anecdotes revealing that women had at all times and in all cultures been interested in fashions.

Although the Revolution wreaked a disastrous impact economically on luxury consumption and the fashion trades, it nevertheless provided a test case of sorts for the editors of the journal, offering conclusive evidence that women's interest in fashion was innately rooted in their femininity rather than in social etiquette and aristocratic privilege.[28] The *Journal de la mode* claimed that although aristocratic women had suffered many losses as the Revolution swept away the imposing titles and the honors which they had shared with their husbands, as women, they still had fashion to fall back on: "There only remains, then, for those who wish to play actively and strike the eyes with a lively glitter, the singularity, the richness, and the elegance of one's costume."[29] The Revolution may have swept away the artifice and corruption of the *ancien régime*, but the journal insisted that it had not hampered women's enjoyment of frivolous adornments; for fashion was a feminine prerogative based in nature, and therefore to be protected by the new régime. As the *Journal de la mode* explained, "Our new form of government does not forbid women to concern themselves with adornment, merely that they combine a certain simplicity with the luxury of the previous times."[30]

The grounding of *la mode* in women's nature and the "natural" desire of the sexes to please one another through adornment constituted only one of several characteristics of *la mode* that the journal uncovered in its attempt to divine the mystery of fashion. As the journal guided its readers through the styles of a given season, it also provided a running commentary on the general nature of fashion. In October 1787, the *Magasin des modes nouvelles* noted the existence of rules governing fashion, "If we would recall all the changes of fashion, it would be easy to convince ourselves that *la mode*, which one calls so variable, is nevertheless regular in her step, and that she is always created in the same way."[31] The journal went on to explain that the principal characteristic of the "regular working of fashion" was the movement of styles from the simple to the complex.[32] The journal repeatedly referred to this "progression" of *la mode* and in July 1789, remarking on the passing of the fashion for elaborately embroidered bodices and skirts, the journal lamented, "Why is it so difficult to stop at a reasonable point and maintain *le parfait milieu?*"[33] The journal's question was rhetorical, for its editors seemed to have a clear idea as to why it was so difficult to stop the evolution of any fashion: the cycles of fashion, which proceeded from the simple to the complex, were propelled by the ceaseless need for variety, whether in the form of wider ruffles, new colors, more elaborate embroidery or narrower skirts.[34] The journal offered, as an illustration of the rule, the example of striped fabric. Once a dress has appeared in a narrow-striped fabric, a medium-striped fabric, and a broad-striped fabric, the fashion could progress no further and must be replaced by a new design.

Although the journal insisted that styles followed a fixed progression, evolving from the simple to the complex, it conceded that there could be variations in this sequence, depending on the particular item of clothing or style. In some cases the journal reported that the first age of a style, the time of its simplest incarnation, was the longest stage: "When you see a fashion begin to get too overburdened with decoration, then you can say: its end is near and shortly it will be destroyed."[35]

And, commenting on the *chapeaux à la Théodore*, that originally had almost no ornamentation but which eventually sprouted bows and plumes, the journal explained, "As long as the embellishments are simple, one would believe that the mode will still last a long time (a long time for her)."[36] But two months later, the journal requested readers not take its pronouncement on the *chapeaux à la Théodore* "too literally." Describing the enduring vogue for striped fabric, the journal explained that the final period of a style's development often witnesses its perfection and the style will last a long time, longer than all of its other periods put together, if it is not destroyed by sudden capriciousness.[37]

The *Magasin des modes nouvelles*'s theory that fashions passed through a "progression of styles," whose course could be roughly, if not specifically, charted, expressed a conception of *la mode* common throughout the later-eighteenth-century discourse on fashion. The *Manuel des toilettes*, a collection of engravings and commentary on men's and women's hairstyles, stated a corollary belief that the progression of fashions paralleled the larger progression of humankind toward perfection. Changing men's hat styles, for example, "reveal how the human race perfects itself. We have worn very small hats; we have worn medium sized ones; we will wear huge ones in the future; and thus in passing from the small to the large, from the average to the fantastic, we can adorn ourselves to attract the attention of women."[38] This projection onto fashion of cyclical, regularly occurring transformations from the simple to the overly elaborate served as an important explanatory device for why fashions change, and reassured readers that *la mode* was really more tame than it might initially seem; protean, enigmatic *la mode* was, in fact, governed by regular, cyclical patterns. Linking changing hat styles to the "progress of the human race" – a kind of pre-Darwinian concept of natural selection through fashion – further naturalized and rationalized fashion; at the same time the press may have fostered the idea that change itself – even revolutionary change – might lead to the perfection of the human race.

The *Magasin des modes nouvelles* also frequently invoked another "law" governing fashion that initially may seem to contradict the belief that fashions followed cycles. In the issue of October 1, 1786, the journal explained that the linear narrative of politics and events shaped *la mode*:

> La Mode, whom detractors have called flighty, inconstant and frivolous, is, however, fixed in her principles; and we believe, in truth, that it is an injustice to treat her with such harshness. We see her constantly seize upon all remarkable events and appropriate them and consign them to her annals, to make them eternal in human memory. What great events, what feats of our warriors, of our magistrates even, has she not made public?[39]

The events that *la mode* seized upon might be routine political events such as the state visit of the ambassadors of Tippoo-Saïb in 1788, which sparked a fashion for dresses of lime-green taffeta with pink spots called *à la Tippoo-Saïb*, or celebrated trials such as that of Marie-Françoise-Victoire Salmon, which inspired the *caracos à l'Innocence reconnue*.[40] In its description of the long-waisted gowns, *caracos à l'Innocence*, the journal claimed that a thousand years hence, "These *caracos* alone will perpetuate the glory of this girl, of her lawyer and the illustrious group who have exonerated her."[41] (Now that is surely a claim for the power of a girl's dress.) The belief that fashions followed a linear progression shaped by events provided a complementary, rather than contradictory, model to the belief that styles followed cycles; the linear political narrative punctuated the cyclical transformation of styles, and was more frequently responsible for the renaming of a dress or the appearance of a fashion in a new color than for creating a wholly new style.

The connection of fashion to current events is perhaps best seen in the journal's chronicle of the Revolution through the eyes of *la mode*. In September 1789, the journal described a new hat that represented the reunion of the three estates, "There can be no doubt, a revolution like the one in France must offer the capital city the inspiration for several new fashions."[42] In November 1789 the journal described buckles made in the shape of the Bastille.[43] And in December 1789, describing a new "*bonnet à la Bastille*," the journal wrote, "We would certainly have been surprised if the fall of the Bastille had not been celebrated by the Marchandes de Modes, and if it hadn't given them the inspiration for several new bonnets."[44] In citing the crucial link between the creation of new fashions and the rush of current events, the journal suggested that the history of fashions could be read alongside traditional annals of history and that fashions themselves played a part in making history, by "eternally engraving" remarkable events in human memory.[45] The reciprocal relationship between fashion and events is underscored in the journal's report that in 1787, responding to Louis XVI's speech to the Assembly of the Notables in which Louis declared his desire to model himself after Henri IV, "Our ladies have read with tenderness this discourse full of sensibility that a father, more than a king, has addressed to his children; and they have tried to keep this speech fixed in memory with the invention of a new style of bonnet, called *à la Béarnaise*, as they have marked almost all remarkable events."[46] Women's decision to wear a new bonnet, *à la Béarnaise*, thus played a part in "fixing" the event of Louis XVI's speech in public memory and in the narrative of history.[47]

When reporting on the inspiration of fashions by political events, the editor of the *Cabinet des modes*, Jean Antoine Brun, could barely suppress his amusement. While conceding a link between fashion, politics, current events, and historical narrative, the journal nevertheless suggested that the creation of new dress and hat styles to commemorate events was worthy of at least light-hearted ridicule. Writing during the first year of the Revolution of a new hat style which represented the union of the three estates, the journal commented, "The origin of this style promises us a long train of new fashions; most important, if this event is any indication, new fashions will mark each essential point of our constitution as it is established and decreed."[48] Typical of the satire of the period, the journal pointed out the ridiculousness of creating fashions to commemorate current events by taking the practice to an absurd extreme, claiming that the *marchandes de modes* of Paris would soon be making hats to comment on each article of the new constitution.[49]

The ambivalence of the editors as to whether they should extol or condemn the connection between fashion and narratives of politics and historical events (with events not only creating fashions but with fashions actually creating historical memory) reveals a moment of transition in the Western conception of the relationship between the history of fashion and the "broader" narratives of history. By the twentieth century the theorist of the sociology of fashion A.L. Kroeber would conclude that there is *no* connection between changes in the contour and silhouette of women's dress styles and historical narrative, and that women's dress independently follows half-century cycles of transformation.[50] For the editor of the Revolutionary fashion press, however, the memory of the politically-charged world of court dress was still a living memory; and in the streets of Paris people could see new Revolutionary identities take shape not only in official badges, tricolor cockades and militant caps of liberty, but in the hats and dresses or ordinary housewives as they tried to find a compromise between private fashion and public virtue.[51]

If the journal found politically inspired fashions slightly ridiculous, it hailed another source of inspiration for women's fashions, events in the world of drama and music.[52] In June 1787 an engraving portrayed a model in a theatrical pose, explaining "Many women desire to act in comedies among their social circle, and for comedies one always chooses dresses that are *à la mode*, because comedies should always express our contemporary manners."[53] Operas, comedies, and celebrated actresses were frequently cited as inspirations for fashions, with fashions seemingly providing a barometer of the public's opinion of the current dramatic and musical offerings in Paris. In April 1787, the journal described the popularity of *poufs* "à la Grande-Prêtresse," inspired by the characters of the Grandes-Prêtresses in Gluck's opera *Iphigénie*. In August 1787 the journal predicted that it would be surprising if the wildly popular opera *Tarare* did not inspire a new fashion.[54] And throughout the journal, Mademoiselle Contat, a popular actress at the Comédie-Française, most famous for her performance in Beaumarchais's controversial and sensationally popular *Marriage of Figaro* (first performed on April 27, 1784), was credited with inspiring hair and hat styles, such as bonnets *à la Bayard*, *à la Suzanne*, and *à la Figaro*.[55]

In its attempt to explain the popularity of Mlle Contat's bonnets the journal suggested at least one reason why women desired to copy the fashions of actresses: "Most of our ladies who have adopted these hairstyles have convinced themselves that they will make conquests as striking [as Mlle Contat's characters had made on stage and Mlle Contat had made off stage], or at the least will have the same seductive aura as Mademoiselle Contat." The journal suggested that fashions adopted from stage costumes took part in the private realm of "conquests," speaking the language of seduction and romance rather than voicing public concerns about the constitution, celebrated trials, and remarkable events such as the storming of the Bastille. The journal emphasized that these theatrically-inspired fashions were intended to participate in a private rather than a public realm by warning readers to use the utmost discretion when emulating the fashions of actresses: "One must have the most modest, decent, naïve, soft, and circumspect tone: the least bit of freedom, the slightest affectation, will give one the look of a prostitute."[56]

While women were cautioned to use discretion in translating an actress's fashions from stage to street, the journal nevertheless presented actresses as arbiters of fashion and possessors of "an exquisite taste."[57] A fashion merchant had only to advertise in the *Cabinet des modes* that she numbered actresses among her clients to assure a steady stream of customers. Mlle Roussaud, a *marchandes de modes* with a boutique near the Comédie-Française, proudly advertised that the Comédie employed her talents in creating new bonnets. In addition, the journal stated that Mlle Roussaud "is the merchant for many actresses, who as actresses, are practically forced to invent the most elegant fashions; she has the advantage of combining her taste with that of actresses."[58]

While the journal accepted women's pursuit of their favorite operatic heroines' fashions, if followed with discretion, the editor objected to the manner in which these fashions were named. In August 1787, the journal complained that women were wearing *chapeaux à la Tarare* and *bonnets à la Figaro* after the male characters in operas when they should name their hats *à la Astasie* and their bonnets *à la Suzanne* in honor of the female characters who had inspired them:

> A complaint that we must make here to the authors of new fashions is that they never name the new fashion after the person who wears it in the theatrical performance. . . .. For example, in *"Tarare"* the divine Astasie should have lent her name to the hat, because she is the heroine . . . . But, completely to the contrary, the male hero of the production lends his name to the fashion . . . . Do men and heroes ever appear on the stage in women's bonnets or hats? This absurdity always makes us indignant.[59]

The editor's complaint that heroines' fashions had been usurped by male names evinces the general tone of the journal regarding women and fashion, on the one hand sympathizing with women while on the other gently chiding them. Although the journal was edited by a man, Louis Edme Billardon de Sauvigny, his name never appeared on its masthead and like many journals devoted to a female audience, the *Magasin des modes nouvelles* maintained the fiction that it was written by a woman. One way of doing this was to appear to take women's side, championing their right to have their hats named after heroines rather than heroes or male playwrights. But the sympathetic but fictitious female editor could not totally mask the influence of the masculine cultural biases in which journals such as the *Magasin des modes nouvelles* took part; while the editor might lend a sympathetic ear to his readers, he made it conditional on their acceptance that their concerns were trivial and that they should not be too shrill in their indignation.

Although the passage on hats *à la Tarare* may have been primarily intended to establish a sympathetic bond between the editor and his female audience, the statement additionally reveals (1) the notion that fashions should be clearly sexed, even in their names (2) a belief that there were, or should be, "rules" for fashion, including general guidelines for how fashions are named, and (3) a desire to acknowledge women's role (in this case actresses') as the creators of fashion and thereby to emphasize the feminine nature of fashion. The issue of naming fashions was one that the editors took especially seriously; giving a new name to an old style was considered tantamount to creating a new fashion. In May 1788 the *Magasin des R.-J. Pothier modes* commented that the new *chapeaux au bateau renversé*, "is only scarcely a new name, and not a new style."[60] The provincial subscriber to the journal did not want to know only what the women of Paris were wearing, but also what these fashions were called: the fashion culture was clearly verbal as well as visual, and the descriptions of the fashions in the journal were as important as the fashion engravings. In August 1788, reporting on the new *robe à la Tippoo-Saïb*, which hardly differed from dresses *à l'angloise* and *à la françoise*, the journal explained, "We must report on names as well as other aspects of the fashion because we must instruct our subscribers in what to call their fashions to demonstrate that they are wearing the newest look."[61] To use twentieth-century parlance, the signifier was as important as the signified, in a culture in which the name made it new and the chatter and banter that accompanied new fashions helped call them into being.

Moreover, even if the actual cut, shape, and style of the dresses, hats, and accessories being worn in Paris had not changed since the previous issue, the journal's discussion of new names supported the vision of a perpetually innovating Parisian fashion culture. In addition, the journal insisted that the slightest new detail might create a new fashion. In May 1786, the *Cabinet des modes* explained, "Appreciators of fashion know that the slightest detail suffices to vary the fashion."[62] Although most of these "small details" concern new types of ribbons and plumes on women's hats, examples were also cited of new men's fashions that were created by the slightest of variations: "Certainly there isn't much difference in men's dress between buttoning the three top buttons and buttoning the three bottom; but the style of the buttoning alone indicates to us the fashion." The journal concluded, "It's a triviality, but a noticeable one."[63]

While the journal acknowledged that there were often no dramatically new fashions to report, it perpetuated the notion that the creativity of the fashionable women of Paris remained fecund and abundant and constantly praised the "riens" that the women of Paris had created. In December 1788 the journal proclaimed, "The whole world knows that the invention of new bonnets and hats by our ladies will never stop . . . . They don't create new fashions all the time, but by varying the bonnets they have already created, they give a look of newness to the old."[64] The changeable, inconstant nature of fashion, which had once seemed terrifying, was presented in the pages of the fashion press as a positive trait: changes in fashion became signs of *la mode*'s fecundity rather than of her inconstancy. The portrayal of a fertile fashion carried with it all of the culture's positive associations of femininity and maternity. This new image of a fertile *mode* (which coexisted in the discourse on fashion with the still powerful image of *la mode* as a fickle goddess) depicted fashion as a benign, maternal force that nurtured commerce. According to this new image, fashion's occasional periods of barrenness, rather than her usual fecundity, were the times society should dread.

The language of procreation – of sterility and fecundity – infused the pages of the journal. When describing an engraving of a new way of arranging ribbons on a hat, the journal commented, "Will this difference be a means of varying, that is to say, will it entirely change the form of our hats; and in creating something new, will it fertilize our journal and make the sterility these items of clothing have been sacrificed to for the past month disappear?"[65] In June 1788, the journal discussed the sterility of fashion in a passage which is worth quoting, not only for its use of the language of procreation, but also for the journal's attempt to explain the relationship between fashion and current events:

> Why is fashion so fertile at some times but so sterile in others? All our subscribers have posed this question since they received our latest issues. Why is fashion so tasteful in one time, while in others is only grotesque and bizarre? This isn't just due to the fickle, inconstant, whimsical, and indecisive nature of fashion. Nor is it because its spirit, used up by its new inventions, cannot produce anything new . . . Isn't her relative sterility and absence of taste a product of the times themselves, which by not creating any remarkable events which one can appropriate, fail to animate fashion's genius, and do not suggest to her new ideas?[66]

The journal's equation of fashionability and fertility suggests a way of understanding why certain periods are fecund in new fashions and others sterile: fashions are inspired by notable events, whether political, such as the fall of the Bastille, or cultural, such as the debut of a new opera. The journal also presented an alternate or complementary model for how and why fashions change, attributing the creation of new fashions to specific individuals, the *marchandes de modes*. Although fashion merchants were inspired by events in choosing the names for their fashions, the principal inspiration for the shape and contour of the garment or accessory occurred in that mysterious place of imagination and frivolity, the mind of the *marchande*. In December 1789, the *Magasin des modes* described in detail the creative process of the *marchandes de modes*: "We know that a *Marchande de Modes* usually takes gauze, or satin, or taffeta, first playing around with every form, trying everything, until she finds the one which is pleasing, and then this style becomes à la mode."[67]

Placing responsibility for the genesis of new fashions in the hands of the *marchandes de modes* was a sound editorial strategy for a journal that catered to the interests of the fashion merchants of Paris; by erecting a cult to the creativity of fashion merchants the journal ensured that its readers would recognize their need for these "artists" and flock to the shops advertised in its pages. In addition, the journal's attribution of new fashions to the *marchandes de modes* served partially to detach *la mode* from the narrative of political and cultural events and place it squarely in feminine hands. Although the journal mentioned public events that had inspired new fashions, the editors unambiguously presented the *marchande de modes* as the very personification of fashion and her boutique as the matrix of *la mode*. This diminished the importance of current events in shaping new styles and affirmed the agency of the feminine caprice (and taste) of the merchant. By the early 1790s, the journal would write, "No longer do events give birth to new fashions; taste alone, or caprice, invents them; and inconstancy successively annihilates them."[68]

Throughout the fashion press the caprice of the *marchandes de modes* was celebrated rather than feared, and the inconstancy of *la mode* presented as benign rather than terrifying. Over time, the journal no longer made sense of *la mode*'s inconstancy and caprice by linking fashion to the narratives generated by court, politics and history, although it did continue occasionally to rely on this framework of explanation. The inconstancy of *la mode* could be even more effectively demystified by linking it to women and taste: what had seemed to be the inexplicable inconstancy of fashion was revealed in the pages of the journal to be merely the caprice of women and a product of women's and, more specifically, the *marchandes de modes'*, taste. Although the grounding of *la mode* in the social group of the *marchandes de modes* and in the commercial setting of their boutiques offered an important means of making sense of fashion and solving the puzzle of who creates *la mode*, at the same time it permitted the fashion press to play the double game of remasking *la mode* by creating a new mystique of feminine taste and caprice. The journal walked a fine line between instructing its readers how fashion worked, and continuing to claim that at heart *la mode* remained an elusive enigma. Fashion was presented both as something that could be purchased in fashion merchants' shops and as an elusive quality shaped by a woman's taste and caprice.

Although the journal's avowed purpose was to portray and describe commodities, its text implicitly suggested that fashion could not be purchased or attained, but was an innate, inalienable quality which the French possessed in greater quantity than other nations, which women possessed more of than did men, and which some women possessed more of than other women. That is to say, at the same time that the journal made clear certain aspects of the connection between *la mode* and the market by explicitly placing the creation of fashion in the hands of a particular group of producers and merchants, it seemed to suggest that at the heart of fashion was an immaterial, un-commodifiable quality, taste.

Part of the journal's "double game" consisted of encouraging its readers to believe that they might possess as much taste in matters of fashion as the renowned fashion merchants of Paris. For every instance in which the journal explicitly stated that fashions were created by the *marchandes de modes*, another counter example attributed the creation of new fashions to a consumer, characterized by the journal as "benevolent author" of *la mode*.[69] In November 1787, when the journal described a new type of blouse, instead of admitting that it simply did not know who had created the new fashion, it suggested coyly that any number of fashionable ladies might have done so:

> It would be too difficult to assign credit for the new fashion for chemises presented in the first plate; we exempt ourselves from any obligation to tell. But certainly a woman of great taste was responsible. Who is she? We don't know. If we took it upon ourselves to make known all the people who have produced and make new fashions each day, we would have to know the names, morals, and manners of all the people in Paris who might have taste; without a doubt no one has the right to demand that of us.[70]

This device of speculating about, but never identifying, the anonymous authors of fashions was used frequently in the journal. It served, in part, to underline the mystery of the process of the creation of fashion, and in part to flatter the journal's readers by suggesting that their "exquisite taste" might one day inspire them to create a new vogue. In the following passage, which accompanied an engraving of a woman dressed *à la Samaritaine*, the reader was allowed a titillating glimpse of the act of creation of a new fashion, and offered the vicarious pleasure of observing a woman of taste designing a new fashion:

> We do not yet know who deserves credit for creating this new style. If the fashion lasts for a long time, and we find out the name of its creator, we shall let you know. Perhaps one invented this fashion because this beautiful season allows a full and spreading skirt and the winds permit, in ceasing to blow, a long veil to float from one's head; maybe the style was invented to mark the change from winter to spring, and to make a kind of allegory; perhaps one was inspired by a theatrical character; or maybe it was only inspired by pure caprice.[71]

No matter who was assigned responsibility for creating fashions, taste rather than expensive fabrics and luxurious accessories was praised as the only solid foundation for dressing *à la mode*. The journal continually advised its readers to "Be pretty, be beautiful; this is a great advantage; but no less important is to exercise one's taste." A woman's taste could permit her to camouflage her defects by embellishing her natural traits; taste consisted "particularly in the choice and assortment of colors, from which comes a pleasant harmony, that diffuses over the whole person."[72] In January 1787, in a passage describing the latest ball gowns, the journal counseled its readers that taste rather than luxury was the key to being well attired: "It is not richness that sets apart these dresses; they do not owe their price to an immense volume of cloth. No, it is taste, the perfect nuance, the shrewd mixing of colors which alone raises their value."[73]

The journal's insistence that taste, rather than the luxurious fabrics and jewels which only those of great wealth could buy, was the most important quality for dressing fashionably served to broaden the potential market for Parisian fashion. The fashionable woman could, "with the simplest cloth, the lightest gauze, make adornments whose value is never in proportion to the price of the materials she uses."[74] Moreover, the journal suggested that wearing the latest fashion in clothing was not of primary importance for enabling a woman to appear fashionable; what was important was that she clothe herself with taste and natural grace:

> Fashions are, then, less the fruits of satiety and of disgust, as the poets say, than they are the children of natural grace. Everyone wants to acquire the radiance with which people of taste shine; everyone believes that it is their clothing that lends them this glow; and everyone then adopts their dress style. But if one does not know how to deport oneself agreeably, the dress, scarcely put on one's body, no longer seduces.[75]

The journal never suggested that elite men and women possessed a monopoly on taste; it organized the economy of taste around sex and nationality, with French women possessing the most refined taste. Thus, the connection made in the late eighteenth century between fashion and taste threatened potentially to sever the link between fashion and rank and wealth: as presented in the pages of the fashion press, any woman, whether aristocrat or shop girl, who possessed a modicum of taste, could accentuate her natural graces and participate in the culture of fashion. Writing during the Revolution, the editor of the *Journal de la mode et du goût* explained that since the practice of decorating one's clothing with precious metals had fallen out of vogue along with the aristocracy, taste rather than ostentation "will be from now on the sole means of distinguishing oneself."[76]

Along with the shift in the late eighteenth century toward the conception that taste rather than hierarchies of rank and privilege provided the foundation for fashion, there was a concomitant shift in the types of concerns about fashion. In the seventeenth century, the *Mercure* participated in a fashion culture that was based on the notion that fashions should express and represent one's social position; thus, for the *Mercure* the most troubling aspect of fashion was its potential to blur class distinctions. But the *Cabinet des modes* rarely mentioned class; instead, its principal worries concerned the appearance in the streets of Paris of clothing of bizarre or bad taste and the scarcity of new fashions. These new worries reveal the extent of the transformation of conceptions of *la mode* in the century between the first coverage of fashion in the *Mercure* and the emergence of a press exclusively devoted to fashion in the late eighteenth century. The late-eighteenth-century fashion press came to the conclusion that taste and the unending passion for variety were the twin pillars that determined the shape of fashion. Ideally, the desire for tasteful fashions and the desire for novelty would complement one another. But the eighteenth-century fashion press acknowledged that the desire for variety often corrupted people's taste and that women too often chose to wear new garments even though they were not tasteful, beautiful, or flattering. In 1789, the *Magasin des modes nouvelles* apologized for presenting a fashion plate of unattractive hat styles: "Certainly the hats that we presented last year were more beautiful than those in this issue: but one must say, they are history. And if these new ones are preferable even though they are uglier, it is because they are newer; it is because they are in fashion."[77]

By the late eighteenth century, what had once been considered the negative potential of the inconstancy of *la mode* and the rage for novelty had been transformed into a treasured resource for the French nation. The *Cabinet des modes* declared boldly, "This rapid variety produces for commerce an advantage that softens all reproaches."[78] An important part of the fashion press's sanctioning of the inconstancy of fashion was the presentation of anecdotes culled from the history of fashion; by insisting that fashions had a history, the journal reminded its readers that fashions had always changed and that change and variety were natural parts of human society. In April 1786, the *Cabinet des modes* explained (perhaps also underscoring that fashion was not incompatible with classical republicanism), "Women's hairstyles have been in all times subject to many revolutions, even in ancient Greek and Roman times. Fashions changed for them, as they do for us."[79]

The fashion press's valorization of the inconstancy of *la mode* was perhaps most marked in the issues published during the first years of the Revolution. The editors of the *Magasin des modes nouvelles* and the *Journal de la mode* suggested that *la mode* and the Revolution were even more profoundly linked than the appearance of *bonnets à la Bastille* would suggest. The change and turmoil of the Revolution were associated by the editors of the journal with *la mode* itself; the journal suggested that *la mode* and women, both of whom were assumed to be in a state of continual flux, had found their ideal environment in the upheaval of the Revolution. The journal explained, "The colors, the form of clothing, bonnets, and

Figure 19 "Robe à l'Egalité," *Journal de la mode et du goût*, 1792, courtesy of the Bibliothèque nationale.

hats change with an inconceivable rapidity; all follow the revolution and feel the effects of the general disturbance; however, the upheaval in which we live, far from harming *le beau sexe*, renders her even more loveable."[80] From its inception the fashion press had tried to harness *la mode* by discerning its laws and understanding how it worked. The preceding passage reveals the ultimate stage in the fashion press's attempt to "tame" *la mode*; even when associated with the tumultuous events of the Revolution, *la mode* was not harmful, but merely churned out fashions for new ribbons and hats more rapidly. As presented in the fashion press, fashion and novelty were not to be feared but to be applauded for making women "plus jolie," and perhaps more modern as well.

The fashion press's avowed purpose was to reveal the glory of French taste and French fashion to the people of Europe, to celebrate, "Paris, this modern Athens . . . the center where all talents, all arts, and all tastes come to perfect themselves and flower . . . and where this *je ne sais quoi* inspires all products with a cachet that the provinces and foreigners can never imitate."[81] In addition to this avowed purpose, the fashion press operated according to the underlying premise that understanding the nature of *la mode* and how fashion operated would allay the French people's fear of this "fickle goddess," and encourage them to accept a prominent role for fashion in their culture. In this, the fashion press took part in the general Enlightenment desire to "unmask" in the belief that knowledge would lead to progress. (The progress the editors of the fashion press hoped for was the material and economic progress of expanding markets and increased consumption.) Paradoxically, the editors of the fashion press wanted their readers to understand that while fashion operated according to some guidelines, it must always remain to some extent a mystery, one that could never be neatly dissected in weighty tomes such as the *Encylopédie* or transparently displayed in a constitution. As the editor of the *Cabinet des modes* wrote in September 1786, "What an error to subject la Mode and her agents to fixed rules, to make them walk with reason! Caprice, delirium, even madness itself . . . those are their laws."[82]

In the seventeenth and early eighteenth centuries, poets who composed verse on *la mode* and satirists of court fashions may have sincerely believed that *la mode* was an enigma; by the late eighteenth century, although the editors of the fashion press could sketch the most important contours of *la mode* and had staked their claim that they understood why fashions piqued the consumer's appetite, they continued to insist that *la mode* was an enigmatic creature of caprice, delirium and folly. The enigmatic nature of fashion had become a useful fiction. By insisting on the mystery of fashion, the fashion press may not have tamed *la mode*, but it did tame the women who consumed fashions by yoking them to a marginal world of the ephemeral, the frivolous and the feminine. Amid the colorful engravings, poems dedicated to "les nouveautés," and "anecdotes plaisantes," the readers of the fashion press may not have noticed that they, rather than *la mode*, were being harnessed by the fashion press to the interests of French commerce and the emerging ideology of femininity and womanhood. By the late 1780s, the empire of fashion was no longer depicted as a despotism, and *la mode* was no longer portrayed as a corrupt, tyrannical queen to dethrone. Now *la mode* had been transformed into a being so gentle, so sweet, and so "naturally" feminine that women would gladly submit to her caprices. And if a woman occasionally dissented from the proclamations of *la mode*, the *Cabinet des modes* reminded its readers that *la mode* was too benevolent to compel anyone to abide by her decrees: "If there are a few rebels who do not wish to submit (because there are some in many empires), and who, by their contrariness, would prefer to renounce all hairstyles and set aside all plumes, . . . my empire is sweet and simple, and I only want to command willing subjects."[83]

Fashion and Domesticity

Considering the liveliness of the debate on luxury, gender, and fashion throughout the *ancien régime* it is perhaps surprising that editors of the late-eighteenth-century fashion press so effectively silenced the debate in the pages of their journal. The *Cabinet de modes* was certainly not alone in its reluctance to condemn women for their interest in fashion. By the late eighteenth century and early nineteenth century tracts and pamphlets decrying the "problem of luxury" participated in a strikingly different discourse than did their early-eighteenth-century counterparts. This formerly serious debate had been transformed into frivolous, bantering literature alternately deploring or upholding women's right to adorn themselves and their homes lavishly. Luxury was now often a term of approval, invoked as an advertising ploy for merchants who proudly began to label their products "de luxe." Historian Ellen Ross contends that the Revolution extinguished the debate on luxury in two ways: first, the Revolution brought to people's attention that problems such as luxury, which had seemed mysterious and rooted in human nature – products of vanity, debauchery, or the passion for novelty – had comprehensible political causes and solutions; second, during the *ancien régime* the debate on luxury had served as a primary outlet for criticizing the regime, but with the Revolution, men and women elected to use overt political means of opposition and no longer had to rely on the genre of the luxury debate.[84]

I would like to suggest an additional reason for the decline of the debate on luxury. The issues of women's nature and women's place had stood at the core of much of the debate on luxury in the *ancien régime*. By the late eighteenth century many of the problems which women's luxury had been accused of causing in society had been "solved" through the ascendancy of a new conception of women, fashion and taste which naturalized women's interest in clothing: the frenzy for fashions was no longer considered a sinful state, harmful to the general health of society and the maintenance of social hierarchies, but rather a natural aspect of femininity, necessary for marital harmony and domestic bliss. The Revolution may have shut women out of the world of electoral politics and representative government, but it reaffirmed their role in the public sphere as consumers. As the editor of the *Journal de la mode et du goût* wrote in April 1791,

> Among people of quality, it is women who have lost the most with the revolution: removed, by their sex, from all employments; no more names, no more imposing titles, and no longer sharing with their husbands the honors of the positions they occupy, are they going to devote themselves to the simple practice of domestic virtues? . . . There only remains for those who wish to participate readily, and to strike the eyes with a lively flash, the singularity, the richness and the elegance of costume.[85]

For the past decade, the dominant paradigm in French women's history has focused on the exclusion of women from active citizenship during the Revolution, placing the blame either on historical contingency or the exigencies of republican ideology. Many women's historians have lamented the eclipse of "twilight of the goddesses" – the power of aristocratic women in salon and court society during the *ancien régime* – by the darkness of revolutionary republican misogyny. Yet recently, historians have begun to revise their interpretations, drawing a more nuanced line between old regime privileges and new regime possibilities. Dena Goodman has suggested that the cultural turn against the dominant role of *ancien régime salonières* predated the Revolution by a decade. Joan Landes's book on gender, representation and the nation suggests that images of erotic and beautiful women played a positive role in helping budding republicans visualize and ally themselves with *La Patrie*. Paul Friedland's work on revolutionary political culture suggests that the theatricality women were so often accused of was not just a feminized atavistic throwback to the Old Regime, but a central part of men's politics in the new regime as well. And Carla Hesse's portrayal of the moral autonomy of eighteenth-century female writers calls into question more pessimistic assessments of the impact of the Enlightenment and Revolution on female of subjectivity and agency. This is an opportune moment to inquire, in what ways did fashion make women modern?[86]

Margaret Darrow has argued that part of the appeal of the new revolutionary model of femininity lay in its avoidance of any association of domesticity with traditional forms of self-denial and stodginess. The late-eighteenth-century wife was encouraged to believe that she could breastfeed her children and devote herself to house and husband while remaining an accomplished, alluring, and fashionable woman. Darrow points out that according to the French model of domesticity the wife was never merely a *femme ménagère* (housewife) but rather the more powerful *maîtresse de la maison* (mistress of the house).[87] These views are echoed in the fashion press and help provide a nuanced explanation of why domesticity and revolution would not have felt like deprivation to many middle- and upper-class women; in the midst of revolution, fashion editors reminded their female audience, theatricality and singularity of fashion would permit women to participate in the broader society and culture outside the home.

The distance that at least some members of French society had traveled by the late eighteenth century from the fear that women's clothing and consumption were socially threatening and morally scandalous is perhaps nowhere more strikingly summed up than in the writings of the social reformer Charles Antoine-Joseph Leclerc de Montlinot, who in 1781 boldly asserted that even working-class women's consumption of *les modes* might benefit society:

This appears strange at first glance, but nonetheless we are persuaded that if one could train all the women of the workhouse to the point of desiring gloves, these women would be regenerated for society, hard-working, and worthy of being mothers . . . . In short, one may say in conclusion that cleanliness gives rise to demands, demands to work, work to thought, thought to the desire for those enjoyments that sustain and augment emulation in all the classes of society.[88]

Certainly the economic collapse of the luxury trades during the Revolution took a devastating toll on the lives of the men and women who worked in the clothing trades. Yet, the seamstresses, linen drapers, tailors, and fashion merchants of Paris, and all those who believed that France's prosperity depended on a thriving trade in luxury goods, must have breathed a sigh of relief upon learning that women's consumption of clothing was no longer considered a threat to husbands and to society at large. The fashion press especially, which had so eagerly championed women's right to consume, celebrated the new harmony of interests between women, their families, and their clothing merchants. As the *Journal de la mode et du goût* wrote in the early years of the Revolution, "If the barbarous practice of covering garments with metal has disappeared, taste has not [disappeared] in France, and it is going to take on a new vigor because it will be from now on the sole means of distinguishing oneself."[89]

National prestige and increasing economic exports stood just as surely at the heart of concerns about women's desire for novelties and fashions in the late eighteenth century as they had at the height of Louis XIV's absolutist state. Yet, the replacement of kings and priests with fashion editors as the legislators of women's fashion may mark the distance between these two cultures of consumption. If the women at Louis's court had struggled to reconcile their taste for new fashions like mantuas with the imperative of costume based on rank, in the dawning world of modern consumption, women would strain to reconcile their taste for fashions with a more nuanced, but no less imperious demand – their sensibility and innate femininity as women. If costume had once starkly marked the aristocrat, clothing was now charged with seamlessly revealing the woman. And it was clear to the editors of the fashion press, who reported with delight that since the abolition of titles and estates in France in 1789, "fashions change even more quickly," or that revealing the inner woman would require even more dresses and styles than clothing the outer aristocrat, even at the height of Louis XIV's reign, ever had.[90]

Conclusion

The clothing of women must have a sex; and this costume must contrast with ours. A woman must be a woman from her toes to her head; the more a woman resembles a man the more she will lose soon enough.

Louis-Sébastien Mercier, *Tableau de Paris*.

Since the invention of fashion in the mid fourteenth century, social critics had worried over the effeminacy of men's fashions. In the early seventeenth century, Jean Polman lashed out at men's flowing hair and long moustaches, asking, "Who would believe that this man is a Christian who is frizzed, curled, and waffled, and whose moustache hits his shoulders; who walks in an affected manner and has an effeminate carriage, and a lewd and wild look?"[91] In the late eighteenth century, although religious critiques such as Polman's were rarely voiced, fops, *petits maîtres*, and *muscadins* were still routinely held up to ridicule.

Although criticism of effeminacy in men's fashions persisted, what is more striking in the late-eighteenth-century discourse on clothing is the number of condemnations of women borrowing from men's clothing styles, of their adoption of men's hats, boots, riding coats and crops, canes, and military-inspired jackets. The Parisian bookseller Antoine-Prosper Lottin charged, "the sex whose timidity and modesty previously created the most beautiful dress today arms its proud eye with a fiery and audacious military air; and her haughty and arrogant head with a ridiculous hat. Oh the charm of novelty: Oh the furor to shine and stand out . . . !"[92] Lottin was, to be sure, a harsh critic of Parisian women's clothing, objecting not only to women's adoption of male styles but, in general, to all pursuits of *la mode*. But even those contemporaries with a more sympathetic eye for women and their fashions were wary of women's appropriation of men's styles. The *Cabinet des modes* was quick to append to its description of a new style of women's riding coat the caveat, "they seem only to adopt such clothing or such manners as men reject them."[93] And the author of the *Manuel des toilettes dédié aux dames* cautioned, "the *cocarde* and the *panache* announce your martial disposition, but at the same time, cascades of gauze and of ribbons mixed with this war-like apparel, remind us that you previously wore pompons. Because in drawing nearer to men, it is necessary not to resemble them completely; you would lose too much in that, my ladies."[94] Louis-Sébastien Mercier's contention that women's clothing must have a sex voiced a commonplace of late-eighteenth-century thought on women and fashion. The author of the *Toilette de dames, ou encyclopédie de la beauté* concurred, "it is necessary that the apparel of women be completely different from that of men, either for hairstyle, shoes, or clothing. This difference should even extend to the choice of fabrics, and a woman dressed in woolen cloth is less a woman than when she is dressed in a transparent gauze, a light mousseline, or a soft and brilliant silk."[95] The desire to fix distinctions between male and female fashions was ultimately registered in a police ordinance of November 7, 1800 that forbade Parisian women to wear trousers without special dispensation.[96]

The ready answer as to why so many eighteenth-century men and women believed in the necessity of difference in men's and women's clothing is that they had adopted a new way of thinking about the sexes that stressed men's and women's difference and complementarity.[97] In the seventeenth century most observers differentiated men from women hierarchically within a one-sex model in which masculinity was the norm, and would have been more concerned by the effeminacy of men's fashions than by the mannishness of women's fashions. But with the acceptance of the two-sex model of difference in the eighteenth century, sartorial transgressions of sexual boundaries became problematic for women as well as for men.

But explanations that rest on the shift from a one-sex to a two-sex model of sexual difference leave unanswered why, of the many ways in which men and women could be differentiated, sartorial differentiation became especially important – and problematic – in this period. Moreover, one is left wondering why this new model of masculinity and femininity was so readily accepted. As I have argued throughout this book, the fashion culture of Paris offers as many riches to historians seeking to understand this transformation to a new model of femininity as it did to contemporaries seeking the latest clothing and accessories. The belief that women's clothing should be fundamentally different from men's was predicated on the belief that women's relationship to Parisian commercial culture – to fashion, consumption, and luxury – was (or should be) fundamentally different from men's. Put another way, even the harshest critics of women's donning of men's styles did not fear that clothing alone would make women "mannish." (A few commentators even admitted that women's pursuit of men's fashions was actually a sign of their femininity since it was in keeping with women's nature to fall under the sway of "the charm of novelty.") Critics' reasons for disapproving of women wearing riding coats and sporting hats were simple and straightforward: these fashions made women visually less appealing to men. Men's pursuit of "effeminate" fashions, on the other hand, was much more threatening to society; for not only did the wearing of these fashions make them look like women, but their very interest in *la mode* made them act like women.

A compromise, however uneasy, was struck in the late eighteenth century between those who believed that luxuries, frivolities, and fashions were beneficial and necessary for French commerce and the French nation and those who believed that the despotism of *la mode* was the bane of humankind: women's desire for fashions was deemed natural, praiseworthy, and even modern, while men's interest in fashions and frivolities was branded foppish, effeminate and decadent. As the editor of the *Magasin de modes* explained in 1787 when commenting on women's latest craze for wearing men's coats, "This evil is much less than that which men were guilty of in previous times in trying to imitate women in their clothing and for a few, in their effeminacy and softness."[98] For many commentators the seemingly "natural" world of sex and gender difference provided a refuge and a strong foothold in the midst of the tumultuous commercial world around them in which traditional hierarchy and the privileges of class and rank were being rapidly transformed.

But what is perhaps more intriguing are the creative ways in which some members of the commercial bourgeoisie used the new model of femininity and the natural complementarity of the sexes deliberately (if not always consciously) to obscure issues of class. For those journalists and merchants who stood to gain most by the expansion of Paris's commercial culture and the growth of the French fashion industry, arguing for the femininity of fashions and suggesting that class not govern how one ought to dress worked to broaden their potential market to include all women. Far from a conservative desire to restore the mores and manners of a bygone day, the men and women who supported this new model which linked femininity, frivolity, and fashion wished to extend France's economy and commercial presence across Europe.

What is perhaps most striking about this new model of the femininity of fashion is its resemblance to a related cluster of commonplaces regarding the Frenchness of fashion. The editors of the fashion press continually contrasted the diffident attitude of the English to clothing and fashion with that of the French arguing, "It is easy to see that variety in fashion is not a characteristic of English men or English women."[99] The author of the *Apologie de la frivolité, lettre à un Anglois* excused the French for their frivolous interest in fashion much as he had excused women for their pursuit of *la mode*, declaring its usefulness for stimulating commerce:

> You claim then, Monsieur, to make a legal case against our nation for its spirit of frivolity; I agree strongly with you that the French genius is more developed towards the agreeable genre than toward great sublime speculations . . . . This taste generally diffused here for works of agreement that you find so futile, is one of the most real advantages that we have over the other peoples of Europe.[100]

This new case for the Frenchness of fashion followed the same lines which had been used to explain and justify women's innate interest in fashions – a peculiar taste for novelty and sense of sight – to argue for both French men's and women's innate disposition to produce and consume fashions. Complementing Mercier's statement that clothing must have a sex, many Parisian merchants worked hard to sell the idea that, when it came to clothing, fashion's nationality was surely French.

Notes

1. The standard introduction to the early-modern French press is Louis Trenard, "La presse française des origines à 1788," in Bellanger et al., *Histoire générale*

de la presse française, 1: 27–376. For works focusing on the Enlightenment and Revolution, see Jack Censer, *The French Press in the Age of Enlightenment* (Cambridge: Cambridge University Press, 1994), Jack Censer and Jeremy Popkin (eds.), *Press and Politics in Prerevolutionary France* (Berkeley: University of California Press, 1987), Harvey Chisick (ed.), *The Press in the French Revolution* (Oxford: The Voltaire Foundation, 1991), and Jeremy Popkin, *Revolutionary News: The Press in France, 1789–1799* (Durham, NC: Duke University Press, 1990). For introductions to the feminine press, see Evelyne Sullerot, *Histoire de la presse féminine des origines à 1848* (Paris: Armand Colin, 1966); "Politique et toilette: Voilà les principales sources de la femme tels qu'ils se dégagent de l'histoire de la presse féminine," *Presse publicité: Hebdamodaire technique de toute la presse* 19 (September 12, 1937): 16–18; Suzanne Van Dijk "Femmes et journaux au xviiie siècle," *Australian Journal of French Studies* 18, no. 2 (1981): 164–78; Sophie Levu, "Le Journal de la mode et du goût, étude d'un journal de mode pendant la révolution" (Maîtrise, Paris I, 1983), and Rimbault, "La presse féminine." Nina Rattner Gelbart's *Feminine and Opposition Journalism in Old Regime France* focuses on one of the most enduring and controversial female journals of the Old Regime. Anne Marie Kleinert, *Die fruhen Modejournale in Frankreich* (Berlin: E. Schmidt, 1980) treats the fashion press, and *Le journalisme d'ancien régime*, CNRS round table (June 12–13, 1981) contains numerous articles on the press.

2. The *Journal de Paris*, also called the *Poste du soir*, first appeared January 1, 1777 and was published by Pierre-Antoine de La Place.

3. *Le courrier de la nouveauté* was unable to attain a privilege or permission and is thus only known to us by its prospectus. The prospectus and two issues, April 1768 and January 1770, of *Le courrier de la mode* survive. Its editor, Boudier de Villemert, was author of *L'Ami des femmes*.

4. See Gaudriault, *Répertoire de la gravure de mode française*.

5. British women's magazines reported on fashion as early as the late seventeenth century with the publication of *Athenian Gazette* (1690) and *The Ladies' Mercury* (1693). But the first thorough coverage of fashions in England began in 1770 with the *Lady's Magazine*. See Alison Adburgham, *Women in Print: Writing Women and Women's Magazines from the Restoration to the Accession of Victoria* (London: Allen and Unwin, 1972), Erin Mackie, *Market à la Mode: Fashion, Commodity, and Gender in the Tatler and The Spectator* (Baltimore: Johns Hopkins University Press, 1997), and Kathryn Shevelow, *Women and Print Culture: The Construction of Femininity in the Early Periodical* (London: Routledge, 1989). The first German fashion magazine, *Journal des Luxus und der Moden*, began publication in Weimar in 1786.

6. The *Cabinet des modes* was published in Paris with permission, and was dedicated to the Countess de Mark. The yearly subscription price was 21 *livres*,

later increasing to thirty *livres*. Nine volumes of the journal are extant and can be consulted at the Bibliothèque nationale, the Bibliothèque de l'opéra, the Bibliothèque de l'arsenal, and the Bibliothèque Forney. Its founder and editor, Jean Antoine Brun, also known as Lebrun-Tossa, became an ardent supporter of the Revolution and contributed to several revolutionary journals. He died in 1837. See Rimbault, "La presse feminine": 86, 92.

7. Throughout his career Louis Edme Billardon de Sauvigny (1736–1812) was influenced by Rousseau and in his writings called for a return to the virtues of a simpler life. In November 1786 he took over the editorship of the *Magasin des modes*. Under Sauvigny's editorship the journal allied itself with the Revolution. See Rimbault, "La presse féminine": 98, and C.D. Brenner, "A Neglected Pre-Romantic: Billardon de Sauvigny," *The Romantic Review* (February 1938): 48–58.

8. See Levu, "Le journal de la mode et du goût".

9. On the French fashion press during the Directory, see Margaret Waller, "Disembodiment as Masquerade: Fashion Journalists and the other 'Realist' Observers in Directory Paris," *Esprit Créateur* 37, no. 1 (Spring 1997).

10. In the following discussion the *Cabinet des modes*, the *Magasin des modes nouvelles*, and the *Journal de la mode et du goût* will be treated as one journal since despite the changing title there is substantial continuity in their format and perspective on fashion.

11. Although historians have relatively little information on which to base precise descriptions of the subscribers to the fashion press, C. Rimbault's research on the catalogs of sale of the books of noblewomen between 1765 and 1780 indicates that the noblewomen of Paris were more likely to subscribe with their husbands to more costly journals such as the *Journal des savans*, *Le mercure galant*, *Le nouvelliste du Parnasse*, *Les nouvelles de la république des lettres*, *L'année littéraire*, and *L'avant-coureur*, whereas bourgeois and provincial women were more likely to subscribe to the less expensive, exclusively feminine journals such as *Journal des dames* and *Cabinet des modes*. Rimbault, "La presse féminine": 119.

12. The systematization of the fashion season progressed remarkably in the century between the first publication of the *Mercure* and the appearance of the *Cabinet des modes*. Whereas de Visé had fretted over the unpredictability of the fashion season, the late-eighteenth-century fashion season worked like clockwork: "On the seventh of this month, everyone put on their fall clothing." *Magasin des modes nouvelles* (September 30, 1788).

13. *Journal de la mode et du goût* (August 1, 1792): 1–2. The influence of the king on fashion was cited only once, when the journal commented on his buttons. *Magasin des modes nouvelles* (April 10, 1788): 115.

14. The October 1, 1789 issue of the *Magasin des modes nouvelles* included two pages of text from Charles IX's sumptuary law on fashions of 1560. Official states of mourning were reported in the journal with precise descriptions of the clothing that should be worn. But there were also several occasions when the journal suggested that mourning dress at court should be scaled back if not dispensed with altogether.

15. *Magasin des modes nouvelles* (February 10, 1787): 66.

16. Ibid. (April 20, 1788): 124.

17. *Cabinet des modes* (July 1, 1786): 128.

18. *Magasin des modes nouvelles* (February 20, 1787).

19. For a description of the proper attire for church, see *Magasin de modes nouvelles* (February 10, 1788): 66; for mother and child fashions, see *Cabinet des modes* (October 15, 1786): 177 and *Magasin des modes nouvelles* (September 30, 1788): 254.

20. Mercier, *Tableau de Paris*, t. 11: 217.

21. *Journal de la mode* (February 25, 1790): 1.

22. *Cabinet des modes* (November 15, 1785): 5.

23. The remaining 24 per cent of the engravings portrayed items such as children's clothing, men's shoe buckles, buttons, carriages, and household furnishings. For a detailed breakdown of the contents of the engravings in the journal, see Rimbault, "La presse feminine," figure 23, "Réparition des Objets des Gravures du Cabinet des Modes," 294.

24. *Journal de la mode* (February 5, 1792): 2.

25. *Magasin des modes nouvelles* (May 20, 1787): 145.

26. Ibid. (May 20, 1787): 145–46.

27. *Journal de la mode* (November 5, 1790): 1.

28. On the luxury trades during the Revolution, see Colin Jones and Rebecca Sprang, "Sans-culottes, sans café, sans tabac: Shifting Realms of Necessity and Luxury in Eighteenth-Century France," in *Consumers and Luxury: Consumer Culture in Europe, 1650–1850*, ed. Maxine Berg and Helen Clifford (Manchester: Manchester University Press, 1999): 37–62.

29. Ibid. (April 15, 1791): 1–2.

30. Ibid. (April 15, 1791): 3.

31. *Magasin des modes nouvelles* (October 20, 1787): 267.

32. Ibid.

33. Ibid. (July 11, 1789): 179.

34. Ibid. (September 30, 1787): 251.

35. Ibid.

36. Ibid.

37. Ibid. (December 10, 1787): 20.

38. *Manuel des toilettes, dédié aux dames* (Paris, 1778): 14–15.

39. *Cabinet des modes* (October 1, 1786): 170.

40. Tippoo-Saïb, sultan of Maïssour in India, sent ambassadors to France in 1787 to conclude an alliance with the French and to ask Louis XVI's aid in expelling the English from India. On the stir caused by the arrival of these two exotic ambassadors, see Elisabeth Vigée-Lebrun, *Mémoires* (Paris, 1984): 60. The *caracos* "*à l'innocence reconnue*" was also called "*à la Cauchoise*" after Mme Salmon's lawyer. *Cabinet des modes* (October 1, 1786): 170; (August 30, 1788): 228.

41. *Magasin des modes nouvelles* (August 10, 1787): 113; *Cabinet des modes* (October 1, 1786): 170.

42. *Magasin des modes nouvelles* (September 21, 1789): 227.

43. *Magasin des modes nouvelles* (November 11, 1789): 257.

44. Ibid. (December 1, 1789): 267.

45. Another way in which the fashion press hoped to participate in the creation of history was by aiding artists in future generations who might use the journal to reconstruct eighteenth-century costume.

46. *Magasin des modes nouvelles* (April 10, 1787) 113–14.

47. For the classic treatment of memory in French culture, see Pierre Nora, *Les lieux de mémoire*, 7 vols. (Paris: Gallimard, 1984–92). On the construction of French national memory see David A. Bell, *The Cult of the Nation in France: Inventing Nationalism, 1680–1800* (Cambridge: Harvard University Press, 2001), Chapter 4.

48. *Magasin des modes nouvelles* (September 21, 1789): 227. Caroline Rimbault suggests that Lebrun continued to write for the *Magasin des modes nouvelles* along with Billardon de Sauvigny under Sauvigny's editorship. "La press féminine": 281.

49. A.L. Kroeber and Jane Richardson, *Three Centuries of Women's Dress Fashions* (Berkeley: University of California Press, 1940).

50. Alice L. Kroeber, "On the Principle of Order in Civilization as Exemplified by changes of Fashion," *American Anthropologist*, 21 (1919): 235–6.

51. For an important and comprehensive analysis of Revolutionary dress see Richard Wrigley, *The Politics of Appearances: Representations of Dress in Revolutionary France* (Oxford: Berg, 2002.)

52. I found no examples in the *Cabinet des modes* of men's fashions inspired by the theater or opera.

53. *Magasin des modes* (June 20, 1787): 170.

54. Ibid. (August 10, 1787): 209.

55. Ibid. (November 20, 1786): 2–3. Louise Contat (1760–1813) was one of the most popular actresses of the late eighteenth and early nineteenth century. In the preface to the 1785 edition of *Le mariage de Figaro*, Beaumarchais described Suzanne's clothing. See, H. Noel Williams, *Later Queens of the French Stage* (New York, 1906): 226–61 and Emile Gaboriau, *Les Comédi-*

ennes adorées (Paris, 1891). On eighteenth-century French actresses, see Lenard Berlainstein, "Women and Power in Eighteenth-Century France: Actresses at the Comédie-Française," in *Visions and Revisions of Eighteenth-Century France*, ed. Christine Adams, Jack Censer, and Lisa Jane Graham (University Park, PA: Pennsylvania State University Press, 1997): 155–90.

56. *Magasin des modes nouvelles* (November 20, 1786): 3. Those fashion engravings that included a background typically depicted a private scene of romantic rivalry or coquettish flirtation between the sexes. For a description of the settings of its engravings and a statement of purpose for choosing these settings, see *Magasin des modes nouvelles* (December 10, 1787): 17.

57. Even Marie Antoinette, ostensibly France's primary arbiter of fashion, sought inspiration from actresses and the theater. Michael Batterbury recounts, "When *Athalie* was performed at the Théâtre Français, Marie Antoinette adopted the straight, loosely sashed gown *à la Lévite* to cover her pregnancy." Michael Batterbury, *Fashion, the Mirror of History* (London: Greenwich House, 1982): 187.

58. *Cabinet des modes* (July 30, 1787): 206.

59. Ibid. (August 10, 1787): 209.

60. *Magasin des modes* (May 20, 1788): 147.

61. *Cabinet des modes* (August 30, 1788): 228. On the semantic system of fashion in the modern world, see Roland Barthes, *The Fashion System*, trans. Matthew Ward and Richard Howard (New York: Hill and Wang, 1983).

62. Ibid. (May 1, 1786): 89.

63. Ibid.

64. *Magasin des modes nouvelles* (December 11, 1788): 9.

65. Ibid. (August 20, 1788): 220.

66. Ibid. (June 30, 1788): 179.

67. Ibid. (December 11, 1789): 273.

68. *Journal de la modes et du goût* (December 25, 1790): 1.

69. *Magasin des modes nouvelles* (November 10, 1788): 284.

70. Ibid. (November 10, 1787): 283.

71. Ibid. (April 11, 1789): 107.

72. *Journal de la mode et du goût* (June 10, 1792): 2–3.

73. *Magasin des modes nouvelles* (January 30, 1787): 57.

74. *Cabinet des modes* (November 15, 1785): 5.

75. Ibid. (July 1, 1786): 121–2.

76. *Journal de la mode et du goût* (June 25, 1790): 1.

77. *Magasin des modes nouvelles* (February 21, 1789): 65.

78. *Cabinet des modes* (May 1, 1786): 94.

79. Ibid. (April 15, 1786): 81–2.

80. *Journal de la mode et du goût* (September 5, 1790): 1.

81. Preface to new volume, *Magasin des modes nouvelles* (November 1786): 1–2.

82. The *Cabinet des modes* explicitly contrasted its vision of *la mode* to the analysis offered in the *Encyclopédie. Cabinet des modes* (September 15, 1786): 163.

83. *Cabinet des modes* (July 15, 1786): 130.

84. Ross, "The Debate on Luxury in Eighteenth-Century France": 185–7.

85. *Journal de la mode et du goût* (April 15, 1791): 1–2.

86. Gutwirth, *The Twilight of the Goddesses*, Goodman, *The Republic of Letters*, Landes, *Visualizing the Nation*, Friedland, *Political Actors*, Carla Hesse, *The Other Enlightenment: How French Women Became Modern* (Princeton: Princeton University Press, 2001).

87. Margaret H. Darrow, "French Noblewomen and the New Domesticity, 1750–1850," *Feminist Studies* 5, no. 1 (Spring 1979): 58. See also Margaret Darrow, *Revolution in the House: Family, Class, and Inheritance in Southern France, 1775–1825* (Princeton: Princeton University Press, 1989).

88. Leclerc de Montlinot, *Etat actuel*, 12. Quoted in Thomas McStay Adams, *Bureaucrats and Beggars: French Social Policy in the Age of the Enlightenment* (Oxford: Oxford University Press, 1990): 197.

89. *Journal de la mode et du goût* (June 25, 1790): 1. (November 10, 1792): 3. Even after the Royal family's flight to Varennes in 1791, Marie Antoinette continued to order elaborate court dresses from Rose Bertin, including a brown silk dress adorned with lace and white satin embroidery to be worn at a party on All Hallows' Eve. Her clothing bill for 1791, although only half of her expenditures in previous years, was still nearly 44,000 *livres*. And after her imprisonment in 1792 she continued to order dresses and have the bills sent to the government of the French Republic. Bernier, *The Eighteenth-Century Woman*: 126.

90. *Journal de la mode et du goût* (August 5, 1790): 2.

91. Jean Polman, *Le voile ou couvre-chef féminin* (Douai, 1635): 93.

92. Lottin, *Discours sur ce sujet*: 9–10.

93. *Cabinet des modes* (August 15, 1786): 145.

94. *Manuel des toilettes dédié aux dames*: 9–10.

95. Caron, *Toilette des dames*: 196.

96. Cited in Perrot, *Fashioning the Bourgeoisie*: 20.

97. For a discussion of the new biology of the incommensurability of the two sexes which was developed in the eighteenth century, see Thomas Lacqueur, "Orgasm, Generation and the Politics of Reproductive Biology," *Representations* 14 (Spring 1986) and *Making Sex*.

98. *Magasin des modes nouvelles* (August 30, 1787): 225.

99. *Magasin des modes nouvelles* (March 1, 1789): 75.

100. Boudier de Villemert, *Apologie de la frivolité, lettre à un Anglois* (Paris: Prault père, 1750): 3–4.

Epilogue: From Absolutist Gaze to Republican Look

From lingerie and dresses to ties and trousers, clothing is so obviously differentiated as masculine or feminine in Western culture that we have perhaps overlooked
the larger significance of the ways in which our entire culture of clothing is deeply
gendered. Even when the discourse on fashion explicitly focuses on class, race,
nationality, or sexual orientation, gendered categories of masculinity and femininity nevertheless make the warp for the discourse on fashion, providing the fundamental fiber of our fashion culture. The diverse ways in which we discuss fashion
– from hygiene and morality to taste and sexuality – are deeply entwined with our
notions of masculinity and femininity. In this way, *la mode* is sexed.

The eighteenth century was a particularly significant moment in the sexing of
la mode, as French society witnessed the emergence of a new fashion culture in
which fashion was deeply associated with femininity and frivolity. In a complex
combination of politics, economics, and sexuality, new notions of masculinity and
femininity were given shape by an explosion of material commodities; at the same
time, new conceptions of gender encouraged the men and women who actively
shaped the commercial revolution to produce more objects – from dressing gowns
to tea kettles – to furnish the newly gendered sphere of family life. From the
courtly fashion culture of Louis XIV, predicated on the sartorial display of both
elite men and women according to an absolutist script, to the association of women
with fashion in the expanding commercial culture of late-eighteenth-century Paris,
this transformation did not always follow a tidy linear narrative: the new synthesis
regarding women and fashion was marked by considerable instability, as witnessed
by the persistence of *petits maîtres*, fops and dandies, and repeated attacks on
women's fashions. Yet, although a remarkably precarious synthesis, the interweav-
ing of fashion, femininity and frivolity, like any synthetic fabric, has proven
remarkably resilient: it has been frayed, unraveled, and even occasionally turned
inside out, and yet continues to clothe our identities as men and women in ways
that are difficult to strip off altogether.

This synthesis is so difficult to discard in part because of the ways in which
bodies and clothing – subjects and material objects – were fused and naturalized
in the eighteenth century. Twentieth-century feminists often talked about our real
bodies, "our bodies, ourselves" beneath our clothes, freed from the corseted vision
of the fashion industry. Yet, just as the past decade of feminist scholarship has

warned us of the pitfalls of conceptualizing a feminist politics on the grounds of a false dichotomy between natural sex and culturally-constructed gender, so also, to distinguish sharply between our "real bodies" and our human-made clothes is to miss the subtle and inseparable play between bodies, gender, identity and fashion. It is to ignore that bodies, as much as clothes, are historically manufactured and that bodies do not exist independently from clothes any more than sex exists apart from gender. Even nudity is, significantly, "the absence of clothing."[1] Since the beginnings of the consumer revolution in eighteenth-century Europe, femininity has been performed within a theater in which living bodies are fused with material objects. Complementing the new medical science of the eighteenth century, which articulated differences between the male and female body through engravings of anatomical cross-sections and skeletons, the emerging fashion culture fixed gender identities through fashion engravings and embodied femininity through clothing.

As we have seen, our modern fashion culture emerged at a moment when men and women were obsessed by the baroque conundrum of the relationship between inner and outer, being and appearance: how can one know if a woman is a good wife or a prostitute, a duchess or a serving girl? How can one know if any person is what he or she claims to be? But did French men and women fear that identities would truly be mistaken? Although the French did not have a well-developed analytical understanding of "class" until the nineteenth century, they were as astute at the semiotics of reading social station as we are in the less hierarchical and more fluid culture of early-twenty-first century America.[2] People in the eighteenth century did not, in fact, mistake fishmongers for duchesses any more than we today would mistake a cleaning woman for a college professor. Instead, their fears about fashion reveal the anxiety that individual identities – and the connection between objects and subjects – had become more complicated than they had once been and that no one sole power – be it king, church, or father – could any longer determine one's identity for life. The early-modern discourse of mistaken identities and fears of transgressive clothing was the explicit language used to express implicit fears about modern identities that no longer used material objects solely to fix social identity but also to express individuality.

By the eighteenth century the availability of fashionable dress to greater numbers of people and the increasing pace of changes in fashion began to complicate the equation between clothing, social role, and individual identity. Because fashion was both more ephemeral and more tightly bound to the individual than mere clothing or costume, it expressed something not only about the individual's external social position, but potentially about his or her inner subjectivity as well. No longer merely a troubling mask or a useful marker of the social man or woman, in a subtle and complicated way modern fashions claimed to make transparent the individual. To put it another way, if the fabric which symbolized seventeenth-century absolutist fashion culture was brocade, a fabric whose stiff contours might either mark the body appropriately or mask it inappropriately, the fashion culture which emerged by the late eighteenth century was symbolized by gauze, a fabric that does not mask or mark but which reveals and mediates between inner and outer in a nuanced spectrum of vices and virtues: purity, piety, sobriety, maturity, reserve, romance, melancholy, playfulness, carelessness, spontaneity, frivolity, coquetry and youth. By the late eighteenth century fashion was conceived as a natural, seamless web between an individual's inner identity and outer garb that no longer merely marked or masked one's public identity. The line between inner subject and object was transformed: clothing was one's identity. And that individual identity was now perceived to be shaped by nature and gender as much as by class and rank.

For both men and women, clothing performed the work of sexing and individuating bodies, a hallmark of both modern liberalism and modern fashion culture. Yet, the connection between clothing and identity was strikingly different for men than for women. As a telling example, men did not wear gauze, but a more solidly woven, manly (and British) fabric, wool. Although the cut and fabric of men's clothing were subtly informed by fashion, by the early nineteenth century men's clothing no longer stepped as quickly to the rhythms and unending changes of details and accessories as women's did. Increasingly in the late eighteenth and early nineteenth centuries, men's clothing looked more like fixed costume or uniform as opposed to women's more capricious fashion. But unlike Louis XIV's courtiers, who were required to wear the costume decreed by the king, nineteenth-century elite men collectively tailored, with remarkable consistency for well over a century, not only their own look – the sober three-piece suit – but a new way of looking at others as well. The Revolution was merely a symbolic marker for a century-long process by which elite French men – republicans and monarchists alike – rejected the absolutist gaze and mastered their own liberal look, through a visual mastery which had political, sexual, social, and racial, as well as sartorial, ramifications. Many men continued to be interested in fashion in the nineteenth and twentieth centuries, but to do so was to risk being labeled a fop or a dandy, to stand outside the proper sphere of manhood, and to deny oneself access to political power in a way that would not have been true in the seventeenth or eighteenth centuries.

A new consensus among gender historians has revealed the deep connections between gender and politics during the French Revolution. Joan Landes's, Sarah Maza's, and Lynn Hunt's pioneering research suggests that the new liberal conceptualization of men's public agency was predicated on essentializing women's nature and removing women from the public realm of politics. Henceforth, women's only link to the public would be through that which was most essential, their maternity as republican mothers.[3] Men's essence was now rooted in the fixed self and their capacity for individual action and moral judgment, while women's was now defined by their relation to men as mothers, wives, and as objects of men's desire.

It is all too easy to fit "the sexing of *la mode*" into this scholarly consensus regarding gender and politics. During the Enlightenment and Revolution, the great surge of energy required to declare liberty from absolutism and *l'infâme* required a certitude about men's power as individuals, as a meritorious elite, and as brothers committed to building a new model of the political community. The rush of political events between 1789 and 1795 witnessed a celebration of masculinity – from the Pantheon's celebration of the male mind to David's celebration of the male torso. Trousers replaced breeches, wigs and powder were exchanged for natural hair, and pastel silks gave way to somber woolens. All were part of what the fashion historian J.C. Flugel has called the "great masculine renunciation," and all helped usher in a masculine revolution that was both libidinal and political.[4] For men, clothing marked their public morality, their participation in the social contract; for women, clothing marked their enclosure in a private sphere of maternity, domesticity, and sexuality, and their bondage by the sexual contract.

This paradigm of the great masculine renunciation is supported by the research of gender historians who argue that by the nineteenth century, women to a much greater extent than men still occupied a world of iconic representation, in which a picture, or a hat, spoke a thousand words. Femininity was spoken in a language that echoed the semiotics of the theatrical absolutist court. As Bonnie Smith has observed in her work on the nineteenth-century bourgeoisie, long after the execution of the king and queen, traces of the Old Regime could still be detected on the bodies of women and in the semiotics of femininity.[5] The spectacular politics of Louis XIV's theater state, founded on an iconic system of representation which played with the relationship between signifier and signified, found a welcome home in the period drawing rooms and fashion revivals of the nineteenth century. In caricatured form one might argue, modern men wrote and debated texts as subjective agents; while traditional women displayed fashion as objectified icons.

To be sure, a feminized culture of clothing aided husbands' and lovers' objectification of women, fetishized the trappings of femininity, and worked to limit women's political and intellectual horizons. At best women who continued to thrill to the experience of being seen were labeled childish exhibitionists. More tragically, from Marie Antoinette to the revolutionary feminist Olympe de Gouge, women who refused to wear the new tightly-laced gender roles prescribed for them were executed. Yet, fashion historians have focused so narrowly on the "great masculine renunciation of fashion" and gender historians so closely on the "great masculine renunciation of women in politics" that they have neglected to assess the more complicated and active roles of women and femininity in both these processes. "The great female acceptance" of fashion begs to be explained, instead of naturalized. And we need to keep open the possibility that, despite revisionist revolutionary historians' claims for the primacy of the text, perhaps a dress really could speak a thousand words

As we have seen throughout this book, the *ancien régime* discourse about fashion and commercial culture – whether in aristocratic women's private letters, guilds' legal briefs, or the new journals that publicized fashion – served as a forum in which French men and women imagined and debated the relationship between the public and private, Frenchness and femininity, the useful and the frivolous, and society and the self. The association between fashion and femininity is no more a "natural fact" than the association of politics with masculinity. Why, then, did late-eighteenth-century women as well as men, accept the new contours of a fashion culture that metaphorically clothed women, whether pregnant or not, in maternity clothes? Why, long after Empire fashion's exaggeration of belly and breast had given way to the Second Empire's cinched waists and Third Republic's flattened stomachs and bustles, did maternity and domesticity continue to be inscribed on women's bodies by their clothing, and femininity continue to be inscribed on their psyches by their relationship to commercial culture? Why did Rousseau's Sophie seem so "right" to eighteenth-century French women? The culture of fashion that emerged in eighteenth-century Paris provides several answers to these deeply political questions.

La mode, as we have seen, was a goddess who thrived not only on fantasy, but also on contradiction and instability. The visual world of clothing in which the purity of white linen shaped the contours of swelling breasts or girlishly-small waists accentuated expanding hips was ideally suited to containing and expressing the new, seemingly contradictory roles of mother and wife, republican and lady.[6] Although anxieties about women, fashion, and theatricality were by no means permanently eradicated from Western culture (even the most skilled dressmaker could never create a dress that so artfully combined contradictions that it permanently silenced the questions: is she a virtuous Madonna or a fallen Magdalene, and is she dressing for her husband or for the public stage?) late-eighteenth-century fashion engravings, shop displays, and *marchandes de modes* showed women how to be republican mothers more artfully and more persuasively than volumes of republican laws, while permitting a degree of personal interpretation that no legal code would tolerate.

The new eighteenth-century distinctions between public and private and masculinity and femininity rested on the belief that women by nature had a duty to seduce men and to produce children; both, ideally, were to take place within the sanctioned confines of monogamous marriage. The tension between erotic sexuality and maternity pervaded eighteenth-century thought – from Rousseauean heroines such as Julie, who was punished for finding amorous fulfillment with one man, Saint Preux, but maternal fulfillment with another, Wolmar, to the memoirs of Mme Roland, who chronicled the tension between her desire to breastfeed her daughter and to aid her husband as wife and political companion.[7] Yet, to see only the tension and incompatibility between maternity and eroticism is to ignore the appeal for women of the new bourgeois fantasy – dished up in best-selling novels like *Pamela* and fashion magazines like the *Cabinet des modes* – that love and reproduction might be conjoined in women's marriage plots and that public and private might be conjoined in their shopping trips.

But how was a woman to seduce and reproduce – from the male perspective, how was she to make her husband happy and make babies? For many French men and women Rousseau's male perspective offered a persuasive answer. Unlike Mary Wollstonecraft, who saw in Rousseau a contradictory mix of appealing republicanism and repellent misogyny, many of his readers repackaged his gender ideology in their own terms and took it as sound fashion advice.[8] As Rousseau's fictional characters portrayed so vividly, desire between the sexes could be heightened, not by the verbal aphrodisiacs of Laclus's jaded aristocratic lovers the Marquise de Merteuil and the Comte de Valmont, but by the visual exaggeration of sexual difference. To heighten difference was to excite desire, but this required a bit of theatricality. Stripping theatricality of its aristocratic taint, Rousseau stressed that the proper wife performed neither for the monarch's gaze nor for the public's, but for her husband's eyes alone. This was a new kind of bourgeois drama, enacted not onstage but in the daily fantasies of men and women across France and it required, like all theatrical productions, costumes. But the theater of bourgeois domesticity demanded costumes that expressed not aristocratic luxury, but individuals' inner subjectivity as men and as women.

The new fashion culture not only redefined women's and men's clothing styles, but reconceptualized the relationship between femininity, fashion, and commercial culture. Fashion and consumer culture were sanctioned for women as a privileged realm in which women might enact theatrical fantasies, not only as a private performance at home under the husband's gaze, but in civil society (if not in political society) more broadly. Stripped of the political associations between fashion, theater, and absolutist politics, every woman could now be an actress. With their identities firmly rooted in biology and nature, women might harmlessly experiment with the range of roles that the dresses and hats available in cities like Paris offered. Denied political power, fashion became a realm in which sensibility, taste, subjectivity, and, dare we say, individuality might flourish.

Men may have conceived of the newly domesticated women as decorative objects, but eighteenth- and nineteenth-century women found ways to value beauty and fashion that were not necessarily destructive to their self-esteem or intellectual pursuits.[9] A fashion culture which had the dual purpose, from the viewpoint of men and manufacturers, of stimulating men's heterosexual desire for women and women's material desire for clothing, might nevertheless be used by women themselves for quite different purposes. Female bonding through fashion might

Figure 20 *Portrait de femme écrivant*, Doucet, courtesy of RMN.

create a homosocial world for women in which gift-giving and the sharing of clothing sidestepped the commercial economy at the same time that caresses of silk and lace created an autoerotic world in which the male gaze was frankly dismissed as impotent. The supposedly natural female desire "to be seen" was often combined with the active desire "to see." Despite attempts to underscore its frivolity, fashion could never be completely severed from the political, for it was too closely associated with the presentation of self and social identity to escape public scrutiny and public import. Not only in the form of Phrygian caps and *sans culottes* but in the fashion for mantuas, hoopskirts, and white muslin gowns, the rebellious *frondeur* in fashion could never be completely contained or silenced.[10]

Women have been as responsible as men for embracing beliefs in essential sexual difference. Seamstresses and female consumers alike helped shape the new culture of fashion and they must have found reassurance in the new correspondence forged in the later eighteenth century between being and appearance, between their identities as individuals and their natural essence as mothers and wives. This reassurance was certainly responsible for quieting the demands and limiting the horizons of generations of women, but it may also have given late-eighteenth-century French women and their daughters and granddaughters after them confidence to become, if not mothers and politicians, then at least mothers and lovers, mothers and artists, or mothers and teachers.[11] It may have given them the confidence to believe that, like Pamela, the eighteenth-century's beloved, spunky, rebellious, and English serving girl, there might be more than one reading to their clothes: for hidden beneath Pamela's petticoats and sewn into the lining of her dresses were literally volumes of words. Eighteenth-century French women did not buy their identities ready-made from kings, priests, medical doctors, or republican philosophers but craftily stitched their own identities and tailored their sense of self, given the cultural matcrials and social tools available to them in expanding commercial cities like Paris.

Ironically, the seemingly definitive answers in the eighteenth century to the baroque enigmas "What is woman?" and "What is *la mode*?" may ultimately have opened the possibility for women themselves finally to pose the modernist question: what do *women* want? The answer would surely be fashionable hats, pretty dresses, and the right to choose whether or not to wear maternity clothes, but would also include a whole lot more as well . . . . At least that's what elusive, insatiable, carefree, vagabond, revolutionary and ever-changing *la mode* would want of women.

Notes

1. As art historian Anne Hollander has observed, depictions of the nude in the West always follow stylistic conventions of the clothed body. Anne Hollander, *Seeing Through Clothes* (New York: Avon Books, 1975).
2. Sarah Maza, *The Myth of the French Bourgeoisie: An Essay on the Social Imaginary, 1750–1850* (Cambridge, MA: Harvard University Press, 2003).
3. Landes, *Women and the Public Sphere*, Maza, *Private Lives and Public Affairs*, see Chapter 2, "The Rose-Girl of Salency," and Hunt, *The Family Romance of the French Revolution*.
4. Flugel, *The Psychology of Clothes*.
5. Bonnie Smith, *Ladies of the Leisure Class: The Bourgeoisies of Northern France in the Nineteenth Century* (Princeton: Princeton University Press, 1981), Chapter 4. Joan Landes' *Visualing the Nation* enriches and complicates our understandings of the ways in which visual culture shaped male and female political allegiances during and after the Revolution.

6. For an insightful theoretical examination of the ability of fashion to express ambivalence and multiple identities, see Fred Davis, *Fashion, Culture, and Identity* (Chicago: University of Chicago Press, 1992).

7. Dorinda Outram, *The Body and the French Revolution: Sex, Class, and Political Culture* (New Haven: Yale University Press, 1989), Chapter 8.

8. Jennifer M. Jones, "Repackaging Rousseau: Femininity and Fashion in Old Regime France," *French Historical Studies* 18 (Fall 1994): 939–61.

9. Ellen Lamberts, *The Face of Love: Feminism and the Beauty Question* (Boston: Beacon Press, 1995): xiii.

10. On debates over the meaning of revolutionary dress, see Richard Wrigley, *The Politics of Appearances*.

11. For an important exploration of the ways female writers and intellectuals in the post-Revolutionary period, deprived of political rights, nevertheless argued for their rights to participate in civil society, see Geneviève Fraisse, *Reason's Muse: Sexual Difference and the Birth of Democracy* (Chicago: University of Chicago Press, 1994). Although Carla Hesse focuses on books and not dress, her analysis of female authors' creation of moral, if not political, autonomy through writing offers important insights for understanding the impact of the market economy on women's relationship to the modern public sphere. Hesse argues, "Capitalism and republicanism were thus pitted against one another with respect to the public role of women. And modern political feminism emerged precisely from the revolutionary conjuncture." Hesse, *The Other Enlightenment*: 155.

Bibliography

Adams, Thomas McStay. *Bureaucrats and Beggars: French Social Policy in the Age of the Enlightenment*. Oxford: Oxford University Press, 1990.

Adburgham, Alison. *Women in Print: Writing Women and Women's Magazines from the Restoration to the Accession of Victoria*. London: Allen and Unwin, 1972.

Akkerman, Tjitske. *Women's Vices, Public Benefits: Women and Commerce in the French Enlightenment*. Amsterdam: Het Spinhuis, 1992.

Allilaire, Jean. *Les industries de l'habillement*. Paris: Société d'éditions française et internationale, 1947.

Apostiolidès, Jean-Marie. *Le roi-machine: Spectacle et politique an temps de Louis XIV*. Paris: Minuit, 1981.

Appadurai, Arjun, ed. *The Social Life of Things: Commodities in Cultural Perspective*. Cambridge: Cambridge University Press, 1986.

Applewhite, Harriet, Darlene Levy and Mary Johnson, eds. *Women in Revolutionary Paris*. Urbana, IL: University of Illinois Press, 1979.

Auerbach, E. "La cour et la ville," in *Scenes from the Drama of European Literature*. New York: Meridian, 1959.

Auslander, Leora. *Taste and Power: Furnishing Modern France*. Berkeley: University of California Press, 1996.

Badiou, D. "Les couturières parisiennes." Maîtrise, Paris I, 1981.

Barker, Nancy Nichols. *Brother to the Sun King: Philippe Duke of Orleans*. Baltimore: Johns Hopkins University Press, 1989.

Barthes, Roland. *The Fashion System*. Trans. Matthew Ward and Richard Howard. New York: Hill and Wang, 1983.

Bataille, Georges. *The Accursed Share: An Essay on General Economy, Vol I Consumption*. New York: Zone Books, 1988.

Batterbury, Michael. *Fashion, the Mirror of History*. London: Greenwich House, 1982.

Becq, Annie. *Genèse de l'esthétique Française moderne*, 2 vols. Pisa: Pacini Editore, 1984.

Beik, William. *Absolutism and Society in Seventeenth-Century France: State Power and Provincial Aristocracy in Languedoc*. Cambridge: Cambridge University Press, 1985.

Bell, David A. *The Cult of the Nation in France: Inventing Nationalism, 1680–1800*. Cambridge, MA: Harvard University Press, 2001.

Bellanger, Claude, Jaques Godechot, et al. *Histoire générale de la presse française*. Paris: Presses universitaires de France, 1969.

Benabou, Erica-Marie. *La Prostitution et la police des moeurs au xviiie siècle*. Paris: Librairie académique Perrin, 1987.

Benhamou, Reed. "Cours Publics: Elective Education in the Eighteenth Century." *Studies on Voltaire and the Eighteenth Century* (1985).

——. "Fashion in the *Mercure*: From Human Foible to Female Failing." *Eighteenth-Century Studies* 31, no. 1 (1997): 27–43.

Berg, Maxine. "Women's Property and the Industrial Revolution." *Journal of Interdisciplinary History* 34, no. 2 (Autumn 1993).

Berg, Maxine, and Helen Clifford. *Consumers and Luxury: Consumer Culture in Europe, 1650–1850*. Manchester: Manchester University Press, 1999.

Berlainstein, Lenard. "Women and Power in Eighteenth-Century France: Actresses at the Comédie-Française," in *Visions and Revisions of Eighteenth-Century France*, ed. Christine Adams, Jack Censer, and Lisa Jane Graham. University Park, PA: Pennsylvania State University Press, 1997: 155–90.

Bermingham, Ann, and John Brewer, eds. *The Consumption of Culture, 1600–1800: Images, Object, Text*. London: Routledge, 1995.

Bernier, Olivier. *The Eighteenth-Century Woman*. New York: Doubleday, 1982.

Berry, Christopher. *The Idea of Luxury: A Conceptual and Historical Investigation*. Cambridge: Cambridge University Press, 1994.

Boileau, Etienne. *Le livre des métiers d'Etienne Boileau*. Ed. René de Lespinasse and Françoise Bonnardot. Paris: Imprimerie Nationale, 1879.

Bonfield, Lloyd. *Marriage Settlements, 1601–1740: The Adoption of the Strict Settlement*. Cambridge: Cambridge University Press, 1983.

Bonnet, Jean-Claude, ed. *Louis-Sébastien Mercier (1740–1814): Un hérétique en litterature*. Paris: Mercure de France, 1995.

Bossenga, Gail. "Protecting Merchants: Guilds and Commercial Capitalism in Eighteenth-Century France." *French Historical Studies* 15, no. 4 (Fall 1988).

——. *The Politics of Privilege: Old Regime and Revolution in Lille*. Cambridge: Cambridge University Press, 1991.

Bourdieu, Pierre. *Distinction: A Social Critique of the Judgment of Taste*. Cambridge, MA: Harvard University Press, 1984.

Bouvier, Jeanne. *La lingerie et les lingères*. Paris: Gaston Doin et Cie, 1928.

Braesch, F. "Essai de statistique de la population ouvrières de Paris vers 1791." *La Revolution Française* (July–December 1912).

Braudel, F. *The Wheels of Commerce*. Trans. Siân Reynolds. New York: Harper and Row: 1982.

Bray, Alan. *Renaissance Homosexuality*. London: Gay Men's Press, 1982.

——. "Homosexuality and the Signs of Male Friendship in Elizabethan England," in *Queering the Renaissance*, ed. Jonathan Goldberg. Durham: Duke University Press, 1994.

Brenner, C.D. "A Neglected Pre-Romantic: Billardon de Sauvigny." *The Romantic Review* (February 1938): 48–58.

Breward, Christopher. *The Culture of Fashion: A New History of Fashionable Dress*. Manchester: Manchester University Press, 1995.

Brewer, John, and Roy Porter, eds. *Consumption and the World of Goods*. London: Routledge, 1993.

Brooks, W.S., and P.J. Yarrow. *The Dramatic Criticism of Elisabeth Charlotte, Duchesse D'Orleans, with an Annotated Chronology of Performances of the Popular and Court Theaters in France*. Lewiston, NY: Mellen Press, 1995.

Brown, Gregory. *A Field of Honor: Writers, Court Culture and Public Theater in French Literary Life from Racine to the Revolution*. New York: Columbia University Press/EPIC, 2002.

Burke, Peter. *The Fabrication of Louis XIV*. New Haven: Yale University Press, 1992.

Campbell, Colin. *The Romantic Ethic and the Spirit of Modern Consumerism*. Oxford: Basil Blackwell, 1987.

Censer, Jack. *The French Press in the Age of Enlightenment*. Cambridge: Cambridge University Press, 1994.

Censer, Jack, and Jeremy Popkin, eds. *Press and Politics in Prerevolutionary France*. Berkeley: University of California Press, 1987.

Champier, Victor, and G.-Roger Sandoz. *Le Palais-Royal d'après des documents inédits*. Paris, 1900.

Chapman, Stanley, and Serge Chassagne. *European Textile Printers in the Eighteenth Century: A Study of Pell and Oberkapf*. London: Heineman, 1981.

Chassagne, Serge. *Oberkampf, un entrepreneur capitaliste au siecle des lumières*. Paris: Aubin-Montaigne, 1980.

Chisick, Harvey. "Institutional Innovation in Popular Education in Eighteenth Century France: Two Examples." *French Historical Studies* 10 (1977): 43–73.

——. *The Limits of Reform in the Enlightenment: Attitudes toward the Education of the Lower Classes in Eighteenth-Century France*. Princeton: Princeton University Press, 1981.

——, ed. *The Press in the French Revolution*. Oxford: The Voltaire Foundation, 1991.

Coffin, Judith. *The Politics of Women's Work: The Paris Garment Trades, 1750–1915*. Princeton: Princeton University Press, 1996.

Colas, R. *Bibliographie générale du costume et de la mode*. Paris: Imprimerie des presses modernes, 1933.

Cole, Charles Woolsey. *Colbert and a Century of French Mercantilism*, 2 vols. New York: Columbia University Press, 1939.

Coppens, Marguerite. "'Au magasin de Paris' Une boutique de modes à Anvers." *Revue belge d'archéologie et d'histoire d'art* 12 (1983): 85.

Cornu, Paul. *Essai bibliographique sur les recueils de mode au xviiie siècle*. Paris: G. Vitry, 1912.

Crawford, Patricia. "'The only ornament in a woman': needlework in early modern Europe," in *All Her Labours*. Sydney: Hale and Iremonger, 1986.

Crow, Thomas. *Painters and Public Life*. New Haven: Yale University Press, 1985.

Crowston, Clare. *Fabricating Women: The Seamstresses of Old Regime France, 1675–1791*. Durham: Duke University Press, 2001.

Cullen, L.M. "History, Economic Crisis and Revolution: Understanding Eighteenth-Century France." *Economic History Review*, 46 (1993).

Czikszentmihalyi, Mihaly and Eugene Rochberg-Halton. *The Meaning of Things: Domestic Symbols and the Self*. Cambridge: Cambridge University Press, 1981.

Darnton, Robert. *The Business of Enlightenment: A Publishing History of the Encyclopédie, 1755–1800*. Cambridge, MA: Harvard University Press, 1979.

——. *The Literary Underground of the Old Regime*. Cambridge, MA: Harvard University Press, 1982.

——. *The Great Cat Massacre and Other Episodes in French Cultural History*. New York: Basic Books, 1984.

Darrow, Margaret H. "French Noblewomen and the New Domesticity, 1750–1850." *Feminist Studies* 5, no. 1 (Spring 1979): 42–65.

——. *Revolution in the House: Family, Class, and Inheritance in Southern France, 1775–1825*. Princeton: Princeton University Press, 1989.

Daston, Lorraine. *Classical Probability in the Enlightenment*. Princeton: Princeton University Press, 1988.

Davis, Fred. *Fashion, Culture, and Identity*. Chicago: University of Chicago Press, 1992.

Davis, Natalie. *The Gift in Sixteenth-Century France*. Madison: The University of Wisconsin Press, 2000.

Debord, Guy. *La société du spectacle*. Paris: Champs libres, 1967.

DeJean, Joan. *Ancients against Moderns: Culture Wars and the Making of a Fin de Siècle*. Chicago: The University of Chicago Press, 1997.

Delpierre, Madeleine. *La mode et ses métiers du XVIIIe siècle à nos jours*. Paris: Musée de la mode et du costume, 1981.

——. *Modes et revolution, 1780–1804*. Paris: Delpierre éditions Paris-musées, 1989.

——. *Dress in France in the Eighteenth Century*. New Haven: Yale University Press, 1997.

De Marly, Diana. *Louis XIV and Versailles*. New York: Holmes and Meier, 1987.

De Nouvion, Pierre, and Emile Liez. *Un ministre des modes sous Louis XVI, Mademoiselle Bertin*. Paris: Leclerc, 1911.

Deslandres, Y. *Le Costume image de l'homme*. Paris: Albin Michel, 1976.

Desplanques, Charles. *Barbiers, Perruquiers, Coiffeurs*. Paris: Gaston Doin et Cie, 1927.

Déville, Etienne. *Index du Mercure de France, 1672–1832*. Paris: J. Schemit, 1910.

Dewald, Jonathan. *Aristocratic Experience and the Origins of Modern Culture in France, 1570–1715*. Berkeley: University of California Press, 1993.

——. "The Ruling Class and the Marketplace: Nobles and Money in Early Modern France," in *The Culture of the Market*, ed. Thomas Haskell and Richard Teichgraeber III. Cambridge: Cambridge University Press, 1993: 43–65.

Dotoli, G. "Il *Mercure gallant* di Donneau de Visé." *L'informazione in Francia nel Seicento Quadernni del Seicento francese* 5 (1983): 219–82.

Douglas, Audrey. "Cotton Textiles in England: The East India Company's Attempt to Exploit Developments in Fashion 1660–1721." *The Journal of British Studies* 8, no. 2 (May 1969): 28–43.

Elias, Norbert. *The Court Society*. Oxford: Blackwell, 1983.

Entwistle, Joanne. *The Fashioned Body: Fashion, Dress and Modern Social Theory*. Malden, MA: Blackwell, 2000.

Erickson, Amy Louis. *Women and Property in Early Modern England*. London: Routledge, 1993.

Fagniez, G. *La femme et la societé française dans la première moitié du XVIIe siècle*. Paris, 1929.

Fairchilds, Cissie. "The Production and Marketing of Populuxe Goods in Eighteenth-Century Paris," in *Consumption and the World of Goods*, ed. Brewer and Porter. London: Routledge, 1993.

Farge, Artlette, ed. *Vivre dans la rue à Paris au xviie siècle*. Paris: Gallimard, 1979.

——. "L'espace parisien au XVIIIe siècle d'après les ordonnances de police." *Ethnologie Française* 12, no. 2 (1982).

——. *Fragile Lives: Violence, Power, and Solidarity in Eighteenth-Century Paris*. Cambridge, MA: Harvard University Press, 1993.

Faure, Edgar. *La banqueroute de Law*. Paris: Gallimard, 1977.

Finn, Margot. "Women, Consumption, and Coverture in England c. 1760–1860." Unpublished paper, Davis Center Seminar, April 1995.

Flandrin, Jean-Louis. "Distinction through Taste," in *A History of Private Life: Passions of the Renaissance*, ed. Roger Chartier. Cambridge, MA: Harvard University Press, 1989.

Flugel, John Carl. *The Psychology of Clothes*. London: Hogarth Press, 1950 (1930).

Forster, Elborg, trans. *A Woman's Life in the Court of the Sun King: Letters of Liselotte von der Pfalz, 1652–1722*. Baltimore: The Johns Hopkins University Press, 1984.

——. "From the Patient's Point of View: Illness and Health in the Letters of Liselotte von der Pfalz (1652–1722)." *Bulletin of the History of Medicine* 60 (1986): 297–320.

——. "From the Garden Snake to the Toad: Madame Palantine on the Ministers of the Grand Siècle." *Cahiers du Dix-Septième: Journal of the Southeast American Society for French Seventeenth-Century Studies* vol. 3, no. 1 (Spring 1989): 243–60.

Foucault, Michel. *The History of Sexuality, Vol. I: An Introduction*. Trans. Robert Hurley. New York, 1978.

Fournier, Edouard. *Variétés historiques et littéraires*. Paris, 1855–63.

Fox, Robert, and Anthony Turner, eds. *Luxury Trades and Consumerism in Ancien Regime Paris*. Aldershot: Ashgate, 1998.

Fox-Genovese, Elizabeth. "The Ideological Bases of Domestic Economy," in *Fruits of Merchant Capital*. Oxford: Oxford University Press, 1983.

Fraisse, Geneviève. *Reason's Muse: Sexual Difference and the Birth of Democracy*. Chicago: University of Chicago Press, 1994.

Franklin, A. *La vie privée d'autrefois*. Paris: Plon, Nouritt et Cie, 1887–1902.

Fried, Michael. *Absorption and Theatricality*. Berkeley: University of California Press, 1980.

Friedland, Paul. "Parallel States: Theatrical and Political Representation in Early Modern and Revolutionary France," in *The Age of Cultural Revolutions: Britain and France 1750–1829*, ed. Colin Jones and Dror Wahrman. Berkeley: University of California Press, 2002.

——. *Political Actors: Representative Bodies and Theatricality in the Age of the French Revolution*. Ithaca: Cornell University Press, 2002.

Gaboriau, Emile. *Les Comédiennes adorées*. Paris, 1891.

Gaines, Jane and Charlotte Herzoz, eds. *Fabrications: Costume and the Female Body*. London: Routledge, 1990.

Garber, Margorie. *Vested Interests: Cross-Dressing and Cultural Anxiety*. London: Routledge, 1992.

Garrioch, David. *Neighbourhood and Community in Paris, 1740–1790*. Cambridge: Cambridge University Press, 1986.

——. *The Making of Revolutionary Paris*. Berkeley: University of California Press, 2002.

Garsault. *L'art de la lingerie*. Paris, 1780.

Gaudriault, Raymond. *La gravure de mode féminine en France*. Paris: Les éditions de l'amateur, 1983.

——. *Répertoire de la gravure de mode française des origins à 1815*. Paris: Promodis, 1988.

Geertz, Clifford. *Negara: The Theatre State in Nineteenth-Century Bali*. Princeton: Princeton University Press, 1980

Gelbart, Nina Rattner. *Feminine and Opposition Journalism in Old Regime France: "Le Journal des dames."* Berkeley: University of California Press, 1987.

Genlis, Mme de. *Dictionnaire critique et raisonné des étiquettes de la cour*. Paris, 1818.

Gigerenzer, Gerd, Zeno Switjtink, et al. *The Empire of Chance: How Probability Changed Science and Everyday Life*. Cambridge: Cambridge University Press, 1989.

Godard de Donville, Louise. *Signification de la mode sous Louis XIII*. Aix-en-Provence: EDISUD, 1978.

Goldberg, Jonathan, ed. *Queering the Renaissance*. Durham: Duke University Press, 1994.

Goldsmith, Elizabeth. *Exclusive Conversations: The Art of Interaction in Seventeenth-Century France*. Philadelphia: University of Pennsylvania Press, 1988.

Goodman, Dena. "Public Sphere and Private Life: Toward a Synthesis of Current Historiographical Approaches to the Old Regime." *History and Theory* 31, no. 1 (1992).

——. *The Republic of Letters: A Cultural History of the French Enlightenment*. Ithaca: Cornell University Press, 1994.

Gordon, Daniel. *Citizens Without Sovereignty: Equality and Sociability in French Thought, 1670–1789*. Princeton: Princeton University Press, 1994.

Grazia, Victoria de, and Ellen Furlough, eds. *The Sex of Things: Gender and Consumption in Historical Perspective*. Berkeley: University of California Press, 1996.

Guillais-Maury, Joëlle. "Une histoire de grisette." Maîtrise, Paris VII, 1980.

——. "La grisette," in *Madame ou mademoiselle? Itinéraires de la solitude feminine, dix-huitième à vingtième siècle*, ed. Arlette Farge and Christiane Klapisch-Zuber. Paris: Montalba, 1984.

Gullickson, Gay. *Spinners and Wavers of Auffay: Rural Industry and the Sexual Divison of Labor in a French Village, 1750–1850*. Cambridge: Cambridge University Press, 1986.

Gutwirth, Madelyn. *The Twilight of the Goddesses: Women and Representation in the French Revolutionary Era*. New Brunswick, NJ: Rutgers University Press, 1992.

Hafter, Daryl, "The Spinners of Rouen Confront English Technology." *Proceedings of the International Conference on the Role of Women in the History of Science, Technology, and Medicine* 1 (Budapest, 1983): 70–75.

——. "Artisans, Drudges, and the Problem of Gender in Pre-Industrial France," in *Science and Technology in Medieval Society*, ed. Pamela O. Long. New York: New York Academy of Sciences, 1985.

——. "Gender Formation from a Working-Class Viewpoint: Guildswomen in Eighteenth-Century Rouen." *Proceedings of the Annual Meeting of the Western Society for French History* 16 (1989): 415–22.

——, ed. *European Women and Pre-Industrial Craft*. Bloomington: Indiana University Press, 1995.

Hanley, Sarah. "The Monarchic State in Early Modern France: Marital Regime Government and Male Right," in *Politics, Ideology and the Law in Early Modern Europe*, ed. Adrianna E. Bakos. Rochester, NY: University of Rochester Press, 1994.

Hesse, Carla. *The Other Enlightenment: How French Women Became Modern*. Princeton: Princeton University Press, 2001.

Hirschman, Albert. *The Passions and the Interests*. Princeton: Princeton University Press, 1977.

Hoffman, Philip T. "The Luxury Guilds of Eighteenth-Century Paris." *Francia* 9 (1982): 257–98.

Hoffman, Philip T., Gilles Postel-Vinay, and Jean-Laurent Rosenthal. *Priceless Markets: The Political Economy of Credit in Paris, 1160–1870*. Chicago: University of Chicago Press, 2000.

Hollander, Anne. *Seeing Through Clothes*. New York: Avon Books, 1975.

——. *Sex and Suits: The Evolution of Modern Dress*. New York: Alfred Knopf, 1994.

Hufton, Olwen. *The Poor of Eighteenth-Century France, 1750–1789*. Oxford: Clarendon Press, 1974.

——. "Women and the Family Economy in Eighteenth-Century France." *French Historical Studies* 9, no. 1 (Spring 1975): 1–22.

Hunt, Lynn. "Freedom of Dress in Revolutionary France," in *From the Royal to the Republican Body: Incorporating the Political in Seventeenth- and Eighteenth-Century France,* ed. Sara E. Melzer and Kathryn Norberg. Berkeley: University of California Press, 1988.

——. *The Family Romance of the French Revolution*. Berkeley: University of California Press, 1992.

Isherwood, Robert. *Farce and Fantasy: Popular Entertainment in Eighteenth-Century Paris*. Oxford: Oxford University Press, 1986.

Jacob, Margaret. *Living the Enlightenment: Freemasonry and Politics in Eighteenth-Century Europe*. Oxford: Oxford University Press, 1991.

Jacque, Jacqueline. "Printed Textiles," in *French Textiles*. Hartford, 1985.

Jaton, Anne-Marie. "Du corps paré au corps lavé: Une morale du costume et de la cosmétique." *Dix-huitième siècle* no. 18 (1986): 215–26.

Johnson, James H. "Versailles, Meet *Les Halles*: Masks, Carnival, and the French Revolution." *Representations*, no. 73 (Winter 2001): 89–116.

Jones, Colin. "Bourgeois Revolution Revivified: 1789 and Social Change," in *Rewriting the French Revolution*, ed. Colin Lucas. Oxford: Clarendon Press, 1991: 69–118.

——. "The Great Chain of Buying: Medical Advertisement, the Bourgeois Public Sphere, and the Origins of the French Revolution." *American Historical Review* 101, no. 1 (February 1996):13–40.

——. *Madame de Pompadour: Images of Mistress*. London: National Gallery, 2002.

——. *The Great Nation: France from Louis XV to Napoleon, 1715–99*. New York: Columbia University Press, 2002.

Jones, Colin and Rebecca Sprang. "Sans-culottes, sans café, sans tabac: Shifting Realms of Necessity and Luxury in Eighteenth-Century France," in *Consumers and Luxury: Consumer Culture in Europe, 1650–1850*, ed. Maxine Berg and Helen Clifford. Manchester: Manchester University Press, 1999.

Jones, Jennifer M. "Repackaging Rousseau: Femininity and Fashion in Old Regime France." *French Historical Studies* 18 (Fall 1994): 939–61.

——. "Coquettes and Grisettes: Women Buying and Selling in Ancien Régime Paris," in *The Sex of Things: Gender and Consumption in Historical Perspective*, ed. Victoria de Grazia and Ellen Furlough. Berkeley: University of California Press, 1996.

Jones, Robert W. *Gender and the Formation of Taste in Eighteenth-Century Britain: The Analysis of Beauty*. Cambridge: Cambridge University Press, 1998.

Jones, Vivien, ed. *Women in the Eighteenth Century, Constructions of Femininity*. London: Routledge, 1990.

Jouhard, Christian. *Mazarinades: La Fronde des mots*. Paris: Aubier, 1985.

Kaiser, Thomas. "Louis *le Bien-Aimé* and the Rhetoric of the Royal Body," in *From the Royal to the Republican Body*, ed. Sarah E. Melzer and Kathryn Norberg. Berkeley: University of California Press, 1998.

Kantorowicz, Ernst. *The King's Two Bodies: A Study in Medieval Political Theology*. Princeton: Princeton University Press, 1957.

Kaplan, Steven. "Réflexion sur la police du monde de travail, 1700–1815." *Revue historique*, 261 (1979): 17–77.

——. *Provisioning Paris: Merchants and Millers in the Grain and Flour Trade during the Eighteenth Century*. Ithaca: Cornell University Press, 1984.

——. "Social Classification and Representation in the Corporate World," in *Work in France, Representations, Meaning, Organization and Practice*, ed. S. Kaplan and C. Koepp. Ithaca: Cornell University Press, 1986.

——. "The Character and Implication of Strife among the Masters Inside the Guilds of Eighteenth-Century Paris." *Journal of Social History*, 19 (1986): 631–47.

Kaplan, Steven, and Cynthia Koepp, eds. *Work in France: Representations, Meaning, Organization and Practice*. Ithaca: Cornell University Press, 1986.

Kaplow, Jeffrey. *The Names of Kings: The Parisian Laboring Poor in the Eighteenth Century*. New York: Basic Books, 1972.

Kates, Gary. *Monsieur d'Eon is a Woman: A Tale of Political Intrigue and Sexual Masquerade*. New York: Basic Books, 1995.

Kavanagh, Thomas M. *Enlightenment and the Shadows of Chance: The Novel and the Culture of Gambling in Eighteenth-Century France*. Baltimore: Johns Hopkins University Press, 1993.

Kelly, Joan. "Did Women Have a Renaissance?" in *Women, History, and Theory: The Essays of Joan Kelly*. Chicago: University of Chicago Press, 1984.

Kidwell, Claudia Brush and Valerie Steele, eds. *Men and Women: Dressing the Part*. Washington, DC: Smithsonian Institution Press, 1989.

Klaits, Joseph. *Printed Propaganda under Louis XIV: Absolute Monarchy and Public Opinion*. Princeton: Princeton University Press, 1976.

Kleinert, Anne Marie. *Die fruhen Modejournale in Frankreich*. Berlin: E. Schmidt, 1980.

——. "La Naissance d'une presse de mode à la veille de la Révolution et l'essor du genre au xixième siècle." *Le journalisme d'ancien régime*, CNRS round table. Lyon: June 12–13, 1981.

Knibiehler, Yvonne, and Catherine Fouquet. *La beauté, pour quoi faire?* Paris, 1982.

Koepp, Cynthia "The Alphabetical Order: Work in Diderot's Encyclopédie," in *Work in France, Representations, Meaning, Organization and Practice*, ed. S. Kaplan and C. Koepp. Ithaca: Cornell University Press, 1986.

Kowaleski-Wallace, Elizabeth. *Consuming Subjects: Women, Shopping, and Business in the Eighteenth Century*. New York: Columbia University Press, 1997.

Kroeber, A.L., and Jane Richardson. *Three Centuries of Women's Dress Fashions*. Berkeley: University of California Press, 1940.

Kroeber, Alice L. "On the Principle of Order in Civilization as Exemplified by Changes of Fashion." *American Anthropologist*, 21 (1919): 235–6.

Kroll, Maria, trans. and ed. *Letters from Liselotte*. London: Victor Gollancz, 1970.

Kuchta, David. "'Graceful, Virile, and Useful': The Origins of the Three-Piece Suit." *Dress* 17 (1990): 118–26.

——. *The Three-Piece Suit and Modern Masculinity: England, 1550–1850*. Berkeley: University of California Press, 2002.

Lacroix, Paul. *XVIIIe siècle, Institutions, usages et costumes*. Paris: Firmin-Didot, 1875.

Lamberts, Ellen. *The Face of Love: Feminism and the Beauty Question*. Boston: Beacon Press, 1995.

Landes, Joan. *Women and the Public Sphere in the Age of the French Revolution.* Ithaca: Cornell University Press, 1988.

——. *Visualizing the Nation: Gender, Representation, and Revolution in Eighteenth-Century France.* Ithaca: Cornell University Press, 2001.

Langlade, Emile. *La marchande de modes de Marie Antoinette, Rose Bertin.* Paris, 1911.

Laqueur, Thomas. "Orgasm, Generation and the Politics of Reproductive Biology." *Representations* 14 (Spring 1986) 1–41.

——. *Making Sex: Body and Gender from the Greeks to Freud.* Cambridge, MA: Harvard University Press, 1990.

Legros. *Suppléement de l'art de la coiffure.* Paris, 1768.

Le journalisme d'ancien régime, CNRS round table. June 12–13, 1981.

Lemire, Beverly. *Dress, Culture, and Commerce: The English Clothing Trades before the Factory, 1660–1800.* London: St. Martin's Press, 1997.

Le Roy Ladurie, Emmanuel. *Saint-Simon and the Court of Louis XIV.* Chicago: University of Chicago Press, 2001.

Lespinasse, René de *Les métiers et les corporations de la ville de Paris.* Paris: Imprimerie nationale, 1897.

Levasnier, G. *Syndicat de l'aiguille: Papiers de famille professionelle.* Paris, 1906.

Levey, Michael. *Rococo to Revolution: Major Trends in 18th-Century Painting.* London, 1966.

Levu, Sophie. "Le Journal de la mode et du goût, étude d'un journal de mode pendant la revolution." Maîtrise, Paris I, 1983.

Lipovetsky, Gilles. *The Empire of Fashion: Dressing Modern Democracy.* Princeton: Princeton University Press, 1994.

Liu, Tessie. *The Weavers' Knot: The Contradictions of Class Struggle and Family Solidarity in Western France, 1750–1914.* Ithaca: Cornell University Press, 1994.

Lougée, Carolyn. *Le paradis des femmes.* Princeton: Princeton University Press, 1976.

Lough, John. *Paris Theater Audiences in the Seventeenth and Eighteenth Centuries.* Oxford: Oxford University Press, 1957.

——. "Women in Mercier's *Tableau de Paris,*" in *Woman and Society in Eighteenth-Century France,* ed. Jacobs, Barber, Block, et al. London, 1979.

Mackie, Erin. *Market à la Mode: Fashion, Commodity, and Gender in The Tatler and The Spectator.* Baltimore: Johns Hopkins University Press, 1997.

Maclean, Ian. *Woman Triumphant.* Oxford, 1977.

Magendie, Maurice. *La politesse mondaine et les theories de l'honnêteté en France au XVII siècle.* Geneva: Slatkine Reprints, 1970 (1925).

Major, J. Russell. *From Renaissance Monarchy to Absolute Monarchy: French Kings, Nobles and Estates.* Baltimore: Johns Hopkins University Press, 1994.

Marin, Louis. *Le portrait de roi*. Paris: Minuit, 1981.

Marion, Marcel. *Dictionnaire des institutions de la France au XVII et XVIII siècles*. Paris: A. et J. Picard et Cie, 1968.

Marion, Rene. "The Dames de la Halle: Community and Authority in Early Modern Paris." Ph.D. dissertation, Johns Hopkins University, 1995.

Marivaux, Pierre de. *Le spectateur Français*, douzième feuille. December 6, 1722.

——. "Lettres sur les habitants de Paris," in *Journaux et oeuvres diverses de Marivaux*, ed. Frédéric Deloffre and Michel Gilot. Paris: Bordas, 1988.

Martin, Morag. "Consuming Beauty: The Commerce of Cosmetics in France, 1750–1800." Ph.D. thesis, University of California Irvine, 1999.

Mauss, Marcel. *The Gift: Forms and Functions of Exchange in Archaic Societies*. New York: Norton, 1967.

Maza, Sarah. "Le tribunal de la nation: Les mémoires judiciares et l'opinion publique à la fin de l'ancien régime." *Annales E.S.C.* 42 (January 1987): 75–90.

——. *Private Lives and Public Affairs: The Causes Célèbres of Prerevolutionary France*. Berkeley: University of California Press, 1993.

——. "Luxury, Morality, and Social Change: Why There Was No Middle-Class Consciousness in Pre-revolutionary France." *Journal of Modern History* 69 (1997): 199–229.

——. *The Myth of the French Bourgeoisie: An Essay on the Social Imaginary, 1750–1850*. Cambridge, MA: Harvard University Press, 2003.

McBride, Theresa. "A Woman's World: Department Stores and the Evolution of Women's Employment." *French Historical Studies* 10 (Fall 1978): 664–83.

McCracken, Grant. *Culture and Consumption: New Approaches to the Symbolic Character of Consumer Goods*. Bloomington: Indiana University Press, 1988.

McKendrick, Neil, John Brewer and J.H. Plumb. *The Birth of a Consumer Society: The Commercialization of Eighteenth-Century England*. Bloomington: Indiana University Press, 1982.

Mélèse, Pierre. *Un homme de letters au temps du Grand Roi: Donneau de Visé*. Paris, 1936.

Melzer, Sara E. and Kathryn Norberg, eds. *From the Royal to the Republican Body: Incorporating the Political in Seventeenth- and Eighteenth-Century France*. Berkeley: University of California Press, 1998.

Mercier, Louis-Sébastien. *Le tableau de Paris*, 12 vols. Amsterdam, 1783–88.

——. *Parallèle de Paris et de Londres*, ed. C. Bruneteau. Paris, 1982.

Merrick, Jeffrey and Bryant T. Ragan. *Homosexuality in Modern France*. Oxford: Oxford University Press, 1996.

Miller, Michael. *The Bon Marché: Bourgeois Culture and the Department Store*. Princeton: Princeton University Press, 1981.

Minard, Philippe. *La fortune du colbertisme: État et industrie dans la France des Lumières*. Paris: Fayard, 1998.

Montespan, Françoise Athénaïs de Rochechouart, Marquise de. *Memoirs of Madame la Marquise de Montespan*. Boston: L.C. Page and Co., 1899.

Montesquieu, Charles de. *Persian Letters*. 1721.

——. *De l'esprit des lois*. Ed. J. Berthe de la Gressaye. Paris: Les belles-lettres, 1950.

Moriarty, Michael. *Taste and Ideology in Seventeenth-Century France*. Cambridge: Cambridge University Press, 1988.

Mui, Hoh-Cheung and Lorna. *Shops and Shopkeeping in Eighteenth-Century England*. Montreal: McGill-Queen's University Press, 1989.

Mukerji, Chandra. *From Graven Images: Patterns of Modern Materialism*. New York: Columbia University Press, 1983.

Munns, Jessica and Penny Richards, eds. *The Clothes That Wear Us: Essays on Dressing and Transgressing in Eighteenth-Century Culture*. Newark, DE: University of Delaware Press, 1999.

Nef, John. *Cultural Foundations of Industrial Civilization*. New York: Harper, 1958.

Nemeitz, Joachim Christoph. *Séjour de Paris*. Leiden: J. Van Abcoude, 1727.

Nora, Pierre. *Les lieux de mémoire*, 7 vols. Paris: Gallimard, 1984–92.

Nord, Philip. *Paris Shopkeepers and the Politics of Resentment*. Princeton: Princeton University Press, 1986.

Oriol, Bernadette Roux. "Maîtresses marchandes lingères, maîtresses couturiers, ouvriers en linge aux alentours de 1751." Maîtrise, Paris I, 1981.

Outram, Dorinda. *The Body and the French Revolution: Sex, Class, and Political Culture*. New Haven: Yale University Press, 1989.

Pagden, Anthony, ed. *The Languages of Political Theory in Early-Modern Europe*. Cambridge: Cambridge University Press, 1987.

Pardailhé-Galabrun, Annik. *The Birth of Intimacy: Privacy and Domestic Life in Early Modern Paris*. Philadelphia: University of Pennsylvania Press, 1991.

Parker, Roszika. *The Subversive Stitch: Embroidery and the Making of the Feminine*. London: The Women's Press, 1984.

Parker, Roszika and Griselda Pollock. *Old Mistresses: Women, Art and Ideology*. New York: Pantheon, 1981.

Pellegrin, Nicole. "Techniques et production du vêtement en Poitou, 1880–1950," in *L'aiguille et le sabaron: Techniques et production du vêtement en Poitou, 1880–1950*, ed. Nicole Pellegrin, Jacques Chauvin and Marie-Christine Planchard. Potiers: Musée de la Ville de Poitiers et de la Société des antiquaires de l'ouest, 1983.

——. *Les vêtements de la liberté, abécédaire des pratiques vestimentaires françaises de 1780 à 1800*. Aix-en-Provence: Alinea, 1989.

——. "L'uniforme de la santé: Les médecins et la réforme du costume." *Dix huitième siècle* 23 (1991): 129–40.

Perrot, Philippe. *Fashioning the Bourgeoisie: A History of Clothing in the Nineteenth Century*. Princeton: Princeton University Press, 1994.

——. *Le luxe, une richesse entre faste et confort, XVIIIe–XIXe siècles*. Paris: Editions du Seuil, 1995.

Popkin, Jeremy. *Revolutionary News: The Press in France, 1789–1799*. Durham: Duke University Press, 1990.

Porter, Roy, and Lesley Hall. *Facts of Life: The Creation of Sexual Knowledge in Britain, 1650–1950*. New Haven: Yale University Press, 1995.

Ranum, Orest. "The Court and Capital of Louis XIV: Some Definitions and Reflections," in *Louis XIV and the Craft of Kingship*, ed. John C. Rule. Columbus: Ohio State University Press, 1969.

Rappaport, Erika. *Shopping for Pleasure: Women in the Making of London's West End*. Princeton: Princeton University Press, 2000.

Ravel, Jeffrey S. *The Contested Parterre: Public Theater and French Political Culture, 1680–1791*. Ithaca: Cornell University Press, 1999.

Reddy, William. *The Rise of Market Culture, the Textile Trade and French Society, 1750–1900*. Cambridge: Cambridge University Press, 1984.

——. *Money and Liberty in Modern Europe: A Critique of Historical Understanding*. Cambridge: Cambridge University Press, 1987.

——. *The Navigation of Feeling: A Framework for the History of Emotions*. Cambridge: Cambridge University Press, 2001.

Revel, Jaques. "Marie Antoinette in Her Fictions: The Staging of Hatred," in *Fictions of the French Revolution*, ed. Bernadette Fort. Evanston, IL: Northwestern University Press, 1991.

Ribeiro, Aileen. *Dress in Eighteenth-Century Europe*. London: B.T. Batsford, 1984.

——. *Fashion in the French Revolution*. London: Holmes and Meier, 1988.

——. *The Art of Dress: Fashion in England and France, 1750–1820*. New Haven: Yale University Press, 1995.

Riley, Denise. *"Am I That Name?" Feminism and the Category of "Women" in History*. Minneapolis: University of Minnesota Press, 1989.

Rimbault, Caroline. "La presse féminine de langue française au XVIII siècle: place de la femme et système de la mode." Thèse de 3ème cycle, Ecole des hautes études en science sociales, Paris, 1981.

Robinson, Philip E.J. *Jean-Jacques Rousseau's Doctrine of the Arts*. Bern, 1984.

Roche, Daniel. *Le Siècle des Lumières en province: Académies et académiciens provinciaux, 1680–1789*. Paris and The Hague: Mouton, 1978.

——, ed. *Journal de ma vie, Jacques Louis Ménétra, compagnon vitrier au XVIIIe siècle*. Paris: Editions Montalba, 1982.

——. "L'économie des garde-robes à Paris, de Louis XIV à Louis XVI." *Communications* 46 (1987): 93–118.

——. *The People of Paris, an Essay in Popular Culture in the Eighteenth Century.* Berkeley: University of California Press, 1987.

——. *The Culture of Clothing: Dress and Fashion in the Ancien Régime.* Cambridge: Cambridge University Press, 1994. Originally published as *La culture des apparences.* Paris: Fayard, 1989.

——. *France in the Enlightenment.* Cambridge, MA: Harvard University Press, 1998.

——. *A History of Everyday Things: The Birth of Consumption in France.* trans. Brian Pearce. Cambridge: Cambridge University Press, 2000.

Ross, Ellen. "The Debate on Luxury in Eighteenth-Century France." Ph.D. thesis, University of Chicago, 1975.

Rothkrug, Lionel. *The Opposition to Louis XIV.* Princeton: Princeton University Press, 1965.

Russell, Douglas. *Costume History and Style.* Englewood Cliffs, NJ: Prentice-Hall, 1983.

Saisselin, Rémy. *Taste in Eighteenth-Century France.* Syracuse: Syracuse University Press, 1965.

——. *The Enlightenment against the Baroque: Economics and Aesthetics in the Eighteenth Century.* Berkeley: University of California Press, 1992.

Sargentson, Carolyn. *Merchants and Luxury Markets: The Marchands Merciers of Eighteenth-Century Paris.* London: The Victoria and Albert Museum, 1996.

Sekora, John. *Luxury: The Concept in Western Thought from Eden to Smollet.* Baltimore: Johns Hopkins University Press, 1977.

Sennet, Richard. *The Fall of Public Man: On the Social Psychology of Capitalism.* New York: Vintage Books, 1978.

Sewell, William. *Work and Revolution in France: The Language of Labor from the Old Regime to 1848.* Cambridge: Cambridge University Press, 1980.

Sgard, Jean, ed. *Dictionnaire des journalistes 1600–1789.* Grenoble: Presses universitaires de Grenoble, 1976.

Shammas, Carole. *The Pre-Industrial Consumer in England and America.* Oxford: Clarendon Press, 1990.

Sharpe, Kevin, and Steven N. Zwicker, eds. *Refiguring Revolutions: Aesthetics and Politics from the English Revolution to the Romantic Revolution.* Berkeley: University of California Press, 1998.

Sheriff, Mary D. *Fragonard: Art and Eroticism.* Chicago: University of Chicago Press, 1990.

——. *The Exceptional Woman: Elisabeth Vigée-Lebrun and the Cultural Politics of Art.* Chicago: University of Chicago Press, 1996.

Shevelow, Kathryn. *Women and Print Culture: The Construction of Femininity in the Early Periodical*. London: Routledge, 1989.

Shovlin, John. "The Cultural Politics of Luxury in Eighteenth-Century France." *French Historical Studies* 23, no. 4 (Fall 2000): 577–606.

Shusterman, Richard "'Of the Scandal of Taste' Social Privilege as Nature in the Aesthetic Theories of Hume and Kant," in *Eighteenth-Century Aesthetics and the Reconstruction of Art*, ed. Paul Mattick, Jr. Cambridge: Cambridge University Press, 1993.

Simon, Jules. *L'Ouvrière*. Paris, 1861.

Smith, Bonnie. *Ladies of the Leisure Class: The Bourgeoisies of Northern France in the Nineteenth Century*. Princeton: Princeton University Press, 1981.

Smith, Jay. *The Culture of Merit: Nobility, Royal Service, and the Making of Absolute Monarchy in France, 1600–1789*. Ann Arbor: University of Michigan Press, 1996.

Sonenscher, Michael. *The Hatters of Eighteenth-Century France*. Berkeley: University of California Press, 1987.

——. *Work and Wages: Natural Law, Politics and the Eighteenth-Century French Trades*. Cambridge: Cambridge University Press, 1989.

Sonnet, Martine. *L'éducation des filles au temps des Lumières*. Paris: Cerf, 1987.

Stafford, Barbara Marie. *Artful Science: Enlightenment Entertainment and the Eclipse of Visual Education*. Cambridge, MA: MIT Press, 1994.

Stanton, Domna C. *The Aristocrat as Art: A Study of the Honnête Homme and the Dandy in Seventeenth- and Nineteenth-Century French Literature*. New York: Columbia University Press, 1980.

Starobinski, Jean, et al. *Revolution in Fashion: European Clothing, 1715–1815*. New York: Abbeville Press, 1989.

Staves, Susan. *Married Women's Separate Property in England, 1660–1833*. Cambridge, MA: Harvard University Press, 1990.

Steele, Valerie. *Paris Fashion: A Cultural History*. Oxford: Oxford University Press, 1988.

Steinbugge, Liselotte. *The Moral Sex: Woman's Nature in the French Enlightenment*. Trans. Pamela E. Selwyn. Oxford: Oxford University Press, 1995.

Sullerot, Evelyne. "Politique et toilette: Voilà les principales sources de la femme tels qu'ils se dégagent de l'histoire de la presse feminine." *Presse publicité: Hebdomadaire technique de toute la presse* 19 (September 12, 1937): 16–18.

——. *Histoire de la presse féminine des origines à 1848*. Paris: Armand Colin, 1966.

Thomas, Chantal. *La reine scélérate: Marie-Antoinette dans les pamphlets*. Paris: Seuil, 1990.

Thompson, Victoria. *The Virtuous Marketplace: Women and Men, Money and Politics in Paris, 1830–1870*. Baltimore: Johns Hopkins University Press, 2000.

Tiersten, Lisa. *Marianne in the Market: Envisioning Consumer Society in Fin-de-Siècle France*. Berkeley: University of California Press, 2001.

Tomaselli, Sylvana. "The Enlightenment Debate on Women." *History Workshop Journal* no. 20 (1985): 101–24.

Trenard, Louis. "La presse française des origines à 1788," in *Histoire générale de la presse française*, ed. Claude Bellanger, Jaques Godechot, et al. Paris: Presses universitaires de France, 1969.

Truant, Cynthia. *The Rites of Labor: The Brotherhoods of Compagnonnage in Old and New Regime France*. Ithaca: Cornell University Press, 1994.

———. "Parisian Guildswomen and the (Sexual) Politics of Privilege: Defending their Patrimonies in Print," in *Going Public: Women and Publishing in Early Modern France*, ed. Dena Goodman and Elisabeth C. Goldsmith. Ithaca: Cornell University Press, 1995.

———. "La maîtrise d'une identité? Corporations féminines à Paris aux XVIIe et XVIIIe siècles." *Clio, Historie, Femmes et Sociétés* 3 (1996).

Trumbach, Randy. *Sex and the Gender Revolution*. Chicago: The University of Chicago Press, 1998.

Van Dijk, Suzanne. "Femmes et journaux au xviiie siècle." *Australian Journal of French Studies* 18, no. 2 (1981): 164–78.

Varron, A. "Créateurs de modes parisiens au XVIIe siècle," *Les Cahiers Ciba* 2, no. 16 (December 1947): 542–75.

Verdier, Yvonne. *Façons de dire, façons de faire: La laveuse, la couturière, la cuisinière*. Paris: Gallimard, 1979.

Vielwahr, André. *La vie et l'oeuvre de Sénac de Meilhan*. Paris: A.G. Nizet, 1970.

Vigarello, George. *Concepts of Cleanliness: Changing Attitudes in France since the Middle Ages*. Paris: Maison des sciences de l'homme, 1988.

Vincent, Monique. "Le *Mercure Gallant*: témoin des pouvoirs de la femme du monde." *Dix- Septième Siècle* 144 (July–September 1984): 241–46.

———. "Donneau de Visé et le *Mercure Gallant*." Lille: Atelier National Réproduction des Thèses, Université Lille III, 1987.

Waller, Margaret. "Disembodiment as Masquerade: Fashion Journalists and the other 'Realist' Observers in Directory Paris." *Esprit Créateur* 37, no. 1 (Spring 1997).

Waquet, Françoise. "La Mode au XVIIe siècle: De la folie à l'usage." *Cahiers de l'association internationale des études françaises* 38 (1986): 91–124.

Waugh, Norah. *The Cut of Men's Clothes*. London: Faber, 1964.

———. *The Cut of Women's Clothes*. London: Faber, 1968.

Weatherhill, Lorna. *Consumer Behaviour and Material Culture in Britain, 1660–1760*. London: Routledge, 1988.

Williams, H. Noel. *Later Queens of the French Stage*. New York, 1906.

Williams, Rosalind. *Dream Worlds: Mass Consumption in Late Nineteenth-Century France*. Berkeley: University of California Press, 1982.

Wilson, Elizabeth. *Adorned in Dreams: Fashion and Modernity*. London: Virago, 1985.

———. *Sphinx in the City: Urban Life, the Control of Disorder, and Women*. London: Virago, 1991.

Wrigely, Richard. *The Politics of Appearances: Representations of Dress in Revolutionary France*. Oxford: Berg, 2002.

Zanger, Abby. *Scenes from the Marriage of Louis XIV: Nuptial Fictions and the Making of Absolutist Power*. Stanford: Stanford University Press, 1997.

———. "Lim(b)inal Images: 'Betwixt and Between' Louis XIV's Martial and Marital Bodies," in *From the Royal to the Republican Body*, ed. Sarah E. Melzer and Kathryn Norberg. Berkeley: University of California Press, 1998.

Index

Index

Mercier, Louis-Sébastien
  distinctions between male and female dress, 201–2
  fashion merchants, 163
  grisettes, 155–7, 159–60
  luxury, 146
  Palais-Royal, 154, 164
  second-hand clothing trade, 163–4
  shops in London, 167
  taste, 114
  women's work in clothing trades, 97–9
merchants
  female, 145–6, 156–8, 161–2
    illustration, 155
Mercure galant, 25–39
  fashion seasons, 33
  gender difference in fashion, 33–7
  royal mourning, 29–30
mode, *see* fashion
modernity, xvii, 74–5
modesty
  female, 84, 88
Monsieur, *see* Philippe d'Orléans
Montaclos, Mme de, 135
Montespan, Marquise de, 11–12, 50–1, 53–5, 60, 64
Montlinot, Charles Antoine-Joseph Leclerc de, 200–1
mourning dress, 29–30

needlework
  discipline, 100
  illustration of girl embroidering, 100
Nemeitz, J.C.
  Séjour de Paris, 152–3
    female merchants, 161, 164
neoclassical art, 118–19
novelty
  discourse on, 150, 179

D'Oberkirch, baronne de
  Rose Bertin, 169
  shopping, 154–5, 165, 167
Oriel, Bernadette
  linen drapers, 157

Pamela, 216, 218
paniers, *see* hoopskirts

Paris
  commercial culture, 145–69 passim
    and fashion press, 27–41, 179–201 passim
  population, 74–5
perruquiers, *see* wigmakers
Philip IV
  Spanish court fashions, 22
Philippe d'Orléans, 19, 47, 52, 56–8
plumassières, *see* feather makers
Polman, Jean
  Le voile ou couvre-chef féminine, 202
Pompadour, Jeanne Antoinette Poisson, Marquise de, 11, 117
prostitution
  clothing workers, 96–100, 156, 158–9, 162
public and private, xvii, 41, 75
public sphere, 75, 179
  shopping, 154–5, 164–5
  women's relation to, 74–5, 164–5

querelle des femmes, 134–5

Ravel, Jeffrey, 13n5
ready-made clothing, 151, 162, 166, 169
Regency culture, 56, 73
Republican motherhood, 215
Restif de la Brétonne, Nicolas-Edmé
  shopping 153–4
  women's work, 99
revendeuse à la toilette, xv, 151–2
Roche, Daniel, 4, 75, 76n4, 86
rococo art, 119
Roland, Mme de, 216
Ross, Ellen, 199
Rousseau, Jean-Jacques, 73
  Julie, 215
  Sophie, 1, 215
  taste, 114, 136–7
  women and clothing production, 81, 97–100
Royal Academy of Painting, 120, 125–6, 130
Royal Academy of Surgery
  training for tailors, 126
Rutledge, James, 1

Saint-Antoine,
  faubourg, 116

Index